JAPAN

ITS HISTORY AND CULTURE

D0388799

Frontispiece:
Sword guard (*tsuba*), eighteenth century; copper and other alloys with gold incrustation. Ht., 3¹⁄₁₆ in. A general (left) is bracing his bow against a rock, while a soldier looks on and another soldier holds a standard. The general is probably Minamoto Yoshiiye, who with his father fought in the bitter Nine Years War beginning A.D. 1051 in northern Japan. He was nicknamed by the soldiers Hachiman Taro, First-born of the God of War. (*Collection of the Newark Museum. Photographs by Keith Scott Morton*)

JAPAN

ITS HISTORY AND CULTURE

W. SCOTT MORTON

McGraw-Hill Book Company

New York   St. Louis   San Francisco   Auckland   Bogotá
Guatemala   Hamburg   Johannesburg   Lisbon   London
Madrid   Mexico   Montreal   New Delhi   Panama   Paris
San Juan   São Paulo   Singapore   Sydney   Tokyo   Toronto

Copyright © 1984, 1970 by W. Scott Morton

All rights reserved. Printed in the United States of America. Except as permitted under the Copyright Act of 1976, no part of this publication may be reproduced or distributed in any form or by any means or stored in a data base or retrieval system, without the prior written permission of the publisher.

Library of Congress Cataloging in Publication Data

Morton, W. Scott (William Scott)
    Japan, its history and culture.
    Reprint. Originally published: New York : Crowell, 1970.
With a new Chapter updating events to early 1984.
    Bibliography: p.
    Includes index.
    1. Japan—History. I. Title.
DS835.M64   1984   952   84-12558
ISBN 0-07-043422-0 (pbk.)

First McGraw-Hill paperback edition, 1984

1 2 3 4 5 6 7 8 9 DOCDOC 8 7 6 5 4

ISBN: 0-07-043422-0

FOREWORD

Japan's history and culture are strikingly individual, but they are no less remarkable for the influence of the cultures of China and the West. Periods of dramatic institutional change have alternated with those of appropriation and domestication of the institutions introduced into Japan, and the end result was usually very different from the import.

In the seventh century Chinese models of government, and especially the figure of the sovereign, were soon modified to fit Japanese realities. The modern monarchy bore even less resemblance to the German pattern on which it had initially been cut. Less strikingly, but no less surely, Japan's Buddhism, Confucianism, art, and literature resonated to emphases different from those of China. Throughout all cultural change a consistent and distinctive sensitivity and selectivity—in views of nature, time, and space and in values of honor, loyalty, and sincerity—distinguished Japan's great tradition of art, letters, and especially poetry.

In modern times the pace of change has quickened and the tide of influence has broadened, but the pattern of selective adaptation of outside example remains visible. The flood of Western influence in the nineteenth century brought a period of tumultuous change. In politics the national resolve to restore autonomy and equality had dramatic influence on the international system. As the first non-Western state to modernize its institutions Japan struggled first to join and then to defeat Western colonialism. It succeeded as it failed, and helped end all colonialisms including its own. Thereafter Japanese leaders and citizens turned to pursue new goals of social justice and economic gain with a vigor that is today transforming the international economic order as thoroughly as the earlier drive to great power status that remade the international political order.

These pendulum swings of enthusiasm should not, however, distract attention from the more important and consistent process of development within Japanese society. The political events that attract the reader's attention illumine, but did not cause, that process. It was one in which Japan moved from an aristocratic, to a feudal, to an urban, and finally to a mass society. Japanese society has been revolutionized without internal revolution in response to modern knowledge and technology, and within a century a society structured on lines of hereditary privilege has been transformed into a mass society with an unusually even income distribution, one in which the prizes are reserved for a meritocracy of talent selected on the basis of educational attainment. As a result Japan's experience of transformation and resilience forces itself upon the attention of the world. It invites a re-thinking of theories and explanations of the modern world that have hitherto been based upon the experience of the Atlantic states.

Professor Morton's brisk narrative provides a pleasing entrance into that experience, and helps to make its outlines accessible to readers in several lands and several languages. One welcomes this new edition and hopes that it will find wide use.

Marius B. Jansen
Professor of History and East Asian Studies
Princeton University

CONTENTS

ILLUSTRATIONS

JAPAN

ITS HISTORY AND CULTURE

JAPAN

Oki

Tsushima Islands

MAEDA

ECHIGO

Iki Hakata
Bay

KANAZAWA

CHOSHU

IKEDA

HIRADO

DAN-NO-URA HIROSHIMA

SHIMONOSEKI

ECHIZEN

HONSHU

HIZEN

ASANO

IKEDA

Lake Biwa

Mt. Hiei SEKIGAHARA

NAGASAKI

Inland Sea

KOBE KYOTO AZUCHI

OTSU

OWARI

Mt. Fuji KOFU

KYUSHU

SHIKOKU

YASHIMA ICHI-NO-TANI

OSAKA

NAGOYA

Shimabara
Peninsula

TOSA

SAKAI

NARA

SHIZUOKA

HAKONE

HOSOKAWA

Awaji
Is.

YOSHINO

KII

KAMAKURA

SATSUMA

Ise
Peninsula

KAGOSHIMA

Tanegashima Islands

HOKKAIDO

SAPPORO

HAKODATE

AOMORI

DATE

NIIGATA   SENDAI

MITO

MITO

TOKYO
KAWASAKI
YOKOHAMA

Names of main islands and city names in Roman capitals
Han or fief names in italic capitals
Other geographical features in upper and lower case type

0   100   200   300
KILOMETERS

I

INTRODUCTION

According to Japanese legends the people of Japan are descended from the Sun Goddess. Not only so, but the land itself is characterized as divine. Looking down from a pine-clad promontory onto the glinting waters and clustered islands of the Inland Sea, or up to the snow-capped cone of Mount Fuji rising out of swirling mist and surrounded at its base by the vivid green of fertile rice fields, it is easy to understand how the early Japanese might have come to feel this sense of immanent divinity. For natural beauty of scenery Japan has few equals. Her people are a distinctive group, conscious of their heritage, having some ties with the mainland but living their separate life as an island people.

The main elements of Japanese higher culture are derived from China. But the Japanese are not alone in this. China has for long been the dominant power all over East Asia, not merely by virtue of her size or her large population, but because of her superior culture. Tibet, Mongolia, Korea, and parts of Southeast Asia, as well as Japan, have been accustomed to look to China as a source of leadership and inspiration, a cultural stimulus, and a cultural storehouse.

Japanese culture is nevertheless distinctive. One of the most intriguing features of the Japanese people is their capacity to borrow and adapt and yet to retain their own individuality and their own style. Thus though they are heavily indebted to China for the shape of their culture, what emerges is distinctively Japanese. They have always shown great powers of converting borrowed material to their special purposes, purposes conceived deep within their own national consciousness, and so of molding a culture that no one could think was anything but Japanese.

These purposes, this style and stamp, do not yield themselves up to superficial inquiry. The student of Japan must submit himself to a soaking process. He must steep himself in all aspects of Japanese history, language, and life, and this is not easy to do, especially if it must be done without the benefit of residence in Japan. The process of assimilating the spirit of an alien culture is always difficult, but special difficulties attend those who want to understand Japan. To the blunt Westerner the Japanese seem to exhibit at every turn a preference for the indirect—indirectness of statement in the language, indirectness in social life for politeness' sake, and indirect rule in politics, exercised through an anonymous group ruling in the name of a figurehead. Nevertheless there is every incentive to study Japan, for rich rewards in the form of the beautiful, the intriguing, the terrible, and the exotic are scattered profusely along the uphill path.

The history of Japan is like her language, apparently simple in the first stages of acquaintance but growing rapidly more complex and subtle the further one penetrates the mysterious regions of idiom and thought-process. So it is also true to say that Japanese history has at first a simplicity of outline but on deeper analysis presents a Sphinx face of stubborn mystery. It seems simple at first because the country is smaller and the span of recorded history shorter than those of the vast neighbor, China. But the intentional indirectness already referred to in the Japanese character and the gulf fixed between Western and Japanese categories of what is important and valuable make it unusually hard for Western scientific history to lay bare the real character of the chain of Japanese historical experience.

However, by a curious and fortunate process of compensation, it seems possible to make a few valid generalizations. Two characteristics of the Japanese that may be mentioned at the very beginning, to reemerge frequently in the course of this story, are their military, feudal qualities and their natural artistic gifts. It may be because Shinto enshrines and fosters both these characteristics that it has, in spite of its primitive nature, remained strong as a religion down the Japanese centuries.

In an attempt to present the history of Japan to those generally unfamiliar with it some use will be made in this book of Japanese terms. The process of explaining and filling out the meaning of these terms will serve to illuminate much that would otherwise remain obscure. An author writing about another culture tends instinctively to introduce those terms in the native language which least lend themselves to direct translation and which most typically illustrate the views that the people of the country hold about their own culture. When the subject is an Asian country, this practice may be of more than ordinary value since Asian history can best be approached in terms of the unity of history, language, and culture.

The scholars of both China and Japan, unaware of the division of disciplines customary in the West, were at one and the same time scholars, philosophers, artists, poets, calligraphers, essayists, and often historians. They did not so much conceive of their culture as a unity as never imagine it could be anything else. And this feeling of theirs, though not all their concepts, percolated down to the common people. Their culture must therefore, even in outline form, be studied through all avenues of art, religion, and economic and social life as well as through the avenues more classic in the West, such as political and military history. By trying to recount the outward events of Japanese history always with an eye to the attitude and stance of the chief actors and of the common folk, we may be able to obtain a truer and more rounded view of the whole. We may be able to arrive at some understanding of that remarkable élan which impelled the vigorous Japanese through their long history and projected them suddenly, by their design but perhaps to their surprise, into the forefront of the twentieth-century world.

INTRODUCTION TO THE
McGRAW-HILL EDITION

For this second edition a further chapter has been added to bring events from 1970 to early 1984 up to date. The importance of economics in this period has caused the main emphasis to fall upon this aspect of contemporary Japan. Some treatment, however, has been given to cultural affairs which were not treated in earlier chapters. A shorter and more up-to-date bibliography has been substituted for the former one, and some events and names have been added to the chronology. A new set of illustrations has been provided.

I am most grateful to Professors Ardath W. Burks and H. Paul Varley for their generous help in preparing this edition. Valrae Reynolds of The Newark Museum, and Allen Wardwell and Robert D. Mowry of the Asia Society, New York, were of the greatest assistance in securing illustrations. Seiichiro Ohtsuka, Japanese Deputy Consul General, and Masakatsu Wajima, both of the Japan Information Center, and Connie O'Keefe of the Japan National Tourist Organization gave me valuable information and fine photographic material.

My editor at McGraw-Hill, Joanne Dolinar, combined efficiency with kindness. Finally, I am grateful to my son, Keith Scott Morton, whose professional skill graces the cover of this book.

New York, April, 1984

2

THE ORIGINS AND EARLY HISTORY
OF THE JAPANESE

The origins of the Japanese people are mixed and obscure. One thing is certain: there were other races, of a non-Japanese character, living on the islands of Japan before the arrival of the Japanese themselves. One of these races, the Ainu, has survived, though precariously, to the present day. The Ainu are of Caucasian type, with white skin and profuse beards. Their totem is the bear and their way of life that of hunters and fishermen. For centuries they dominated the northern section of the islands, but they are now reduced to a small group living in Hokkaido (see Plate 2).

The Japanese, on the other hand, are of Mongolian race, smaller in stature, with the typical Mongolian features of the fold in the eyelid, a yellow tinge in pigmentation, black hair, faces on the whole flatter than the Caucasian type, high cheekbones, and limbs proportionately short in relation to the trunk. This last feature helps to conserve body heat which would otherwise be dissipated by long extremities. This, along with the eyefold which may offer protection against snow glare, is thought by some to point to a reservoir of Mongolian peoples living in prehistoric times in the Siberian North.

But within the Mongolian family at least two more exact areas of origin may be distinguished for those peoples who mingled to form the Japanese race. The first is Central Asia. The evidence for this is to be found not only in the physical type already mentioned but also in the language. Japanese in its syllabary (consonant followed by vowel) and in certain roots shows some similarities to Hungarian-Magyar and to Finnish. All three probably stem from a common Central Asian source. The second area of origin for one of the Japanese strains is the South China region. This is indicated by certain physical features, such as the comparatively small size, yellower skin, and delicate bone structure of the Japanese, which correspond more closely

[5]

to the people of South China than to those of North China. Certain items of diet, notably the use of wet rice, also point to a South China origin. There is a third possible strain in the Japanese people, namely one stemming from Southeast Asia and the Pacific islands; but this is controversial. The main argument for it is found in the form of architecture used in old Japanese farmhouses and in the Shinto shrine buildings, for example at Ise. In all these and in the huts of the dwellers in Malaysia and Polynesia the main roof beams at the gable ends are not sawed off but allowed to project at the top for a considerable distance in the form of an X. It has been objected to this theory that the islanders could never have covered the distance from the South Pacific islands to Japan in open boats and without navigational aids. But the use of a simple coconut shell device for a sextant, with a water level within it to maintain the artificial horizon, might well have allowed adventurous mariners to complete the journey to Japan successfully. Present-day Polynesians in outrigger canoes with similar navigational devices are known to be able to sail immense distances with remarkable accuracy.

What of the land itself in which these people mingled and established themselves? Japan consists of four large islands, running from north to south and then bending in a curve to the west, as follows: Hokkaido, Honshu (the main island), Shikoku, and Kyushu, as well as innumerable small islands. Their total area is about the size of the state of California. If superimposed on the east coast area of the United States, Japan would extend as a narrow sickle curve from the Canadian border to the northern edge of Florida. Honshu greatly exceeds the other three main islands in size, so much so that on the superimposed map it alone would run from the latitude of New York to that of Atlanta, Georgia. The climate exhibits differences corresponding to this long north-south range, from deep winter snows in Hokkaido to semitropical vegetation in Kyushu.

A large proportion of the country is mountainous, leaving only 17 percent of the surface area available for agriculture, with a small extra margin to be squeezed out of the hill slopes by terracing (see Plate 3). The three chief agricultural plains of Japan are the Kanto Plain around Tokyo, about 5,000 square miles in extent, the Nobi Plain around Nagoya, and the Kansai Plain around Nara, Kyoto, and Osaka at the eastern end of the Inland Sea. The latter two are each only about one-tenth the area of the Kanto Plain.

Abundant rainfall and assiduous industry have enabled the Japanese to survive on the products of their farming, but these have always had to be supplemented by the produce of the sea—fish, shellfish, and edible seaweeds. A study carried out by Japanese scientists during World War II demonstrated that seafood and a small amount of meat, rice, and vegetables, especially the vitamin-rich *daikon* or giant radish, would provide an adequate diet at extremely low cost.

It has been noted that the island situation of Japan is similar to that of Great Britain and that, as a consequence, there are certain parallels to be found in the history of each. Both are islands near enough to a great continent to receive cultural stimuli but just sufficiently isolated to evolve their own ways of life, tolerably free from hostile invasion. Both have developed strong navies, doubtless from reservoirs of skill gained in fishing and trading. Finally, both in modern times have had to make strenuous efforts in manufacture and export trade in order to feed their island populations.

In one respect Japan differs geographically from Britain; her islands with mountains two miles high are perched on the edge of a cleft in the ocean floor five miles in depth known as the Tuscarora Deep. Stresses appear to be thus set up which make Japan extremely liable to earthquakes, some of great severity. There are also a number of active volcanoes in the islands. The perfect cone of Mount Fuji is that of an extinct volcano (the last eruption occurred in 1707); but Mount Asama, for instance, is still active, and alarming sulphurous jets of steam pour out of many fissures in the mountains of Central Japan.

In mineral resources Japan is comparatively poor. She has very little iron or oil. Coal is scarce and not of superior quality and only copper is fairly abundant. Premodern Japan was, however, amply supplied from the forest slopes with the woods of various kinds she needed for the construction of houses, temples, and the mansions of the great, in addition to boats and implements of all kinds. Her short, fast-flowing rivers give little help in transportation but provide modern Japan with ample sources of hydroelectric power.

Japan is a comparative latecomer in the development of civilization, since cultural movements reached her after passing eastward from Central Asia and China. There are three sources of information about ancient Japan, namely archaeological evidence; Chinese written records, which are reliable but scanty; and Japanese mythology, which is voluminous but difficult to interpret, since the undoubted historical traces within it are hard to disentangle from the legendary material.

There are only a few evidences of Old Stone Age remains in Japan. The first major culture is dated as Mesolithic or Middle Stone Age in its earlier stages, beginning around 3000 B.C. This culture is known as the Jomon, from the Japanese word for "cord pattern" which distinguishes its hand-thrown pottery—that is, pottery not made on a wheel. The Jomon people used stone weapons and lived in sunken-pit dwellings of a kind which are also reported to have existed in early China. They did not practice agriculture but lived by gathering roots, nuts, and small game from the forests and shellfish from the shore. Large mounds of discarded shells are associated with their sites. These sites are most plentiful in the east and north of Japan, a probable indication that the Jomon people survived longer in these regions.

The next culture group appears much later, between 300 and 100 B.C. and is known as the Yayoi, from a site in Tokyo where the early discoveries were made, although in fact this culture was strongest in west Japan. They produced wheel-made pots and certainly practiced agriculture of quite an

[7]

advanced type, in irrigated rice fields after the Chinese pattern. They apparently used both bronze and iron together, and thus Japan cannot be said to have gone through a separate Bronze Age period. Presumably Japan, being on the edge of the Asian civilized area, received bronze metal techniques slowly and late, while iron, with its immense technical advantages for weapons and tools, moved more rapidly and caught up with bronze in Japan. Among the Yayoi archaeological remains are mirrors, bells, swords, and spears of bronze, the last being ceremonial weapons; but a few tools and actual weapons made of iron have also been found.

The Yayoi people still used pit dwellings and left shell mounds behind them; but in two respects they show a remarkable affinity with historical Japan, namely in their method of agriculture and in the thatched roofs over the primitive dwellings. These thatched roofs are clearly depicted in the designs on the large, ornamental bronze bells that are a distinctive feature of Yayoi culture.

About the middle of the third century A.D. the Tomb culture was superimposed upon, though it did not altogether replace, the Yayoi culture. The Tomb culture is marked by the building of stone burial chambers and huge earthen mounds, reaching 1,500 feet in length and 120 feet in height. These tombs and tumuli are similar to burial places in Korea and Northeast Asia and indicate further continental influence in addition to what must have come over to Japan in the earlier periods. The tombs are also indicative of a powerful aristocracy able to command large numbers of workers in their construction. Associated with these tombs are the well-known *haniwa* pottery figures of very hard light-brown or reddish clay representing men, houses, and animals, especially horses. Many of the men are depicted wearing elaborate armor and helmets, and carrying swords whose actual counterparts are known to have been of iron (see Plate 1). The greatest number of these tombs are found in the Yamato area, and some of the richest of these were almost certainly tombs of the early emperors of the historic imperial line. But the Yamato people do not begin in Yamato but farther west, and their movement is the first decisive episode traceable, though but faintly, in Japanese history.

The Chinese of the Han Dynasty, in their confident phase of military expansion, established a colony in Korea in 108 B.C., conquering a native dynasty that had already absorbed considerable Chinese influence. The Han Chinese thus became more closely aware of Japan, and the visit of a Japanese envoy to the Han court is recorded in A.D. 57. But it is in the Chinese records of the Wei Dynasty, a smaller state subsequent to the Han, that we first find some concrete details about Japan, which confirm the other sources and add facts not otherwise known. The *Wei chih* of about A.D. 292 (about the time when the Yayoi and Tomb cultures were overlapping) speaks of the Wa (dwarf) people of regions easily identified as Kyushu and West Japan. These people are said to have lived in one hundred "countries" or tribes, of whom thirty had contact with the Wei court. They are portrayed as having respect for law and as being careful to observe social differences, traits that have persisted in Japanese society. Some social distinctions were indicated by tattooing and other body marks. They are described, moreover, as being fond of liquor and as practicing agriculture, spinning, weaving, and fishing. The Chinese records state that the rulers are sometimes male and sometimes female, one powerful sovereign being a certain Queen Himeko or Pimiko, meaning "Daughter of the Sun." This alternation between female and male rulers may indicate a change from matriarchal to patriarchal society. Early Japan shows a number of instances of female rulers. Shamanism, or contact with the spirit world through mediums subject to trances, is known to have been a feature of ancient Japanese religion, and indeed of the early religion of East Asia as a whole. Notions that women are peculiarly subject to emotional states leading to trance may, in addition to a general matriarchal tradition, have made them seem especially desirable as priestess-sovereigns in Japan. Among these queens the Himeko mentioned in the Wei records seems to have been a particularly notable ruler toward the end of the third century A.D.

The Shinto legends, the third source of information about early Japan, represent a primal pair, Izanagi, the male god, and Izanami, his consort, standing on the rainbow bridge of Heaven and dipping a spear into the ocean beneath. Drops of water falling from the tip of the spear congealed to form the sacred islands of Japan. In another version the islands were produced from the union in marriage of the god and goddess. In any case they descended to live on the islands, and had children who were the gods and goddesses of the land. The last god to be born was the Fire God and his birth caused the death of Izanami. Izanagi went to seek her in the underworld but found that her body had already decayed. When he returned to the light of day, it was at the "Even-Pass-of-Hades" in Izumo, in the west part of Honshu, the main island, opposite Korea. He purified himself from the pollution of death by washing in a river in Hyuga in Kyushu, and various deities were then born from his person, Amaterasu the Sun Goddess from his left eye, Tsukiyomi the Moon Deity from his right eye, and Susanowo the Storm God from his nose. The Moon Deity plays no prominent role in the subsequent story, but the Sun Goddess and the Storm God, her brother and later her consort, become the most important figures in the Japanese pantheon.

The legends represent Susanowo as an unruly fellow, constantly making trouble. For instance, he broke the boundaries of his sister's rice paddies, a heinous crime in any agricultural community, especially one employing irrigation. He slew the piebald colt of Heaven, flayed it, and insolently threw its skin into the Weaving Hall where the Sun Goddess was working with her maidens. For these deliberate acts of lawlessness and ritual defilement (the blood on the horse skin was defiling), he was banished, some accounts say to the nether regions, others say to Izumo. In Izumo Susanowo, "His Swift Impetuous Male Augustness," rescued a maiden by slaying an eight-tailed dragon, having first made it drunk by providing eight vats of wine. In one of its tails he discovered a sword, which became part of the jewel-mirror-sword regalia of Japan. Meantime the Sun Goddess, having been mortally offended by her brother's actions, shut herself up in a cave. Men and gods, distressed by the sun's absence, tried to persuade her to come out, but in vain. At length one of the goddesses uncovered herself and performed an obscene dance on an upturned tub and all the denizens of Heaven laughed uproariously. The Sun Goddess, overcome with a woman's curiosity, put her head out of the cave to see what was happening. The sight of a mirror further intrigued her, and she was seized and brought out, so that once again all the world could rejoice in her light.

These tales reflect the primitive nature worship of a people with some humor and strong feelings, and they have many elements—such as the importance attached to sunshine (Amaterasu), storms and rainfall (Susanowo), eclipses (Amaterasu hiding in a cave), and fertility rites (the dance on the tub)—in common with similar cults all over the world.

Some Shinto legends, in addition to referring to such specific geographical locations as Izumo and Kyushu, also contain references to actual political and military events, thus giving valuable clues to history. Kyushu, an island lying to the south and west of the rest of Japan and also near Korea, would be the first place encountered by incomers from South China and Korea. Archaeological research in fact points to Kyushu as an early site of Japanese civilization; and this is confirmed in the legend which relates that the divine grandson of Amaterasu, Ninigi-no-mikoto, came down from Heaven onto a mountaintop in Kyushu. His great-grandson, in turn, Jimmu-tenno, led an expedition eastward along the south coast of the main island. This expedition slowly worked its way up the Inland Sea and its members established a domain in the Yamato region, which includes the Ise peninsula, today the site of the most sacred and revered shrines of Shinto (see Plate 8).

Section XLIV of the *Kojiki* (the "Record of Ancient Things"), the earliest written collection of the legends and dating from A.D. 712, represents this move as being the result of a definite decision.

> The Emperor Jimmu and his elder brother took counsel saying, "By dwelling in what place shall we most quietly carry on the government of the Empire? It were probably best to go east."

But the advance was not an undisputed one.

> When His Augustness Jimmu-tenno made his progress and reached the great cave of Osaka [not the modern Osaka], earth-spiders with tails, [namely] eighty braves or robber-chiefs were in the cave awaiting him. . . . He commanded that a banquet be bestowed on the eighty braves.[1]

[1] *Kojiki*, Sections XLIV and XLVIII, both passages in B. H. Chamberlain translation.

Eighty butlers, each armed with a sword, were appointed to wait on the braves, and when Jimmu-tenno gave the signal by starting to sing, the butlers set upon the braves and slew them.

This picturesque account may be transposed into something like history by reasonable conjecture as follows: warlike clans, headed by what ultimately became the imperial Yamato clan, deliberately decided to leave Kyushu about the first century A.D., in all probability in search of better agricultural land, and made their way gradually along the coast of the Inland Sea. This journey probably took more than one generation in time, for they met with resistance from the original inhabitants (earth-spiders equal pit dwellers). The ancient records call Jimmu-tenno (Divine-Warrior Emperor) the first *human* emperor of Japan, descended from divine emperor ancestors. This may be taken as a signal that "historical," individually recognizable events, such as a migration or invasion, have now begun to occur.

Dating in this whole early period is highly conjectural and does not become even moderately reliable until after A.D. 400. The traditional date in the *Kojiki* for the establishment of the throne in Yamato by Jimmu-tenno, at the end of the migration from Kyushu, is 660 B.C.; but this probably antedates the events by some seven to eight hundred years. The migration, it is conjectured, started in the first century A.D. and the imperial clan may have been established as rulers in the Yamato region by the third century or possibly the fourth.

When the position of the imperial clan was sufficiently stable, they began promulgating a version of the early legends which exalted the place of the Yamato ancestress, the Sun Goddess, over the Storm God ancestor of the Izumo clan or clans. For instance, Onamuji, an Izumo monarch or god, agreed to serve the Yamato dynasty if a palace or temple were built for him and he were suitably worshiped. His son, Kotoshironushi, supported the claims of Yamato and was greatly honored in Ise as a result. However, traces of the early importance of the Izumo region, geographically opposite the source of immigration and higher civilization in Korea, could not be effaced altogether even from the slanted Yamato records; witness the entitlement of Susanowo, the Izumo Storm God, to the regalia sword by his prowess, and the elaborate care taken in the records to prove him unworthy of leadership by recounting all his misdeeds and consequent banishment.

Notwithstanding the importance of Yamato, there is evidence that Izumo had a higher level of culture, for a hundred skilled workers in clay are said to have been brought from Izumo to Yamato by one Nomi-no-Sukune. He was the reputed inventor of the *haniwa* clay figures used to take the place of human sacrifices previously buried alive in a standing position at the funerals of the great.

The Yamato-Izumo rivalry may also be the reflection of a transition from matriarchy to patriarchy. If this is so, the interpretation would be somewhat as follows: patriarchy, as represented by the male god of Izumo, was becoming dominant in society over the whole country, but matriarchy (the female divinity of Yamato) was the older tradition and its followers were able to assert its seniority in the field of religion and sacred sovereignty. Heads of families were male figures; yet the headship of the nation was still entrusted from time to time to empresses up to the end of the Asuka Period in 710, but only rarely thereafter.

The whole process of recording and editing the legends indicates that long before A.D. 712, the date of publication of the *Kojiki*, and probably before 300, the approximate date of the Queen Himeko, of the Chinese records, the Yamato clan leader had become the dominant figure in Japan. Starting simply as *primus inter pares*, he reached the point of claiming a paramount role, a position to be dignified by the name of emperor after the Chinese model. It is this family that has provided in unbroken line the emperors of Japan from the beginning of the Christian era to the present day. Even if allowance is made for freedom in marriage rules and recourse to adoption, this is a remarkable record of solidarity and respect for tradition, one that is unmatched in the history of any other modern nation.

The religion of Shinto, although based on quite primitive animism and nature worship, has survived strongly into modern times. Its strength seems to derive from the natural, almost unconscious way it embodies for the Japanese people their deep feelings for nature and their strong love of country.

Shinto has no founder, no inspired scriptures, no moral code. At first it did not even have a name. The word *shinto* means "the way of the gods" and is a term borrowed from the Chinese language long after the legends mentioned above had become a part of the native folk tradition. The same ideographs in Japanese can be read *kami-no-michi*, and the word *kami* can mean "gods" or simply "those above." To understand the term, Westerners must divest their minds of the ideas of holiness and otherness associated with God in Judeo-Christian tradition. *Kami* are of a simpler sort and their divinity is associated with anything remarkable or extraordinary in nature: a high mountain; an odd, lone tree; a venerable man; even a queer form of insect life—anything, in fact, to which the term "mana" or the Latin *numen* might be applied. An example of the feeling inspired by *kami* would be the sense of awe yet pleasurable thrill experienced by a child who, in climbing up through a sunlit wood, suddenly comes upon a dark cave in a rock overhung with fir trees.

These gods are worshiped before shrines without images in a simple ritual, with hand clapping and bowing. The gods' presence does produce awe in the worshiper, but Shinto on the whole is a sunny rather than a somber religion. Sir George Sansom refers to this fact in discussing the racial origins of the Japanese:

> It may be that, to wayworn tribes from arid regions of Korea and northern China or inhospitable Siberian plains, the genial climate of Japan, with its profusion of trees and flowering shrubs, its fertile soil, and its wealth of running streams, was so pleasing as to make upon them a profound impression,

stored up in the racial consciousness as a pervading sentiment of gratitude. Certainly their religion was, as Aston says, a religion of love and gratitude rather than of fear, and the purpose of their religious rites was to praise and thank as much as to placate and mollify their divinities. The very names given in their mythology to their country—the Land of Luxuriant Reed Plains, the Land of Fresh Rice Ears of a Thousand Autumns; and to their gods—the Princess Blossoming-like-the-Flowers-of-the-Trees, and Her Augustness Myriad-Looms-Luxuriant-Dragonfly-Island—testify to their strong sense of the beauty and richness of their environment.[2]

In accordance with the conception of *kami*, the notion of *tsumi*, crime or sin, in Shinto is connected with ritual impurity rather than with moral guilt. Ritual impurity or pollution is associated with blood, wounds, death, menstruation, sexual intercourse, and childbirth. The word *kega* signifies both "wound" and "defilement." Lustration or symbolic washing, including rinsing the mouth, is necessary before an act of worship can be performed. There are elements of taboo and animal fetishism in early Shinto which are strongly reminiscent of primitive religion in Africa and elsewhere. For example, a goddess in a birth hut thatched with cormorant feathers was spied upon by her husband as, at the moment of giving birth, she turned into her original shape, that of a crocodile. She was vexed at his behavior, but the pair nonetheless remained faithful to one another and exchanged love poems. The god's poem shines with the Japanese poetic pleasure in nature:

His Augustness Fire-subside said, "As for my younger sister, whom I took to sleep [with me] on the island where light the wild-duck, the birds of the offing, I shall not forget her till the end of my life."[3]

Such were the beliefs of the early Japanese. Their political center was firmly established by the third century A.D. or earlier in the fertile land of the Yamato region. The north of the main island was still in possession of the Ainu, but the central and western portions of Japan were controlled by that amalgamation of peoples we know as the Japanese. Their society consisted of a number of semi-independent clans, or *uji*, under the general leadership of the Yamato clan. Each *uji* claimed descent from a common ancestor, worshiped the god of the clan and was united under a clan chief. This aristocracy of chiefs, however, already had distinctions drawn within it. The *Nihongi*, a book of early chronicles dating from 720, or shortly after the *Kojiki*, distinguishes between the Omi of imperial and the Muraji of nonimperial descent. The Muraji in turn were divided into those who spoke of their descent from "heavenly deities" and others descended from "earthly deities." This last distinction is thought to refer in the former case to clans who joined the Yamato in conquest and in the latter to clans who were forced to submit.

There were also corporations, *be* (or *tomo*, "attendants"), which developed within or were attached to certain *uji*. These groups of workers

2 G. B. Sansom, *Japan, A Short Cultural History* (London: Cresset Press, 1946), pp. 46–7.
3 *Kojiki*, Section XLII, B. H. Chamberlain translation.

corresponded closely to the corporations of the late Roman Empire, such as the *navicularii* (seamen) or *pecuarii* (cattlemen), being in both instances hereditary in families but not related throughout the corporation by ties of blood. In early Japan there were *be* of carters, seamen, mountain wardens, and others. The heads of the corporations were ennobled and became important enough to rival the clan aristocracy. One reason for their importance was undoubtedly the fact that land was more plentiful than labor in early Japan and skilled workers of all kinds were in demand. Not only did the workers ply their trade but the corporation as a whole supported itself by working the land granted to it. Some *be* engaged in agriculture only, and the attachment of either an agricultural or an artisan *be* was of great benefit to the *uji* concerned and to its chief.

Several corporations were associated with the imperial clan and their heads became nobles of high rank. Among these were the great military groups, the Otomo (Great Attendants) and Mononobe (Corporation of Arms). Others attached to the emperor's house had religious functions, such as the Nakatomi (Medium Ministers), Urabe (Corporation of Diviners), and Imibe (Corporation of Abstainers). The original functions of the Imibe, as mentioned in the Chinese records, reveal more about the taboos of early Shinto. "They appoint a man whom they style 'mourning-keeper' [professional abstainer]. He is not allowed to comb his hair, to wash, to eat meat, or to approach women. When they are fortunate, they make him valuable presents; but if they fall ill or meet with disaster, they set it down to the mourning-keeper's failure to observe his vows and together they put him to death." [4]

Workers in certain specialized crafts could only be obtained from China and Korea, among them brocade weavers and scribes. Such skilled men were readily welcomed in Japan, and their leaders, along with refugee aristocrats fleeing the internal troubles of the mainland, seem to have been accepted without question into the ranks of the Japanese nobility. As Reischauer and Fairbank have pointed out,[5] a book of noble genealogies of 815 shows that over 33 percent of 1,182 families of the Yamato nobility were of foreign, that is, mainly of Korean, origin.

There are indications both in archaeology and legend of the existence of close ties and a significant two-way traffic between Korea and early Japan. Korean records support the connection, in rather a negative sense, when they mention twenty-five attacks by Japanese on the coasts of the kingdom of Silla from the first to the fifth century A.D. More specifically, the Japanese established a bridgehead on the south tip of the Korean peninsula at Mimana in 369 which they maintained in permanent occupation until 562. From this base a considerable Japanese force moved against the king of Koguryŏ in

<hr>

[4] James Murdoch, *A History of Japan* (New York: Frederick Ungar, rev. ed. 1964), Vol. I, pt. I, p. 40.

[5] Edwin O. Reischauer and John K. Fairbank, *East Asia, The Great Tradition* (Boston: Houghton Mifflin, 1958), p. 471.

391. The king of Paikche, the third of the kingdoms into which Korea was divided, was grateful for the help of the Japanese, who already had a reputation as warriors, against his Koguryö enemy. Sending gifts of peace in return for aid in war, he dispatched to the Japanese court some scholars trained in the Chinese classics, who brought with them a copy of the *Thousand Character Classic* and possibly also a copy of the *Analects* of Confucius.

Thus the Yamato kingdom by the fifth century or earlier was sufficiently centralized to exercise some control in Japan from the Kanto Plain to Kyushu and was interfering actively in the affairs of Korea, while itself deriving benefit from the Chinese culture that Korea had to offer. China was beginning to exert that strong cultural influence which all the countries on her periphery would sooner or later feel. The next stage of Japanese history was to see an extension of the Chinese influence to Japan in such a marked degree that all subsequent Japanese civilization would be affected by it.

3

The INTRODUCTION OF
Chinese Thought AND Culture

Asuka Period: 552–710

A boat from Korea pulled in to the shores of Japan and the gangplank was arranged with extra care. A large casket shrouded in yellow silk was ceremoniously borne off and placed with reverence on a palanquin carried on the shoulders of the highest retainers of the Soga clan. Accompanied by gongs, banners, ceremonial umbrellas, sutras (scriptures), and chanting priests in saffron robes, the image of Shaka Butsu (Buddha) in gold and copper was solemnly conducted on a long ceremonial progress to the capital of the day. It was in the Yamato region of central Japan, but we do not know exactly where, since it changed with each emperor's reign.

The official date for the introduction of Buddhism to Japan on this occasion is 552, when the image and accompanying cult objects were sent as a gift from the king of Paikche in Korea in the hope of receiving in return military aid against his enemy, at this juncture the king of Silla. Doubtless images, sutras, and priests had arrived via Korea before this date. Certainly Chinese Confucian classical texts and Korean scribes had been introduced into Japan, as we have seen, before 400. As a religion, as a system of thought, and as the bearer of elaborate and artistic ritual, Buddhism was immensely impressive to the Japanese. It came as the revelation of a depth and significance in life and death at which they had not previously guessed, and the spirits of many Japanese responded to the beauty and solemnity of its worship. But it arrived in Japan only after a long pilgrimage from the country of its origin.

Buddhism arose in northern India in the sixth century B.C. through the experiences of a prince, Sakyamuni (or Gautama). According to legend, Sakyamuni was carefully protected by his father and sheltered from the world during childhood and youth. He was happily married, but as a young man became suddenly acquainted with suffering. Leaving the palace on four successive days by different gates he met a beggar, then a sick man, then heard the cries of a woman in childbirth, and finally saw a corpse in a funeral procession. Affected by these encounters, he determined to find the cause and solution of suffering in the world. He gave up his former life, bade farewell to his family—an action more readily accepted in India than in the West—and joined a band of Hindu ascetics. Self-inflicted suffering brought him no nearer his goal, and leaving the ascetics he sat down under a bo tree to meditate. In spite of temptations, represented in Buddhist art by seductive maidens dancing around him, he persisted until at length enlightenment came to him and he saw through the *maya*, illusion, of this world and attained inner harmony. Perceiving that desire is what holds men down, leads them into suffering, and chains them to the constant wheel of rebirth, he obtained release and became Buddha, the Enlightened One.

Buddha then went on to bring the way of enlightenment to any who would listen and gathered round him a group of disciples. His most famous early sermon was preached in the deer park at Benares. In this and subsequent talks he developed the summary of his way in the Four Noble Truths and the Eightfold Path.

Thus Buddhism arose out of Hinduism and was intended in part as a reform of Hinduism. Buddha rejected, for instance, such well-known Hindu tenets as the predominant role of the Brahmins, the caste system, and the value of extreme asceticism (though not of spiritual discipline). Significantly, he neither required nor inculcated belief in a personal god nor indeed in any god at all.

This new faith, with its combination of deep philosophy and practical, ethical appeal, made great progress in India and reached its peak there in the third century b.c. under the great Emperor Asoka (ruled 273–232 b.c.). Asoka as a matter of policy sent missionaries with the trading caravans which went to other countries, and in particular is said to have sent his son to secure the conversion of Ceylon. But a change was taking place and a new form of Buddhism began to arise which did more to satisfy certain deep religious longings of its adherents. One essential point in this new form was its concept of the Bodhisattva, a merciful being who is ready to pass beyond this life into nirvana, the blessed state of release beyond desire or fear, but who turns back to the world of men vowing not to accept his own release till all have been saved. In the course of time these Bodhisattvas, such as Kuan Yin (Chinese) or Kannon (Japanese), became the hearers of prayer, were paid divine honors and virtually turned into gods. All are in essence incarnations of Buddha. It was this form of Buddhism, the Mahayana or Greater Vehicle, which was disseminated over most of East Asia, China, Korea, Japan, Mongolia, and Tibet, as opposed to the form nearer the original, Hinayana, the Lesser Vehicle. Hinayana, or as its followers prefer to call it, Theravada Buddhism (the way of the Elders), has remained strong in Ceylon, Burma, and certain parts of Southeast Asia. Both forms have died out in India, the country of their origin.

Buddhism reached China via central Asia and is said to have been introduced in the first century A.D. during the Han Dynasty. It did not develop markedly, however, until the fourth century in North China and was at that period also brought to the Korean peninsula. The religion spread rapidly in the sixth century because of the strong support accorded it by the Northern Wei and Liang dynasties in China, and this is the point which corresponds in date to the official introduction of Buddhism into Japan. Throughout China's history the Confucian literati tended to oppose Buddhism, often strongly though rarely violently, as a foreign importation inimical to the Chinese way of life. This may explain why Buddhism, though present, did not develop during the confident, centralized Han Dynasty, but did on the other hand burgeon strongly during the succeeding period of divided kingdoms. Then the disturbed conditions weakened the influence of the literati at the same time as they caused the general run of men to look for a source of comfort and strength beyond the present world.

In Japan the new faith was involved in controversy from the start. In the formal account given by the *Nihongi* of the first reception of the image presented by the king of Paikche, the emperor said: "The countenance of this Buddha which has been presented by the western frontier state is of a severe dignity such as we have never at all seen before. Ought it to be worshiped or not?"

The Soga family were for Buddhism, the Mononobe and Nakatomi, both of whom had official duties in the Shinto national cult, were against its introduction. A compromise was reached in which the Soga were given authority to set up Buddhist worship as a kind of religious experiment. A plague broke out, which was attributed to the wrath of the national deities, the new image was thrown into a canal and its temple burned. After further vicissitudes Buddhism was strongly supported by the new Emperor Yomei, son of a Soga mother, in 586. Unfortunately he died in the following year and the Soga were once again faced with a crisis. Their chieftain, Soga Umako, decided to appeal to force and won a definitive victory over the Mononobe at the battle of Shigisen in 587, upon which the Mononobe withdrew their opposition. Buddhism then became somewhat rapidly established among the aristocracy, to the point where there was actual rivalry in the erection of temples. It was to be some time, however, before the new faith was adopted to any marked degree by the mass of the people.

After a series of dynastic quarrels, Soga Umako, now very powerful, placed the Empress Suiko on the throne and arranged that her nephew, also of Soga descent and the second son of the former Emperor Yomei, should become regent. This young man of twenty-one, Prince Shotoku (Shotoku Taishi, 572–622), was on any showing one of the most remarkable figures of Japanese history. He was universally respected for his learning and beloved for his goodness. He was a devout Buddhist and studied under a monk from a region of Korea that had close connections with the strongly Buddhist Sui Dynasty in China. When the famous monastery and seminary of Horyuji was founded in 607, Prince Shotoku built within its grounds his residence and chapel, named Yumedono, the Hall of Dreams (see Plate 11). But he also had a Confucian tutor for the Chinese classics, which were becoming highly valued in Japan for their lessons in statecraft.

Prince Shotoku is notable above all for his policy of leading Japan to adopt Chinese models in the spheres of politics, religion, and art. This he accomplished in three ways: the promulgation of a constitution of seventeen articles; the adoption of "cap ranks" at the Japanese court; and the sending of the first official embassy to China in the name of the ruler of a united Japan in 607.

The constitution was not a constitution in the Western sense at all, but rather a collection of maxims to guide and exhort those engaged in government along ethical lines derived mainly from Confucian sources in China. It was a high-level policy directive couched in general terms. There is doubt as to whether Prince Shotoku was actually the author or whether it was written slightly later by some of his followers and piously ascribed to him. It certainly seems to represent his thinking and was probably issued to prepare the way for that reform in government and administration along Chinese lines which is known to have been favored by Prince Shotoku and which actually took place in 645, twenty-three years after his death, under the name of the Taika Reform. The aim of the constitution may be summed up by the words in Article XII: "In a country there are not two lords; the people have not two masters. The sovereign is the master of the people of the whole country." [1] In these parallel phrases so beloved by the classical authors, Prince Shotoku's party sought to move away from the traditional Japanese view of the Yamato leader as a paramount chief among chiefs and toward the Chinese bureaucratic pyramid with a sole ruler at the summit.

The institution of ranks at court, designated by different colors and materials in the ceremonial caps, was also intended to strengthen the central government. Apparently minor in itself, the new rule was a first, and perhaps cautious, attempt to substitute for the native Japanese pattern of hereditary aristocracy the Chinese system of officials appointed for merit, and therefore in theory able to be dismissed for demerit. The theory is estimable, but the Japanese reformers were never able to carry it fully into practice.

The third achievement of Prince Shotoku was more successful and indeed of prime importance for the future of Japan. The embassy to China organized in 607 was led by one Ono-no-Imoko, who carried a letter to the Sui emperor at Lo-yang which began: "The Emperor of the sunrise country writes to the Emperor of the sunset country." This phraseology, though impeccable in its style, was scarcely of a tone calculated to win friends at the Chinese court. A second visit, in which the humbler attitude of a vassal was adopted, proved more successful and the Japanese ambassador returned

---

[1] Murdoch, *A History of Japan*, Vol. I, pt. 1, p. 124.

with the Chinese books which it had been Prince Shotoku's object to secure, and more important, with assurance that an official relationship was now established between the two countries.

These first embassies were succeeded by some fourteen others, extending over two centuries—the last took place in 838—and included among their personnel officials, students, Buddhist priests and laymen, artists, craftsmen, and secretaries. Among the most distinguished of the latter-day visitors to China was Kibi-no-Mabi, who spent seventeen years at Ch'ang-an, the T'ang dynasty capital. He is said to have brought back from China the art of embroidery; the *biwa* or four-string lute; and the game of *go* or Chinese chess, favored by Japanese warriors as a training in military strategy. He is also supposed to have invented *kana*, the Japanese syllabary of simplified Chinese characters used for phonetic purposes only. He was one of the very few in Japanese history who came of common stock and rose to the highest rank by native ability, becoming Minister of the Left (principal minister) in 766.

It is evident that Prince Shotoku was important in his own person as the initiator of a deliberate policy of sinicization, or conforming to Chinese models. But he was also significant as a symbol of certain trends that were to reappear frequently in Japanese history. In the first place, as regent he exercised the effective rule but only indirectly, in the name of his aunt, the empress. Later the practice of having a titular ruler and an actual ruler became the common, almost standard, procedure. In many cases indeed the practice of indirect rule was carried further and the policy of the actual ruler was determined by a small and undefined group of advisers who remained in the background. Though they may have had no known or named leader, their consensus often was too powerful for the ruler to ignore. In the second place Prince Shotoku led the movement for the conscious introduction of new forms of religion, philosophy, art, and political organization into Japan. This custom of cultural and technological borrowing is recognized as a Japanese trait even by those who have no close acquaintance with Japanese history. But what is not so widely recognized is the distinctive manner in which the Japanese have always been able to assimilate borrowed material and make something of their very own out of it. They frequently succeed in improving upon the original. Buddhism itself provides a major example, for there the leadership in speculative thought and in the creative influence of the religion upon the arts gradually passed from China to Japan. The whole process took centuries because Buddhism was not easily grasped. In modern technology, Japanese mastery and advance has been much more rapid, but the principle of thorough assimilation and intelligent application is the same.

The Japanese who went in search of the new religion and the new arts could not fail to be immensely impressed with the magnificence of T'ang China. In A.D. 618 China entered upon a period in which she became the largest, best organized, and culturally most advanced nation in the world. (In Europe, at this time, the Western Roman Empire was in ruins and the Eastern half, though still great, was no rival to China. The great Islamic civilization was just about to come to birth.) The Japanese visitors must have been both delighted and overawed by the splendors of the T'ang capital at Ch'ang-an (the modern Sian in northwest China). They copied its city planning in the rectangular grid pattern of city streets when they came later to build their new capital at Heian (Kyoto). Nothing in their own experience had prepared them for the sight of the imperial processions, when the T'ang emperors made official tours to show the flag, accompanied by the court ladies, officials, army regiments, and wagon trains bearing tent pavilions, tapestries, silk hangings, furniture, porcelain dinner services, golden cups, and the infinite amount of paraphernalia used in Chinese court life. It is said the retinue took two or three days to pass a given point.

The Japanese were fortunate to be visiting China just before and during the T'ang Dynasty, for this was the period when China was most hospitable to foreigners and most open to new ideas. Armenians, Jews, Koreans, Arabs, men from Central Asia, and Nestorian Christians of the Asian tradition which traces its spiritual ancestry back to Christ's disciple, Thomas—all were to be found in the streets of Ch'ang-an. What the Japanese took home with them from this stimulating and enlarging experience were two basic systems of thought, both by now thoroughly Chinese, namely Confucianism and Buddhism. Japan had earlier received Chinese Buddhism by way of Korea; now she was receiving greater knowledge of the religion and its various sects directly from China. The influence of Confucianism, though less spectacular than that of Buddhism, had a marked and lasting effect upon Japanese political thought and institutions.

These systems of thought did not come to Japan alone, for they brought with them new ways, a new life style, and a degree of sophistication unknown hitherto in Japan. They were accompanied by a number of arts and crafts. Carvers of wood, workers in lacquer, artists skilled in painting on silk and on paper, weavers of brocade, potters, and bronze casters of remarkable proficiency all began to migrate from Korea and China to satisfy the new religious and artistic demands of the Japanese aristocracy. These artists and craftsmen, some prominent, some anonymous and of humble origin, settled down, intermarried with Japanese, and in time contributed an important creative strain to Japanese life. This was eagerly taken up and developed by the Japanese themselves, who were as a people more than usually sensitive to the beauty at this time being created at the centers of Chinese civilization.

But the group of craftsmen most far-reaching in their influence on the future were the writers and scribes. A religion as developed and as philosophical as Buddhism depended to a much greater degree than the native Shinto upon the written word for its transmission and propagation (see Plate 13). The first scribes were foreigners, but soon the Japanese themselves were copying out the sutras destined for the libraries in the new temples. Before long, even the aristocrats were toiling over the difficult script, for it became a social hallmark at court to be able to read and write Chinese. At once the value of a written script became evident in fields other than the religious. The new possibility of keeping accurate and permanent records, particularly tax records, led in turn to an increase of power and of centralization in the government.

Meanwhile in the political arena the power of the Soga, which had been instrumental in placing Prince Shotoku in a position to influence affairs, continued unabated. Some twenty years after the prince died in 622 this power was being exercised in an obnoxious and overbearing manner by Soga Emishi and his son, Soga Iruka. There was more than a suspicion that they were attempting to arrogate the powers of the emperor to themselves. Opposition gathered in 644 under the leadership of Prince Naka-no-Oye (later the Emperor Tenchi, 661–71), a discontented Soga clansman, and the great Kamatari, the head of the Nakatomi family. Soga Iruka was killed at court, reportedly in the very presence of the Empress, and Soga Emishi was later executed. Effective power passed to Prince Naka-no-Oye, although he did not become emperor until later. He is said to have met Nakatomi Kamatari through an ancient equivalent of the game of soccer, and the two are known to have attended lectures by the same Confucian teacher and to have plotted the overthrow of the Soga in a garden under cover of discussion of the Confucian classics. Kamatari became the confidential adviser to the Prince and actually the chief power in the land. He was known by the sobriquet of Kuromaku, "Black Curtain," a theatrical phrase meaning "stage prompter." Later he was given a new family name, Fujiwara (wisteria), in remembrance of the wisteria garden where the plotting took place. He was thus the founder of the great Fujiwara family which was to dominate Japanese court life for centuries, without a rival in controlling the national destiny from 857 to 1160, and still influential in the imperial circle right up to the nineteenth century, even though power had passed to the Shogunate.

As soon as the anti-Soga coup had been successfully carried out, Kamatari and Prince Naka-no-Oye proceeded to put through the Taika Reform of 645. The name means "great change" or "great reform" and its provisions were in fact definitive for all subsequent Japanese history. Here a thoroughgoing attempt was made to impose upon Japan a governmental system similar to the bureaucratic administration of China, which the Japanese rightly judged had contributed greatly to China's centralized authority and manifest cultural success. All the land of Japan was declared to belong to the emperor. The great land-owning nobles continued to live on their existing territory, but this was technically at the emperor's pleasure. In return they were given court rank and offices as provincial or lesser governors, or as other officials of the emperor, to exercise administrative functions and to receive emoluments corresponding to their rank and office.

The main provisions of the reform edict were four in number:

Article I abolished private holdings of land and of corporations of agricultural workers.

Article II set up the "Inner Provinces" or metropolitan region, with appointment of the necessary officials, and provided for an improved system of communications, roads, and bridges with the outer provinces.

Article III provided for registers of the population for the purpose of allotting rice land to farmers at so much land per "mouth" in the family, for assessment of taxes, and for the appointment of local headmen.

Article IV did away with the old taxes and introduced a new system of taxation. This included taxes on agricultural produce, on textiles, a tax in lieu of corvée or compulsory labor (although in certain instances the corvée was retained), and military service. Those called up for military service were exempt from other taxes, but the soldier went at his own expense and the service was often arduous.

The working of the new tax structure, in common with other features of the reform, was only gradually evolved and was probably not applied fully and equally in all parts of the country. Further regulations and modifications were made at intervals over the next half century, culminating in the Taiho Code of 702. The Taiho Code provided Japan with what she had never previously possessed, a code of law and a formal system of government administration. The Code of 702 was actually a revision of law codes of a Chinese type issued earlier and an adaptation to Japanese conditions of the T'ang administrative system.

The organization of the government under the Taiho Code may be summarized as follows:

1. The central government was in two parts, the Department of Worship (Jingi-kan) taking precedence over the Department of State (Dajo-kan).

2. The Department of Worship took charge of the great national religious ceremonies, of the upkeep of shrines and the recording of oracles. Its sphere was Shinto, not Buddhism.

3. The Department of State was headed by the Great Council of State, presided over by the chancellor (*dajo-daijin*), and consisting of four great councillors (*dainagon*) and three lesser councillors (*shonagon*). The Great Council was the ultimate authority to advise the emperor on all civil and military affairs of state. Routine administration was divided up among the various ministries and officials below.

4. Under the chancellor was the minister of the Left (*sadaijin*), the senior minister in charge of all branches of administration.

5. His deputy and junior minister was the minister of the Right (*udaijin*).

6. Four ministries were associated with the office of the Left, viz., the Ministry of the Center, the official channel from the Throne to the lower levels of administration; the Ministry of Ceremonial; the Ministry of Civil Affairs; and the Ministry of People's Affairs.

7. The four ministries associated with the office of the Right were the

Ministry of Military Affairs; the Ministry of Justice; the Ministry of the Treasury; and the Ministry of the Imperial Household.

The fact that this scheme was closely modeled on the T'ang system goes far to explain a circumstance curious to Western eyes, namely that the ministries of the Right, concerned with war, justice, finance, and the imperial household, were subordinated to the Ministries dealing with ceremonial and civil matters. As a matter of record, military and judicial affairs emerged as of paramount importance under the Kamakura Shogunate, in the twelfth and following centuries. In the seventh and eighth centuries, however, neither Japan as a whole nor the imperial house appeared to feel threatened by war, nor was there open military rivalry between the clans. The reformers were therefore able, in their enthusiasm for things Chinese, to institute a system which was surprisingly nonmilitary in its orientation. The Taiho Code also placed much emphasis on the promotion and regulation of court life and comparatively little on the affairs of the common people. Of the eight ministries, only half—namely the ministries of People's Affairs, Military Affairs, Justice, and the Treasury—were concerned with the nation as a whole. The Ministry of Civil Affairs, which might seem to be concerned with the people, in fact dealt with such miscellaneous and mainly court matters as the marriage and succession of high officials, omens, funerals, reception of foreign envoys, music, and the registration of Buddhist temples and monks. The nature and extent of the government's interest in the life of the common man may be judged from the list of duties of the Ministry of People's Affairs. These included the census, forced labor and exemption therefrom; relief of the distressed; maintenance of bridges, roads, and harbors; collection of taxes; and management of granaries and land tax in grain. The Treasury had charge of the public accounts, weights and measures, commodity prices, the mint, and the lacquer, weaving, and other industries. It must be borne in mind that this was an ideal scheme; thus when "the maintenance of bridges, roads, and harbors" is mentioned, improvement in communications may in fact have been very limited.

Although Japan was indebted to China for the general shape of its political structure, there were nevertheless some very significant differences between the systems of the two countries. First, the primacy of the Department of Worship was a distinctly Japanese innovation, apparently designed to preserve the sacred functions of the emperor intact. No forfeiting of the "mandate of Heaven" by unworthy rulers and the consequent right of the people to revolt was even envisaged. (An interesting linguistic point preserves clearly early Japanese attitudes on the importance of the priest-king nature of the emperor's office: the word for "religious affairs," *matsurigoto*, is also the word for "government.") The second, and greatest, difference lies in the methods of recruitment and appointment of officials. In China the T'ang emperors had improved and regularized a system begun under the Han of entrance to the bureaucracy by public, competitive examination, which opened the way for a very gradual but significant infiltration of fresh talent from the non-gentry classes into the government service. In Japan examinations were of little importance. Exemption from them was granted to sons of noble families and the whole official system as constituted tended merely to perpetuate the power of the former clan and aristocratic leaders with little change. An edict of 682 openly stated that the considerations in selecting men for office were to be birth, character, and capacity, in that order. Third, the matter of exemption from the taxes set up in the Taika Reform and provided for in the Taiho Code presented peculiar difficulties in Japan and was to have most unfortunate results later on. Stated simply, the problem was that tax exemption was granted to estates held either by government officials or by religious foundations, mainly Buddhist temples and monasteries. Since both these categories were numerous and tended to increase, the effective tax base of the country was constantly being narrowed and the burden of raising revenue tended to fall on fewer and fewer persons. In effect the hardship fell on those least able to pay, since such burdens are always shifted downward onto the peasants.

There is evidence that the census at the time of the Taika Reform was meticulously compiled and the distribution of land at so much per person or "mouth" made with reasonable fairness. But the situation altered, changes in ownership came about, tax exemptions were granted, and the redistribution of land at intervals, as originally planned, proved too difficult to carry through. Even in China little was done to redistribute land to maintain correspondence with family and population changes.

Nevertheless the Taika Reform and Taiho Code marked a clear stage of advance in the Japanese political field. In theory the authority of the emperor was increased and in practice some centralization and strengthening of governmental power took place. Without this Japan could not have undertaken her course of future development as effectively as she did.

4

THE STIMULATING EFFECT
OF CHINESE CULTURE

Nara Period: 710–794

In 710 the capital of Japan was fixed for the first time and located at Nara in the fertile plain area at the base of the Ise Peninsula and near the east end of the Inland Sea. In the early days of the Yamato kingdom there had been no single capital. Each successive emperor had simply been accustomed to conduct the government from his own residential estate, both for convenience and in order to avoid the ritual pollution attaching to the house of his dead predecessor, according to Shinto belief. Buddhist and Confucian doctrine now rendered the moving of the palace site unnecessary, and the elaboration of court life and religious architecture made it virtually impossible. This settlement of the center of government ushered in the Nara Period (710–794).[1] At this time the engrafted shoots of Chinese culture and especially of Buddhism began to flower and soon to bring forth fruit which was truly indigenous and Japanese in nature.

Buddhism continued to grow and to attract to its ranks an increasing number of devotees, mainly from the upper ranks of society. Genuine religious motives were at times mixed with political ambitions, for the fortunes of Buddhism did at first ebb and flow with the fortunes of such families as the Soga. But soon the new religion was so thoroughly established that it was no longer dependent on the favor of one or two clans. The court was generally a staunch supporter of Buddhism, and the Taika reformers, following Prince Shotoku, took the same line. There is no doubt that the profundity, comprehensive orderliness, and moral challenge of this religion, as well as its artistic and ritual accompaniments, held an attraction, even a

---

[1] It should be noted that Japanese chronology differs from that of China and most other countries in being marked not by dynasties (for there is strictly but one dynasty or ruling family) but by periods, whose names are generally the names of the geographical seats of power, *e.g.* Nara, Kamakura, Edo.

fascination, for the Japanese. In the long run Buddhism exercised a refining and civilizing effect upon the rude warriors of early Japan. It revealed to them the power of gentleness and opened up perspectives on the problems of life, death, and suffering in ways that Shinto was quite incapable of doing.

A concrete example of this kind of influence may be seen in the image of Miroku Bosatsu, the Buddha who is to come, in the Chuguji Nunnery in Nara, dating from the eighth century. This serene figure has a simple, dignified pose—erect but not stiff, calm and self-possessed. His unseeing eyes show him to be absorbed in meditation, yet fully awake and aware. The facial expression, the archaic smile, the middle finger extended to the chin suggesting the formation of an idea in the mind, all give an impression of tenderness and gentleness, of quiet inward bliss. When the figure was first seen, the effect on peasants and nobles alike must have been overwhelming.

One obvious measure of the growing influence of Buddhism is the rise in the number of monasteries, monks, and nuns. By 624, two years after the death of Prince Shotoku, and just over seventy years from the official introduction of Buddhism, Japan had 46 monasteries, 816 monks, and 569 nuns. By 692 the 46 monasteries had become 545, and the lavish donations of the court tended to make Buddhism almost the state religion. It never in fact attained that status in any official way; the great Shinto court ceremonies were always maintained, and emperors and nobles supported both Shinto and Buddhist institutions; but the rapid spread and firm hold of Buddhism are well attested.

The sense of exclusiveness and the necessity of deliberate choice that cause Western man to adhere to one religion only are notably absent in East Asia. Neither the Chinese nor the Japanese people have difficulty in regulating their lives by the ideas of more than one faith at the same time. An official might therefore attend a national festival such as the New Year ceremonies, conducted according to Shinto rites, but have a Buddhist service celebrated for the repose of his mother's soul, and apply Confucian canons to his government administration, without the least sense of inner contradiction.

Although the ennobling effect of Buddhism has been mentioned, it is hardly surprising that there is also evidence of the element of superstition in the spread of the new faith. For instance, one of the earliest known examples of printing in the world is to be seen in the distribution by the Empress Suiko of 100,000 copies of a Buddhist charm to ward off disease during an epidemic in the year 770.[2] This incidentally provides an excellent

[2] The discovery of a still earlier example of printing took place on October 14, 1966, in the stonework of a Buddhist pagoda in the Temple of Pulguksa at Kyongju in South Korea, the ancient capital of the kingdom of Silla. The material was the twenty-foot scroll of a sutra, printed from twelve woodblocks and translated from Sanskrit into Chinese by Mi T'o-hsien, who is known to have lived in the T'ang capital of Ch'ang-an between 680 and 704 A.D. The date of the printing must therefore fall between 680 and 751, the date of the building of the temple.

historical example of the kind of emergency circumstances that favored both the expansion of Buddhism and the wider use of the new technology of printing, since that was the only conceivable method of reproducing the enormous number of 100,000 examples of a charm in time to counter the disaster of an epidemic.

The art of writing was called to the aid of Shinto as well as of Buddhism. At the very beginning of the Nara period the ancient Shinto legends were written down in the *Kojiki* (712) and the *Nihongi* or *Nihonshoki* ("Chronicles of Japan," 720), to which reference has already been made. These works show clearly the combination of Chinese with native elements, the matter being purely Japanese but the form mixed.

The *Kojiki* employs Chinese characters phonetically to represent the sounds of the Japanese language, while the *Nihongi* uses Chinese characters in the Chinese language. The former, it may be imagined, results in a text which is extremely difficult to read. (The simplified *kana* syllabary does not appear until the ninth century.) Painstaking work by the great scholar of late Tokugawa times, Motoori Norinaga (1730–1801), made the text and its meaning more readily available to modern scholars. The language of these works is copied from the rather high-flown style of the Chinese dynastic histories, for they were deliberately written to exalt the prestige of the imperial house. In addition to tracing the descent of the emperors from the Sun Goddess, they supplied elaborate genealogies to strengthen the claims of the landholders of noble family and those who had acquired office under the Taika Reform.

A different type of literature from this same period is represented by the famous collection of poems called the *Manyoshu* ("Collection of a Myriad Leaves"), probably compiled by Tachibana no Moroye (fl. 738–756), a high official who was a protégé of the Fujiwara. The poems, emanating from the court aristocracy from the earliest times to the year 760, deal with many topics such as love of Japan (No. 2), Nature and Man (No. 13), the sadness of banishment (No. 23), and a mallard duck waking (No. 1744). A great number are poems of love, on an absent husband (No. 59), proposal to a maiden (No. 1726), "How can I live alone?" (No. 1728), "to his wife" (No. 1782), and one of the more moving, "She dwells so deep in me" (No. 1792). Already at this early stage there is evident the preference for extremely short, lapidary statement of a theme and the evocation of a mood by a swift parallel from Nature that is to distinguish all subsequent Japanese poetry. Noticeably absent from Japanese, as from Chinese, verse is the grand epic style. Grandeur in language and theme is to be found in the military prose romances such as the *Taiheiki*, but not in poetry, either early or late.

The following examples, quoted in full, will give some idea of the nature of the *Manyoshu* poems.

Had he been at home, he would have slept
Upon his dear wife's arm;
Here he lies dead, unhappy man,
On his journey, grass for pillow.[3]

—Prince Shotoku, sixth/seventh century

YEARNING FOR THE EMPEROR TENJI

While, waiting for you,
My heart is filled with longing,
The autumn wind blows—
As if it were you—
Swaying the bamboo blinds of my door.

—Princess Nukada, latter half of seventh century

The above are poems by famous figures at court, but the two following anonymous poems reflect the simpler life of the people. The first sounds as if it might have come from the *Greek Anthology* or Catullus, but perhaps this is just because the theme is universal.

(UNTITLED)

The vivid smile of my sweetheart
That shone in the bright lamplight,
Ever haunts my eyes.

DIALOGUE POEM

Where others' husbands ride on horseback
Along the Yamashiro road,
You, my husband, trudge on foot.

Every time I see you there I weep,
To think of it my heart aches.

My husband, take on your back
My shining mirror, my mother's keepsake,
Together with the scarf thin as the dragon-fly's wing,
And barter them for a horse,
I pray you, my husband.

Envoys

Deep is the ford of the Izumi.
Your travelling clothes, I fear,
Will be drenched, my husband.

What worth to me my shining mirror,
When I see you, my husband,
Trudging on your weary way!

---

[3] "Grass for pillow" henceforth is a literary phrase meaning "on a journey away from home."

By her husband
If I get a horse, my beloved,
You must go on foot;
Though we tread the rocks,
Let's walk, the two of us, together.[4]

The religion of Buddhism is the dominant factor in the history of the whole Nara period, not only in the realms of religion and culture but also in those of economics and politics. The reign of the Emperor Shomu, a zealous supporter of Buddhism, includes the Tempyo Period (729–748), famous in art history, when some of the most renowned and graceful of Buddhist statuary in wood and metal was executed. By the time of Shomu's reign the faith was sufficiently established and self-confident to reach some accommodation with the native Shinto belief. The Buddhist monk Gyogi (670–749) taught that the Shinto divinities were avatars or manifestations of Buddha, thus laying the foundation of what was to become in the twelfth century Ryobu Shinto (Dual Shinto). On this theory Amaterasu, the Sun Goddess, was worshiped as Vairocana, the great cosmic Buddhist deity who ruled over a world of light.

Gyogi also devoted himself to collecting alms for the erection of a huge bronze statue of Buddha as Vairocana, the Daibutsu, "Great Buddha," of Nara. This image was erected by the Emperor Shomu with Gyogi's help, in fulfillment of a vow made by him when a severe epidemic of smallpox, which had started in Korea, spread to Japan, seriously threatening the court and the inhabitants of Nara in 735. The casting of the image was an immense and costly effort for a country of Japan's resources, as it was fifty-three feet high, weighed over 500 tons, and was gilded with 500 pounds of gold. The head and neck, over twelve feet high, were cast in one piece. After seven unsuccessful attempts the casting was finally accomplished and the image dedicated in 752 in the vast hall of the Todaiji Temple amid great splendor and enthusiasm. Four years later some of the ritual objects used at the dedication ceremony were laid up in the Shosoin, a treasury made of large wooden logs, that still survives with its contents intact. This remarkable treasury containing also personal belongings of the Emperor Shomu was erected and given to the Todaiji by the Emperor's widow. Its contents include weapons, pictures, musical instruments, and land and population registers of Japanese origin, as well as pottery and metal work from China, Central Asia, and possibly Persia.

It was also during Shomu's reign that the Chinese monk Ganjin arrived in Nara after five unsuccessful attempts to reach the country and established the first *kaidan* or ordination platform in Japan. His was the Ritsu (San-

---

[4] These translations are taken from *The Manyoshu, The Nippon Gakujutsu Shinkokai Translation of 1,000 Poems* (New York: Columbia University Press, 1965), Nos. 20 (III.415), 29 (IV.488), 944 (XI.2642), and 871–74 (XXIII.3314–17). The *Manyoshu* reference numbers are in parentheses.

skrit, Vinaya) sect, and this sect with five others formed the group known as the Nara sects, as distinct from other Buddhist sects introduced at later periods.

Just prior to the Nara Period the Horyuji (see Plate 10), the temple already mentioned in connection with Prince Shotoku, was rebuilt. It had been destroyed by fire and was reconstructed in 708 in the same style as the original of 607. The Kondo, or Golden Hall, of this temple is a massive but beautifully proportioned structure representing the best of T'ang architecture, and is probably the oldest existing wooden building in the world. The Horyuji, Todaiji, and Kofukuji temples at Nara (the last associated with the Fujiwara family) and the great temples of Kyoto, founded in the next period, the Heian, all contain a number of common features setting the standards for temple architecture as required by the elaborate cult of Mahayana Buddhism, features that are impressive still and must at the time have had an awesome effect upon the Japanese worshippers. These include, first, the great worship hall with an immense roof expressing majesty and solemnity, high and spacious within, yet yielding a suitably dim vision of the great image of the deity. The image combines the remoteness of calm contemplation with the nearness of compassionate concern in a manner that only the Buddhist master-craftsmen have been able to convey. Leading up to the great hall is the ceremonial gateway with its guardian deities, while to one side or to the rear are the dwellings of the monks. An essential feature is the library, for the scriptures of Buddhism are not one book but many. There are storehouses, such as the Shosoin, for the temple treasures, and many additions made in later years, schoolrooms, offices, gardens, and guest chambers, usually laid out and maintained with order and precision. The arrangements show many similarities to European medieval monasteries. Often but not invariably there is a pagoda, a monument which has no functional use but which serves, with its images in niches and its vertical lines broken by delicate roofs and topped by Buddhist symbols at the peak, to focus the attention of the worshipper on the transcendental or heavenly aspects of the faith. (See Plate 12).

It is obvious then, on the architectural evidence alone, that the emerging centralized government in the person of the emperor and his court spent large sums of money during the Nara Period on the endowment of the Buddhist religion and its priesthood. This fact provoked considerable opposition on the grounds that the Buddhist clergy were becoming too powerful and exercising an altogether excessive influence over the emperors and over what could now begin to be dignified by the name of national policy. At one time, no fewer than 116 priestly exorcists were attached to the court. One Nara temple alone possessed forty-six manors with 5,000 acres of the best land, tax free. The temple domains tended constantly to increase because peasants, to escape taxes, preferred to "commend" their land to a temple and pay rent, since the rent was far less than the taxes.

A reaction against the monasteries was precipitated in the 760's by the misconduct of a Buddhist monk, Dokyo, who managed to ingratiate himself with the Empress Koken by his flattering interpretations of dreams and portents. Despite the efforts of the Fujiwara family to dislodge him, Dokyo became her confidant, her chancellor, and perhaps her lover. He even aspired to be emperor, but the Empress was unwilling to take the ultimate step of legitimating his claims, and at her death in 770 he immediately fell from favor.

The Council of State read the warning signs in this incident. They had watched Buddhist power increase at court through the reigns of four empresses, and they now refused to allow another woman to ascend the throne, a precedent followed almost undeviatingly through the remainder of Japanese history. Koken, also known as Shotoku, was thus the last empress with the exception of two unimportant female rulers in the seventeenth century. The succession passed in 781 to Kammu (781–806), who proved to be a strong emperor.

Three years after Kammu's ascent to the throne, the decision was taken to move the capital to Nagaoka, a short distance to the north, this time not for reasons of ritual purity but, in part at least, to remove the court from the baleful influence of the great monasteries at Nara. Such a move probably took considerable courage, since it involved braving the unknown dangers of the wrath of the Lord Buddha, which were doubtless stressed by those with vested interests in the old capital. The Emperor Kammu, an able statesman, was well qualified to undertake the task.

The capital remained at Nagaoka, for only a decade. The Emperor's brother was involved in the murder of the official in charge of the building, was banished, and died of starvation in exile. It was felt that his spirit was haunting the new capital, so Kammu, after careful consultation with the geomancers (experts in the study of the influence of topography on the spirit world), chose a new site, that of modern Kyoto, and settled there in 794. Kyoto was to remain henceforth the seat of the emperor until 1868, when the transfer of the palace to Tokyo coincided with the decision to modernize Japan.

The new capital bore a grand name and had a grand plan. Called Heiankyo, Capital of Eternal Tranquillity, it was laid out in a grid design, as Nara had been, along the lines of the magnificent contemporary capital of T'ang China, Ch'ang-an. But Japan had nothing like China's resources and in fact not all of the ground within the planned rectangle of the city was taken up or built upon. And yet the very considerable effort made was one more concrete sign that Japan meant seriously to follow out in her own way the course of Chinese civilization. She planned to adopt wherever possible a civilian and bureaucratic rather than a military and tribal approach to life and government.

5

The JAPANESE PATTERN

Early Heian Period: 794–857
Late Heian or Fujiwara Period: 858–1158

In the Heian Period Japan clearly came of age. The shorter Early Heian Period is distinguished by the reduction of new territory in the east and north to central control and by new developments in Buddhism. The longer Late Heian Period is noted for the dominance of the great Fujiwara family and for an unusual elegance of taste in the life of the court, accompanied by achievements in prose literature fit to rank with the best that has been produced anywhere in the world. Yet at the same time, outside court circles, profound changes took place in the Japanese countryside which shifted the basis of power to a new warrior class.

At the outset of the Heian Period the Emperor Kammu was compelled to devote attention not only to the founding of two new capitals in succession but also to some distant but pressing problems created by the movement of the Ainu people in the north of Japan. The good rice lands of the Kanto Plain had been gradually settled by the more adventurous Japanese pushing east and then north. They had to farm with one hand and fight with the other, for their advance was disputed by the Ainu, who had held this land since Neolithic times. Kept at a keen edge by constant practice, the prowess of the men of the east was celebrated in early Japan, and they were frequently enlisted for the fourth to sixth century wars in Korea in which Japanese took part. Although there was Ainu resistance, many of these people coexisted peacefully with the incomers. Some of the more warlike Ainu in the far north, aided by Japanese who were not willing to submit to central government control, started a rebellion in 776 and attacked the frontier town of Taga, near the modern Sendai. Raids and counterraids continued, usually ending in ignominious defeat for the government forces. The militia system supplied soldiers from the central rather than the frontier regions, men of little skill and low morale, and the commanders from Heian were more ornamental than useful as generals. The pervading orientation of the Chinese type of government adopted under the Taika Reform did not foster the fighting spirit in either the troops or their officers. In 783 Kammu reprimanded the commanders publicly and instituted a new campaign. At length a fully competent deputy commander, Sakanouye Tamura Maro, was found. He achieved brilliant successes in 795 and again between 800 and 803, when he had full command. Garrison strongholds were built in the extreme north at Izawa and Shiba, and Tamura Maro was rewarded by being granted the title of *sei-i tai-shogun*, barbarian-subduing generalissimo. He was thus the first holder of a title that was to be the most coveted among military men for the next ten centuries.

At about the same time, in 805 and 806, some twelve years after the establishment of Heian, a twin event occurred which was to be of great significance in the development of Buddhism in Japan, though it was not to free the new capital from the political tensions that religion had brought to the old one at Nara. In those years two prominent scholar-monks, Saicho and Kukai, each at the height of his powers, returned to Japan from a period of study in China.

Saicho (later granted the honorific title of Dengyo Daishi) returned to his former settlement on Mount Hiei to the northeast of Heian. His monastery, Enryakuji, founded before Heian was built, enjoyed great prestige because it served to protect the capital from malign influences coming from the Demon Entrance, the unlucky direction of the northeast. Moreover certain Shinto deities were worshiped as mountain gods. Saicho, anxious not to offend the Shinto faith, particularly in the home region of Yamato where it was strongest, paid reverence to one of these deities as Sanno, King of the Mountain. Thus Indian Buddhism, Japanese Shinto, and Chinese geomancy all had a part in the spiritual protection his monastery offered the capital. Saicho on his return from China brought the new doctrine of the Tendai sect to Japan. The word *tendai* means "heavenly platform," and the reference is to a platform for ordination. The new sect gained an important advantage when the emperor granted it the right to ordain Buddhist priests on a par with the older Nara sects. Tendai favored mountain retreats for their value as an aid to the contemplative life. Its doctrine was comprehensive and marked by a certain practical quality congenial to both Chinese and Japanese minds, as opposed to the extreme flights of speculation to be found in the Buddhism native to India. For example, it conceived of the rewards of paradise and the punishments of hell in a definite way, in contrast to the Buddhist emphasis on the difficult concept of nirvana, release into nonbeing. The sect flourished exceedingly, for in later years there were some 3,000 temples, small chapels, and monasteries scattered over the Mount Hiei range.

The other returning monk, Kukai (or Kobo Daishi), went to Mount Koya in the Yamato region, some distance southeast of the capital, and there introduced the Japanese form of another important sect, the Shingon or True Word. The title implies a gnostic idea of knowledge within knowledge, the True Word being the special possession of this sect. Later development took place, as might be expected, in two directions, high philosophical refinement of esoteric doctrine and lower popular belief in special charms or mantras. This sect also became powerful, and serious rivalries grew up between the two, often disturbing the peace of the realm. The monasteries on Mount Hiei in particular frequently became a threat to the tranquillity of the capital. A division between the Mount Hiei monasteries and a branch of the same sect at Miidera on Lake Biwa led in 891 to the recruiting by each side of guards, in reality little more than bullies or strong-arm men, a sinister development in the peaceful religion of Buddhism. A later emperor, Go-Shirakawa, once sadly remarked, "There are three things which I cannot control, the fall of the dice, the flow of the River Kamo, and the turbulent monks of Mount Hiei."

Most of the Heian Period was dominated by the great Fujiwara family. Their influence began even before the location of the capital at Nara, with Fujiwara Kamatari, founder of the line and architect of the Taika Reform. His son, Fubito, with the aid of a committee, was responsible for the promulgation of the Taiho Code in 702. Fubito's four sons died in 737 in an epidemic of smallpox but not before they had become the progenitors of the four main branches of the family. In course of time and not without internal disputes, the Hokke branch from the north emerged as the leaders of the Fujiwara, who now began to rise to a position of supremacy which eclipsed all other clans. They were able to do this first of all by their control of land, the perennial basis of political power in Japan, as more and more small landowners "commended" plots of land to the Fujiwara in order to enjoy their protection. But the primary means used by the Fujiwara to maintain their political dominance was one which the Soga had used to a lesser degree before them, namely constant intermarriage with the imperial house. The Fujiwara arranged for their daughters, wherever possible, to become the wives or concubines of the successive emperors. Since a Fujiwara was thus usually the father-in-law of the reigning sovereign, he was able, whether officially or unofficially, to exert an enormous influence upon affairs. "The real power of the Fujiwara was attained," in one of Sansom's lapidary phrases, "not by usurping but by protecting the throne."

The point of time generally reckoned as the beginning of the unquestioned supremacy of the Fujiwara is the year 858, when Fujiwara Yoshifusa became *sessho*, regent, for the nine-year-old Emperor Seiwa. He was the first regent not of imperial blood and he remained in virtual control of the state until 872. He was succeeded as regent by his nephew, Mototsune, who was first *sessho* and then *kampaku*, an office sometimes translated as civil dictator. (The *kampaku* continued to act as regent even after an emperor had attained his majority, speaking on behalf of the ruler and issuing commands in his name.) When Mototsune in turn died in 891, his son Tokihira was only twenty-one and no new appointment to the position of *kampaku* was made. The young Emperor Uda, one of the few not born of a Fujiwara mother, preferred to depend for advice on a brilliant official named Sugawara Michizane, formerly a professor of *kambun* or written Chinese. Michizane rose to high rank and favor, but the Fujiwara were just biding their time. After a brief eclipse until 899 they reasserted themselves and secured the office of minister of the Left, relegating Michizane to second place as minister of the Right. But that was not enough; Michizane was soon given a post in Kyushu, almost equivalent to a sentence of banishment, and died there in 903, it is said of a broken heart. The tale has a curious sequel. Soon after Michizane's death lightning struck the palace, blinding rainstorms took place over long periods, fires broke out, and important persons died. These dire occurrences were ascribed to the vengeful ghost of the unfortunate Michizane. He was restored posthumously by imperial decree to all his rank and titles. The natural disasters however continued, so a temple was erected for his worship; he was enshrined as the God of Learning and Calligraphy and was given the title of Heavenly Deity in 986.

During his lifetime Michizane was invited to lead one of the long series of embassies to China, but he declined on the grounds of the disorders attending the decline of the T'ang dynasty, and, further, arranged that such cultural visits be discontinued. The Japanese apparently now felt they had acquired all that China could usefully offer; the next step was to work out in greater fullness their own indigenous culture on the basis of the riches they had already received.

The zenith of Fujiwara glory was reached in the person of Michinaga, who was the most powerful figure at court from the year 995 until his death in 1027. His father and his two brothers had already been regents. He never took the title himself, but he scarcely needed to, for his daughters were consorts to four emperors, though that involved one of the rulers marrying his own aunt. Two emperors were Michinaga's nephews and three his grandsons. A brilliant man and leader of a brilliant society, he was not without a sense of his own value, for he boasted in a poem that he was "master of his world, like the flawless full moon riding the skies." [1]

Michinaga built a Buddhist monastery, the Hojoji, and dedicated the Golden Hall in it (to the repose of his own soul) on the occasion of his retiring from public life and taking the tonsure. (In the manner of the time he still exercised influence after this from within the monastery.) There was a dazzling ceremony of dedication and a sumptuous entertainment to follow, attended by the emperor and all the court. Jeweled nets hung down from the branches of plants around the pond on which floated jewel-adorned boats, while peacocks strutted on the island in the center of the pond. The Golden Hall itself had pillars that rested upon masonry supports shaped like huge elephants, a roof ridge of gold and silver, a golden door, and rock crystal foundations.

Michinaga was an adherent of the Jodo or Pure Land sect of Buddhism.

[1] G. B. Sansom, *A History of Japan to 1334*, (Stanford, Calif.: Stanford University Press, 1958), p. 174.

The school was brought into prominence in Japan in the tenth century by a learned monk, Eshin. It stressed neither elaborate ritual nor arduous study of abstruse doctrine; repetition of the sacred formula, "Namu Amida Butsu," calling upon the Buddha of infinite compassion, was sufficient for salvation and would insure being reborn in the Western Paradise or Pure Land. It was thus a religion of faith alone and not works, and made a strong appeal to the common people and the unfortunate. It found a response also among the aristocrats and warriors, for even the educated Japanese inclined to a faith involving feeling rather than one of abstract speculation. To this day the branches of this sect command the largest following of any in Japan. When Michinaga was dying he followed the Jodo practice of his day by holding in his hand a thread attached to an image of Amida Buddha, so that he might be drawn into the Western Paradise.

One of the ladies of the court to whom Michinaga at one time paid more than passing attention was the Lady Murasaki Shikibu, lady-in-waiting to the Empress Akiko and authoress. Girls were not supposed to attempt the study of Chinese, but Murasaki picked up a knowledge of the language when her brother was having his lessons. It was now no longer acceptable for nobles and courtiers to hand over to scribes the task of writing; it was expected that a man of position would be able to write in a calligraphy that was aesthetic and a style that was civilized and elegant. The two systems of writing, one basically Chinese, the other using simplified symbols derived from Chinese to stand for Japanese sounds, had by this time been developed. Murasaki used the latter, *kana*, form of script in writing the famous *Genji Monogatari* ("Tale of Genji"), a novel of remarkable insight that ranks as the greatest work in Japanese literature. It was composed about the year 1008.

This long tale of the loves of the young Prince Genji is filled with a sensitivity, an appreciation of beauty, and a wistful Buddhist melancholy that lend it universal appeal, in spite of the fact that it deals with a small, closed court society with very specialized tastes in a time and an atmosphere remote from our own. In her ability to portray the least vibration of the human heart, Murasaki is the equal of Jane Austen and Charlotte Brontë. Man can write tales of action and intrigue, but perhaps it requires a woman's intuitive discrimination and patience to unravel the timeless motives and responses at the heart of human life. The following passage could well apply to a woman in any century or any land.

> The lady, when no answer came from Genji, thought that he had changed his mind, and though she would have been very angry if he had persisted in his suit, she was not quite prepared to lose him with so little ado.
>
> But this was a good opportunity once and for all to lock up her heart against him. She thought that she had done so successfully, but found to her surprise that he still occupied an uncommonly large share of her thoughts.[2]

[2] *The Tale of Genji*, by Lady Murasaki, tr. Arthur Waley (New York: Doubleday Anchor Books, 1955), p. 58.

As to the tinge of Buddhist melancholy in the *Tale of Genji*, a Japanese critic of the year 1200 noted the presence of the quality *aware*, which may be translated "sadness," "sensitivity," "that which is emotionally moving." The word *aware* begins as an exclamation of wonder or delight, a reaction to what has been called the "ahness" of things, goes on to mean that peculiar sadness just mentioned, and ends in modern Japanese as plain "wretched," "pitiable." But the high point of the word's significance is in Heian times when "the sadness of things" was very present to men's minds. Vergil's well-known line, *Sunt lacrimae rerum et mentem mortalia tangunt* ("There are tears in everything and the affairs of mortal men touch the heart"), reflects almost the exact feeling of the phrase *aware no mono* and of the spirit of the *Tale of Genji*, in spite of the lightness and frivolity of its topic.

An acquaintance with this novel is essential for the understanding of Heian, and indeed Japanese, aesthetics. The following quotations, from Arthur Waley's incomparable translation,[3] give the flavor of the novel and the feeling of the times. Here is Murasaki's account of Genji's meeting with a mysterious girl, Yugao.

> He had come in a plain coach with no outriders. No one could possibly guess who he was, and feeling quite at his ease, he leant forward and deliberately examined the house. The gate, also made of a kind of trellis-work, stood ajar and he could see enough of the interior to realize that it was a very humble and poorly furnished dwelling. For a moment he pitied those who lived in such a place, but then he remembered the song, "Seek not in the wide world to find a home; but where you chance to rest, call that your house"; and again, "Monarchs may keep their palaces of jade, for in a leafy cottage two can sleep."
>
> There was a wattled fence over which some ivy-like creeper spread its cool green leaves, and among the leaves were white flowers with petals half-unfolded like the lips of people smiling at their own thoughts. "They are called Yugao, "Evening Faces," one of his servants told him; "how strange to find so lovely a crowd clustering on this deserted wall!" And indeed it was a most strange and delightful thing to see how on the narrow tenement in a poor quarter of the town they had clambered over rickety eaves and gables and spread wherever there was room for them to grow. He sent one of his servants to pick some. The man entered at the half-opened door, and had begun to pluck the flowers, when a little girl in a long yellow tunic came through a quite genteel sliding door, and holding out towards Genji's servant a white fan heavily perfumed with incense, she said to him, "Would you like something to put them on? I am afraid you have chosen a wretched-looking bunch," and she handed him the fan. (See illustration, Plate 19.)
>
> • • •
>
> Having arranged for continual masses to be said on the sick woman's behalf [Genji had been visiting his foster mother, a nun, who was ill, and who lived in the house next door to the mysterious lady], he took his leave,

[3] Pp. 68–92 *passim*.

ordering Koremitsu to light him with a candle. As they left the house he looked at the fan upon which the white flowers had been laid. He now saw that there was writing on it, a poem carelessly but elegantly scribbled: "The flower that puzzled you was but the *Yugao*, strange beyond knowing in its dress of shining dew." It was written with a deliberate negligence which seemed to aim at concealing the writer's status and identity. But for all that the hand showed a breeding and distinction which agreeably surprised him. "Who lives in the house on the left?" he asked.

. . .

[Intrigued, Genji replies in verse] "Could I but get a closer view, no longer would they puzzle me,—the flowers that all too dimly in the gathering dusk I saw." [Through arrangements made somewhat unwillingly by Genji's faithful servant, Koremitsu, the couple meet.] Their room was in the front of the house. Genji got up and opened the long sliding shutters. They stood together looking out. In the courtyard near them was a clump of fine Chinese bamboos; dew lay thick on the borders, glittering here no less brightly than in the great gardens to which Genji was better accustomed. There was a confused buzzing of insects. Crickets were chirping in the wall. He had often listened to them, but always at a distance; now, singing so close to him, they made a music which was unfamiliar and indeed seemed far lovelier than that with which he was acquainted. But then, everything in this place where one thing was so much to his liking seemed despite all drawbacks to take on a new tinge of interest and beauty. She was wearing a white bodice with a soft, grey cloak over it. It was a poor dress, but she looked charming and almost distinguished; even so, there was nothing very striking in her appearance—only a certain fragile grace and elegance. . . .

"I am going to take you somewhere not at all far away where we shall be able to pass the rest of the night in peace. We cannot go on like this, parting always at break of day." "Why have you suddenly come to that conclusion?" she asked, but she spoke submissively. He vowed to her that she should be his love in this and in all future lives, and she answered so passionately that she seemed utterly transformed from the listless creature he had known, and it was hard to believe that such vows were no novelty to her.

. . .

[They made the move.] It was now almost daylight. The cocks had stopped crowing. The voice of an old man (a pilgrim preparing for the ascent of the Holy Mountain) sounded somewhere not far away; and as at each prayer he bent forward to touch the ground with his head, they could hear with what pain and difficulty he moved. What could he be asking for in his prayers, this old man whose life seemed fragile as the morning dew? NAMU TORAI NO DOSHI, "Glory be to the Saviour that shall come"; now they could hear the words. "Listen," said Genji tenderly, "is not that an omen that our love shall last through many lives to come?" And he recited the poem: "Do not prove false this omen of the pilgrim's chant; that even in lives to come our love shall last unchanged."

Then unlike the lovers in the "Everlasting Wrong" who prayed that they might be as "twin birds that share a wing" (for they remembered that this story had ended very sadly), they prayed, "May our love last till Maitreya comes as a Buddha into the World." But she, still distrustful, answered his poem with the verse: "Such sorrow have I known in this world that I have small hope of worlds to come." Her versification was still a little tentative.

. . .

[But the story ends tragically. Yugao dies suddenly and mysteriously.] Her breathing had quite stopped. What could he do? To whom could he turn for help? He ought to send for a priest. He tried to control himself but he was very young, and seeing her lying there, all still and pale, he could contain himself no longer and crying, "Come back to me, my own darling, come back to life. Do not look at me so strangely!" he flung his arms about her. But now she was quite cold. Her face was set in a dull, senseless stare.

. . .

[Yugao's body had to be taken away.] A faint light was already showing in the sky when Koremitsu brought the carriage in. Thinking that Genji would not wish to move the body himself, he wrapt it in a rush-mat and carried it towards the carriage. How small she was to hold! Her face was calm and beautiful. He felt no repulsion. He could find no way to secure her hair, and when he began to carry her it overflowed and hung towards the ground. Genji saw and his eyes darkened. A hideous anguish possessed him.

The length of these quotations from the novel of Lady Murasaki is justified not only by the intrinsic beauty of the language but also by the fact that they cast a fascinating light upon the attitudes of the court nobles during that long era when they were the ruling councillors of the Empire of Japan. Here we see them in their casual moments, at play not at work; but it is obvious that these men have moved far from the position of the tribal warriors who were their ancestors. They move in a society with elaborate rules of etiquette and highly refined tastes. Indeed they carry this refinement to the point of preciousness, with a Japanese tendency to exaggeration and extremes. It is surely a little overdone, not to say banal, to end a paragraph of such emotional depth and haunting beauty as the one containing the prayer "May our love last till Maitreya comes as a Buddha into the World" with the sentence "Her versification was still a little tentative." This was scarcely surprising, for Yugao was only nineteen. But the ability to write sophisticated verse was in those days an important social hallmark, and in this as in all else Lady Murasaki faithfully mirrored her times. It almost seems that the primary civilizations of the Greeks and the Chinese had an instinct of restraint and avoidance of extremes that was never quite shared by the derived civilizations of the Romans and the Japanese.

Although the persons reflected in these tales, written, be it noted, sixty years before the Norman Conquest, produced a remarkable indigenous civilization from alien and native elements and set the standard for the future at least in matters of taste, they belonged to the upper crust of society, small in numbers, dwelling mainly in the capital. They were probably even more limited in the range of their contacts within their own nation than the courtiers of the Sun King in seventeenth-century France. And as in Louis XIV's

France, the narrow but brilliant civilization of the court was becoming perilously separated from its agricultural base. The continual absence of the landlords in the capital and the heavy tax burdens placed on some manors while so many others were granted tax exemptions for one reason or another (see the end of Chapter 3) created an unstable situation over most of the countryside. Too many *shoen*, or manors, belonging to officials, nobles, and the Buddhist church were claiming exemption from tax, whether or not they had a valid title to exemption. The very officials who should have enforced the payment of taxes were at the same time the great landowners who gained most from tax exemption, both for themselves and for the smaller farmers who placed land under their protection in return for a fee much less than the tax. With the drying up of tax sources, the organs of the government faded in importance, the scope of their administrative authority shrinking along with their revenues. Thus, the highly centralized government, established on the Chinese model by the Taika Reform, gradually decayed in late Heian times and the way was prepared for a new military class destined to control the future.

One of the greatest losses in potential tax revenue was from land newly brought under cultivation. New land, particularly in the east and north, had been brought continuously into use by many enterprising lords and Buddhist abbots over a long period of time. Reclamation of land from the wilderness implies at least a rudimentary use of capital. The addition of irrigation canals and the control of water levels in the rice fields required tools and labor along with a high degree of planning and control (see Plate 5). Japanese resources apparently were sufficient to meet these needs and were intelligently used. Records of the seventh and eighth centuries show crown gifts of thousands of iron hoes and spades to high officers and to monasteries for expansion of the cultivated area. In 722 the Court ordered the reclamation of three million acres of new land as national policy. But incentives had to be offered, and so the new land was excluded from taxation and reallotment under the Taika Reform. This tended further to invalidate the old reform system and to withdraw from the exchequer the most important source of new revenue.

Considerable change also took place in the legal and administrative system. Developments and early revisions in the Taiho Code had been gathered together in two sections, the *ryo*, or administrative and civil codes, and the *ritsu*, or disciplinary and penal regulations. But revisions continued to be made to suit changing conditions and these were compiled in various collections from 820 onward, ending in 967 with the Engishiki, which aimed at fixing administrative procedure in permanent form. Both the Engishiki and the other collections came to have the force of statutory law, in some cases even superseding the original codes. Herein lay a double irony. At the very time that the process of change in law reached its climax in the Engishiki, the whole administrative system was being shunted aside to make way for the personal rule of the Fujiwara. And thus it was the descendants of Fujiwara Kamatari, founder of the Fujiwara family and chief author of the Taika Reform, who served mainly to render that reform defunct.

A curious, though it must be admitted almost inevitable, process set in whereby the *mandokoro*, the secretariats or estate offices of the great families, and particularly of the Fujiwara, began to assume the functions of government offices and to maintain such administrative liaison as there was between different parts of the country. For example, a letter written by a Fujiwara clerk might affect the tax returns of a whole province owned by the family, and would take precedence over a government order through the old channels. This was in a sense bound to happen because the whole Chinese machinery of the Taika Reform and the Taiho Code was alien to the structure of Japanese society, both agrarian and aristocratic. The peasants made the complicated bureaucratic system of periodic reallotment of land completely unworkable by their fierce attachment to their own plots of carefully irrigated rice paddy. Indeed even in China, its country of origin, the full program of periodic redistribution had not been found practicable. The aristocrats nullified the system of public service and promotion by allowing the offices to become hereditary and thus open to no competition on merit. An extreme example was the appointment simply on the basis of pedigree of a young man of seventeen to the office of Commander of the Metropolitan Police Bureau in 1025. The Emperor Toba later gave the qualifications for this same post as good family, good sense, knowledge of precedent, good looks, high Court rank, and wealth.

In the end the administrative scheme of government offices became a dead letter, although the titles attached to some of them were retained by court nobles right down to the nineteenth century. Three of the old government offices, however, did remain active. Originally they were of minor importance, but being functionally valuable they grew during the tenth century while the rest declined. They were:

1. The Board of Audit, Kageyushi. These "release commissioners" received and audited the accounts of an official leaving office before he was released from his responsibilities. The outgoing official had likewise to submit a report to his successor. In the course of time the whole matter of appointing and dismissing officials, including the creation of new offices and what we would call job descriptions, devolved upon this office. This, however, is not to imply that in appointments they acted independently of the great Fujiwara officers of state. Financial and fiscal affairs continued to be handled through this office as a result of their auditing function.

2. The Bureau of Archivists, Kurando-dokoro. This office began as the emperor's private treasury and archives. The officials in it had the responsibility of drawing up the imperial rescripts and edicts and thus had to know something of the emperor's mind. Originally without executive powers, the bureau increased greatly in importance and authority as the Fujiwara found it useful for getting things done without going through channels. For the

intelligent and ambitious it offered such good chances of promotion that it became known as Toryumon, the Gateway of the Ascending Dragon.

3. The Commissioners of Police, Kebiishi-cho. At first a metropolitan police establishment, its jurisdiction was later extended to the provinces, while its authority covered judicial as well as strictly police matters. The Bureau of Archivists and the family Mandokoro of the Fujiwara may be compared to the private secretariat of the Roman Emperor Augustus, known as *ab epistulis*, and his accountant's office, *a rationibus*, which soon became in effect no longer private household offices but important administrative departments of the government under Augustus and his successors, replacing the official Senate machinery.

The successor of the great Fujiwara Michinaga was Fujiwara Yorimichi, who became regent in 1017 and continued in the office for fifty years, during the reigns of three emperors. In spite of this impressive display, however, the power of the Fujiwara was beginning to pass its peak, and when Go-Sanjo became emperor in 1068 it received a check. The new emperor's mother was not a Fujiwara lady, and he himself had been miserably treated by Yorimichi when a youth; he decided he would rule on his own. He established a Land Record Office to try to deal with the problem of the manors and counter the trends so harmful to central administration. He abdicated of his own will in 1072 and intended to continue to rule through his son, Shirakawa, but unfortunately died in the following year at the early age of thirty-nine.

It was this son, the Emperor Shirakawa, who, in the last decades of the eleventh century, first successfully carried through the curious device known as *insei*, "cloister government." Japanese emperors, and indeed other Japanese dignitaries up to the present day, have a heavy burden of ceremonial duties. The practice, therefore, grew up in the Heian court of early abdication and retirement. The usual way to retire was to take the tonsure and live as a Buddhist monk. This act was not irrevocable and many government officials and some emperors returned from the monastery to reenter active political life. (The word *in* means a quiet apartment in a monastery, and by a common Japanese practice the word is transferred from the place to the occupant, Go-Sanjo being known after his abdication as Go-Sanjo In.) Shirakawa, however, seems to have begun the practice of placing on the throne a child emperor, who would give no trouble, and continuing to direct affairs of state from the cloister, with more personal freedom and less obligation to fatiguing ceremonial. He was in this way able to retain his mystic authority as retired emperor, but use as his advisers and mouthpieces independent persons of his own choice, outside the official hierarchy. This ingenious device offered the retired emperor several advantages, not least of which was a means to circumvent the Fujiwara, whose whole object for centuries had been to become an indispensable part of the official order, but who had little excuse to interfere in the unofficial arrangements of a retired person who was sheltered by the umbrella of the church, although they continued to serve and usually to direct the titular emperor.

The institution of the *insei* is of sociological and anthropological as well as historical interest, for it is one more move away from matriarchy and toward patriarchy. The installing of empresses had previously been abandoned. Now the emperor was no longer influenced by the men related to his mother and his wife or concubine, the Fujiwara, but by his father, the retired emperor. It seems that sheer biological accident made the shift to the *insei* form easier. After the death of Michinaga the Fujiwara ladies died young or gave birth to girls almost exclusively or were childless. Divisions within the Fujiwara clan further weakened their position, for Fujiwara Yoshinobu, a dissident clansman, opposed the regent, Fujiwara Yorimichi, and supported Go-Sanjo in his claim to the throne, from which resulted a major check to Fujiwara ambitions.

The *insei* emperors were long-lived. Shirakawa ruled as actual emperor from 1072 to 1086, then abdicated and continued to govern from the cloister for forty-three years more, until his death in 1129. During this long period no fewer than three emperors occupied the throne but ruled in name only. The Emperor Toba ruled for sixteen years in the titular position, then on the death of Shirakawa six years after his own retirement held the power of abdicated emperor for twenty-six years. Go-Shirakawa (*Go* in effect means II, "the second") was emperor for three years and then ruled from the cloister for thirty-four years more. Thus the 120 years from 1072 to 1192 are spanned by the rule of only three emperors, and of this period these three ruled as cloistered emperors for 104 years or all but sixteen of the total. Nevertheless it must be made clear that the effective period of *insei* control was in fact limited to seventy years, from 1086, the abdication of Shirakawa, to 1156, the death of Toba. Thereafter the power lay with the warring clans. Go-Shirakawa survived by his cleverness in playing off one side against the other in their rival claims to be the protectors of the Throne, but the real authority no longer lay with him or his advisers. The great period of civilian, and highly civilized, rule by the court nobles was almost over. Armed warriors, cruder and of coarser grain, but more efficient and sometimes wise and far-seeing, were in process of asserting their right to rule in the name of the emperor.

The process was a gradual one, fostered by the continuance of disturbed conditions in the countryside. Skirmishes and revolts broke out as landowners sought, in the absence of a law centrally enforced, to defend their territories or to increase them. As early as 935 a large-scale armed rebellion against the Throne was initiated by Taira Masakado in the eastern region of Japan. During the early tenth century, powerful landowners in the provinces were for all practical purposes supreme in their own domains. They were often given imperial appointments as vice-governors, since the governor was generally an absentee living at the capital, and this gave them virtual control in their own regions. About 935 Taira Masakado began attacking his uncles and other members of the Taira family in order to add to his lands. Encouraged by victories over them and then over government forces sent to subdue him, he secured aid from powerful allies and after some years controlled no fewer than eight of the eastern provinces. In 940 he sent a letter to the chief minister, Fujiwara Tokihira, in which he claimed the title of emperor for himself. But this was also the year of his nemesis, for he was attacked by powerful forces at the request of the emperor. He expected help from his allies, who had mustered over 8,000 troops, but they refused to join him. He was completely defeated and his head put on view in the capital to discourage others.

At the same time in Western Japan, Sumitomo, who might be described as a pirate chief, wrought havoc in the Inland Sea with a force of 1,000 small ships until defeated in 941.

Nearly a hundred years later in 1028 the vice-governor of Shimosa Province, Taira Tadatsune, overstepped his bounds and attacked two neighboring provinces. After some unsuccessful attempts to crush Tadatsune, the government called on the most famous general of the day, Minamoto Yorinobu, to quell the revolt. Yorinobu had only to move in the direction of the rebel; so great was his prestige that he did not need to attack. Tadatsune gave himself up. The loyal troops of the clans who suppressed these uprisings were later to be the support of the new military dictatorship, but at this point they were still willing to be the "claws and teeth" of the Fujiwara, who were to remain the leaders of an elegant and cultured society at the capital until well into the twelfth century.

6

THE RISE OF THE WARRIOR CLASS AND THE GEMPEI WAR

End of the Heian Period: 1158–1185

In this period the center of gravity in Japanese political power shifted from the emperor and his court nobles to the heads of warrior families; from the capital, Kyoto, to the country estates; and from those who held ancient, hereditary titles and ruled under the form of a civil administration of Chinese type to those clan leaders, old and new, who could carve out land and power for themselves by a sword and a strong right arm. In the conservative tradition of Japan all the old features remained—emperor, nobles, titles, and the ancient capital—but they gradually became increasingly empty symbols, for the authority lay elsewhere. As the court became less powerful and as the nobles drew less income from their estates, the country squires were the gainers, not only in money but in knowledge of affairs. These country squires, many of whom started out as estate managers for absentee nobles, had been able to acquire control of land and of the all-important labor force to work the land and to provide a stalwart body of armed retainers.

The name of the war between two great houses with which this period ended is compounded from the Chinese form of their names, "Gen," in native Japanese form "Minamoto," and "Hei," in Japanese "Taira." The compound for phonetic reasons emerges as "Gempei." Other families of military prowess were involved, but these two, the Minamoto and the Taira, were the chief. The period is still known as the Heian, but leadership was clearly passing from the Fujiwara to the warrior families. The Taira were the most powerful at the end of the Heian Period. The next era, the Kamakura Period, began when the Minamoto became the dominant power in the state.

The origins of both the Taira and the Minamoto go far back in Japanese history. The Taiho Code, doubtless foreseeing large families in the imperial household where wives and concubines were the rule, decreed that descendants of the emperors in the sixth generation were to be deprived of the rank of prince, were to take a family name and start on their own. This rule was observed and began to come into effect in the late ninth century. A younger son of the Emperor Kammu (died 806) had been appointed governor of Hitachi in eastern Japan. His descendants increased their lands and possessions and in due course became an independent family with the name Taira. Taira strength in the eastern part of the country continued to be considerable, for Taira Masakado controlled eight provinces before he was defeated in 940. In a subsequent rebellion led by a Taira, that of Tadatsune in 1028, it is significant that the leader of the government forces sent to suppress the rising was of the rival house, Minamoto Yorinobu.

Taira fortunes rose steeply a hundred years later, for then Taira Tadamori gained the ear of the retired Emperor Shirakawa, and strongly supported court policy, especially where the Minamoto could be made to appear in the wrong. Tadamori rendered special aid to the government by controlling piracy in the Inland Sea in 1129. He controlled piracy rather than suppressing it, for he was not above making some deals to his own advantage with local magnates who held coastal property and combined piracy with more legitimate activities. It was largely owing to the success of Tadamori that the center of Taira power moved from its place of origin in the east to central and western Japan. Tadamori, though head of a warrior house, was far from being a mere rough soldier. He was a clever and experienced politician, something of a poet and not a little sought after as a witty and accomplished companion by the ladies of the court. His younger kinsman, Taira Kiyomori, became a still more powerful figure and dominated the government for twenty years during the second half of the twelfth century.

The Minamoto family also arose on account of the Taiho Code rule, the various branches being distinguished by the inclusion of the name of the particular emperor from whom they reckoned descent, *e.g.*, Saga-Benji, Uda-Genji, and so on. The branch that ultimately succeeded in assuming general leadership of the clan was that of the Seiwa-Genji (Seiwa reigned 858–876), though each branch retained a high degree of independence. The Seiwa-Genji reckon their origin as a separate branch of the family from the year 961. The Minamoto gave aid and service to the Fujiwara from the beginning, and the great Fujiwara Michinaga (died 1017) depended heavily on Minamoto Yorimitsu and Minamoto Yorinobu, so much so that their enemies referred to them as "running dogs" of the Fujiwara. This derogatory term, however, does not do justice to their qualities as both soldiers and courtiers. The military reputation of the Minamoto was greatly enhanced by Yorinobu's son, Yoriyoshi, and by his grandson, Yoshiiye. Both were involved in bitterly fought wars in the north, known as the Early Nine Years' War and the Later Three Years' War. The Early Nine Years' War was brought on through the ambitions of the Abe family.

This family had for some time held the post of northern commander-in-chief and commissioner for the Ainu, and in 1050 one Abe Yoritoki began exacting taxes and attaching property to which he was not entitled. The governor complained to Kyoto and Minamoto Yoriyoshi was appointed to bring the Abe clan to heel. When Abe Yoritoki was killed in the course of the protracted campaigns, his son, Sadato, a man of immense strength and courage, took his place. After an unsuccessful Minamoto attack on a stockade fortress, Sadato's men broke out in a surprise attack and pursued the Minamoto forces in a thick snowstorm. Among the few who escaped slaughter on this occasion were Yoriyoshi and his fifteen-year-old son, Yoshiiye, who had followed his father to the wars. Yoriyoshi, undismayed, collected another force, and attacked Sadato again. He diverted the water supply of the fortress and managed to set fire to the stockade. After incredible privations, Sadato finally surrendered.

The story of the Later Three Years' War is somewhat similar. In this case the Kiyowara family, who had aided Yoriyoshi and the government side in the last war, themselves began to exceed their authority and mishandle affairs in the north. This time Minamoto Yoshiiye undertook the commission to discipline the Kiyowara in 1083. Difficult terrain, biting cold, and considerable slaughter on both sides made the campaign a desperate one. A certain youth of sixteen received an arrow in the eye. Pausing only to break off the shaft, he fired an arrow of his own back at his opponent and hit him. Then he collapsed on the ground; but when a friend came to pull the arrow out, and put his foot on the youth's face to get a better purchase, the wounded youth threatened to kill him. To trample on a warrior's face was an insult which could only be avenged by death. Finally Yoshiiye's brother brought reinforcements from Kyoto and with this aid he defeated the Kiyowara. Yoshiiye became a national hero, so much so that the government had to try to put a stop to numbers of farmer-soldiers "commending" their lands to him, not because he was powerful at court but because they wanted to be feudal retainers of so admired a warrior.

These wars in the far north were not in themselves of first importance, though obviously the government was unwilling to allow widespread disobedience even at a distance. But they were significant in the national development because they were hard training schools in the military virtues and in the forging of those intimate bonds of loyalty between leaders and men that would mark the national ethos from that point right up to the present. Yoshiiye, we are told, would assign seats each evening in the barracks to his soldiers in the Three Years' War, the higher places for the brave and loyal, the lower for those who had flinched from the battle. Courage and loyalty, both for good and ill, were soon to outshine all other virtues. Not for nothing had Yoshiiye, when fighting as a youth with his father, been nicknamed by the soldiers "Hachiman Taro," or "Firstborn of the God of War." (See frontispiece.)

A further disturbance, the Hogen Insurrection, took place between 1156 and 1158, led this time by one of the Fujiwara themselves, Fujiwara Yorinaga. At the deaths of the Emperor Konoye in 1155 and the retired Emperor Toba the next year, an acrimonious dispute broke out over the succession. A woman's name was put forward but did not gain support at court. The Regent Tadamichi, who was Yorinaga's elder brother, and the powerful Taira Kiyomori took the side of the man who eventually succeeded as the Emperor Go-Shirakawa, while Yorinaga turned to support another retired emperor, Sutoku. The matter came to an open breach. Yorinaga raised troops and, with Sutoku, fortified a palace in the city of Kyoto, but their forces were heavily outnumbered. Sutoku's palace was burned and Yorinaga himself killed. The insurrection was not on a large scale and never had much chance of success. Its importance was that it was an omen of things to come, the overwhelming power of the military clans.

Although both the Taira and the Minamoto had their share of power and authority in the provinces, the Taira became the dominant force in the state through the influence of Taira Kiyomori, who became chief of his clan in 1153 and was virtually without a rival until his death in 1181. The groundwork had been laid by the capable and diplomatic Taira Tadamori. Kiyomori was a younger kinsman but not a son of Tadamori. In fact there was a whisper of an imperial sire. In any case Kiyomori gained the ear of the ex-emperor Go-Shirakawa and used to the full his position at court, his increasing wealth, and his clan influence in the region of the Inland Sea. Some of his work there in the construction of harbors, dredging of channels, and development of trade with China was of permanent value to the country.

During the wars in the far north and the power plays at court, life went on fairly peaceably for farmers and the little people in much of the country. There was one rather ominous feature of this period which gravely disturbed the life of all in and around the capital but did not greatly affect the provinces, and that was the endemic warfare conducted by the soldier-monks attached to some of the great monasteries. The situation was particularly bad during the period of the cloister government, in the century 1080 to 1180. In many cases the outbreaks were occasioned by disputes over the appointment of abbots or the right to ordain monks. They seem not to have been the deliberate policy or choice of the leading church dignitaries themselves but to have stemmed rather from the sectarianism and crowd psychology of the somewhat ignorant lay brothers who made up the regiments of temple guards. They were a nuisance rather than a serious threat, but occasionally, as in the Teiji Rising in 1160, their participation did affect the outcome of a revolution or palace plot. A determined military leader from time to time was able without any difficulty to scatter their ill-organized forces; yet many leaders were most unwilling on grounds of conscience or superstition to proceed to extreme measures against those who claimed the protection of Buddha. The soldier-monks were not slow to take advantage of this fact and would sometimes exercise a form of spiritual blackmail by bringing a sacred image with them. If their demands were not met, they would leave the image in its palanquin where it stood on the street and return to their temple. This was thought to expose their enemies to the wrath of the god, particularly if anything were to happen to the image. They would have their demands granted and be begged to come and remove the image to its resting place in the temple.

The last quarter of the twelfth century shows increasing signs of a declining regime, less and less able to keep order. There are notices of famine, great fires in the capital, some of them due to deliberate arson, and piteous tales of infants and their dead mothers and corpses lying unburied in the streets. There was an understandable air of pessimism abroad, and this in turn was linked to a doctrine of Buddhism prevalent at the time. Popular preachers spoke of a prophecy which the original Buddha Sakya had uttered, predicting that there would come a degenerate age in which men would forsake the Law. It was widely felt that the time of the Latter Day of the Holy Law (Mappo) had now arrived and men were exhorted, by believing in the simple creed of the compassionate Amida Buddha, to save themselves from this untoward generation. The strong presence of Taira Kiyomori doubtless served to prevent even worse disasters; but events seem to have passed the point where one man could patch them up. Taira Kiyomori was not a popular figure, and the Minamoto rivals were always seeking an opportunity to supplant him. Three such attempts were made, the first and the last being the most serious.

In the first, the Heiji Rising of 1160, a Minamoto and a Fujiwara took advantage of Kiyomori's absence from Kyoto to seize the persons of the Emperor and the ex-Emperor. Their coup seemed to have succeeded, but they were slow to follow up their advantage. Kiyomori returned and acted with his usual decisiveness. He gathered Taira reinforcements and engineered the escape of the ex-Emperor. The Emperor was disguised as a lady-in-waiting and reached the Rokuhara headquarters of the Taira in Kyoto in safety. The Minamoto leader defended the Great Palace with great bravery but was finally driven out. The final blow to the Minamoto forces was delivered by an army of soldier-monks from Mount Hiei. Go-Shirakawa and Kiyomori were back in the saddle.

The second attempt, the Shishigatani Affair, in 1177, was a plot hatched by leaders who hated Kiyomori and was named for the remote country mansion in which the conspirators met to lay their plans. But a junior member of the Minamoto house revealed the plot and the conspirators were ruthlessly dealt with. The subjection of a Buddhist monk to torture to extract information created a particularly bad impression. It is thought that a serious illness was beginning to embitter Kiyomori and affect his judgment.

The third attempt came in 1179, two years before Kiyomori's death. A call to arms was raised by Minamoto Yorimasa, himself an old man. He was, in a sense, a transitional personality illustrative of the changing times. A poet and a courtier, he had abandoned an earlier military career, and had commended himself to Kiyomori as a safe and reliable supporter by taking no part in the Heiji Rising. But apparently clan loyalty was still the dominant factor in Yorimasa's character; and it is certain that Kiyomori was becoming more morose and tyrannical. In any event, in May 1180 Yorimasa sent messages to Minamoto leaders and to the monasteries which Kiyomori had specially alienated. He was joined by a son of Go-Shirakawa, Prince Mochihito, whom Yorimasa planned to make emperor. Kiyomori received word of the plot, brought in reinforcements to the capital, and put a close guard on the person of Go-Shirakawa. Prince Mochihito retreated to the monastery of Miidera to escape arrest, but had to move on in the direction of Nara. Minamoto Yorimasa, who was now with him, had the bridge at Uji partially destroyed to foil the Taira pursuers. Some of them managed to ford the river and a battle ensued outside the Byodo-in temple (see Plate 9). Yorimasa received an arrow wound, and urged the Prince to escape, while he himself, to avoid capture, committed *harakiri* in due form right in front of the beautiful Phoenix Hall of the monastery. The Prince was later captured and killed and Kiyomori had the remnant of the insurgents ruthlessly suppressed. Yorimasa's call to arms against the Taira therefore seemed abortive and premature; but it was the last straw. The Minamoto were now burning to avenge the numerous defeats and insults Kiyomori had inflicted upon them.

In the same month of June 1180 in which he had defeated Yorimasa, Kiyomori attempted to secure the persons of the Emperor and the ex-Emperor more closely under his control—always the key to the legitimacy of a regime —by removing the whole court to his own seat at Fukuwara. This move was not a success. The place did not seem to suit the health of the young Emperor, who had never been strong, and Kiyomori was unable to keep an eye on events at the capital, where he knew there was mounting opposition to himself. So Kiyomori returned to Kyoto, taking the whole court back with him, at the end of the year 1180.

The shadows were gathering rapidly. Kiyomori fell sick of a serious disease and, in spite of the counsel of his sons and advisers, he seems in a kind of madness to have decided on burning the monasteries of Todaiji and Kofukuji, two of the most ancient and honorable, though by no means peaceful, shrines of Buddhism. By the spring of 1181 he was running a high fever, and on March 21 he died.

The issue was now out in the open and the battle joined in earnest and on a large scale between the Taira and the Minamoto; the Gempei War had begun. Kiyomori had lived to hear of two engagements and had made his sons swear everlasting enmity to Minamoto Yoritomo, the new head of the Minamoto clan. In the first of these battles, a minor one, Yoritomo with only a small force had been halted and turned back in September 1180 at Ishibashiyama as he moved from his eastern base toward the capital. Completely undeterred, he went on gathering forces, claiming that he was the legitimate protector of the Throne and that the dead Prince Mochihito had called upon him to subdue the enemies of the state. In the second battle of 1180, that of the River Fujikawa in Suruga Province, he was more successful, defeating a Taira force in a night attack.

The battles of the Gempei War, which lasted from 1180 to 1185, were fought on several fronts. The Minamoto moved in on the capital from their bases in the east and from the north in the early stages of the war, while the Taira, who had local strength in west Japan and on Shikoku Island, moved in these directions when they were forced to abandon the capital. The Taira were also stronger on the sea than the Minamoto. The Minamoto had the intangible but important advantage of being a rising star, whereas the long dominance of Kiyomori had made the Taira unpopular. Since there was some dissension among the various Minamoto leaders, it is well to note their names and relationships. Minamoto Yoritomo was the commanding general, though perhaps a better statesman than a strategist. His brother, the dashing Yoshitsune, was the best military tactician on either side. Noriyori, the brother who came between the first two in age, also played a significant part in the war. Two other Minamoto generals of great importance were Yoritomo's uncle, Yukiiye, and his first cousin, Yoshinaka, a competent leader, but one who tried to play his own hand and failed.[1] It was a war of young generals, for Yoshitsune and Yoshinaka both died at the age of thirty. Yoritomo's famous father, Yoshitomo, had been killed at the age of thirty-seven, in the course of the Heiji Rising. Yoritomo himself, after winning the war and designing the peace, died at the comparatively early age of fifty-two.

Following the opening battles in 1180, there was a lull in the fighting during the winter of 1181, but the Taira were able to defeat Minamoto Yukiiye on the Sunomata River in the province of Owari, not very far distant from Kyoto, during the month of May. The Taira were not really able to exploit this victory, and the Minamoto went on recruiting support. The struggle then moved to the north where, in the autumn of the same year, the Minamoto this time were victorious in Echizen under the able Yoshinaka, Yoritomo's cousin.

Very little fighting took place during the whole of 1182, when famine and disease affected large parts of the country. When warfare resumed in early summer of 1183, Taira Koremori was at first successful in reducing certain enemy strongpoints, but his fortune changed when he moved further north to Etchu Province. Koremori, with superior numbers, was encamped on the slopes of Mount Tonami. Minamoto Yoshinaka, in a carefully coordinated move, surrounded his army by night, confused it by a series of prodding surprise tactics, and at length put the whole host to flight. This defeat was disastrous for the Taira, since Yoshinaka was now able to move unimpeded toward the capital from a northerly direction, while Yukiiye with another force advanced upon it from the east.

At this point the Minamoto gained a considerable psychological advantage, for Go-Shirakawa, the ex-emperor, threw in his lot with them. He went ostensibly on a religious pilgrimage to Mount Hiei, close by the capital

[1] It may simplify the mastery of Japanese names to note that most consist of four syllables and that the component parts divide into two two-syllable pairs, which correspond to two Japanese characters. Many of these two-syllable pairs repeat within a family in various combinations. Surnames are placed first and given names second.

but far enough away to put him out of reach of the Taira and within the protection of soldier-monks. From this vantage point he was soon brought back in triumph to the capital by Minamoto Yoshinaka's army. Go-Shirakawa was no doubt tired of the heavy-handed "protection" of the Taira, particularly under the domineering Kiyomori, now deceased; but he also had an eye to the main chance, reckoning the imperial house would be better off under Yoritomo, with whom he had secretly been in contact. Portraits of the long-lived Go-Shirakawa show a heavy head, with large nose, small beady eyes, and a full, down-drawn mouth—the impression is of a crafty man rather than a great one. But there was dire need of shrewdness in the imperial player in this poker game, where others held the main cards of brute force and money and he only those of prestige and his natural wits.

Taira Munemori, chieftain of the clan since his father Kiyomori's death, had now no choice but to retire to the west, and this he did, taking with him the child-emperor Antoku and the imperial regalia. The establishment of the Minamoto in place of the Taira as the dominant power in the capital ushers in the second and final phase of the Gempei War, in the early autumn of 1183.

At first things went well for the Taira. Their retreating army was a formidable force and succeeded in defeating a pursuing detachment of inadequate strength at Mizushima. More important still, Yoritomo had to settle a matter of serious dissension within his own Minamoto ranks. Yoshinaka, now in charge in Kyoto, was plotting to carry off Go-Shirakawa and set up his own regime in the north. Go-Shirakawa himself revealed the plot to Yoritomo, who promptly dispatched his two brothers, Noriyori and Yoshitsune, again Yoshinaka. In an episode famous in Japanese romances Yoshinaka was brought to book near the renowned Bridge of Uji, where Yorimasa had made his last stand in 1180, and killed after desperate resistance.

The Taira had established a base in friendly territory at Yashima on the island of Shikoku, and were hopeful of being able to restore their fortunes. As the first stage of a possible move back to Kyoto, they took advantage of their naval superiority to cross over the Inland Sea to a point on the north shore at Ichi-no-tani, where they erected excellent defenses along the road running between mountains and sea. But Yoshitsune with great skill devised a plan to turn the terrain to the advantage of the attacking Minamoto forces. Leaving the bulk of his army under the command of Noriyori, he led a small party of disciplined cavalry round through the hills and took up position by dawn above the Taira left flank at Ichi-no-tani. Quieting their restless horses, Yoshitsune and his men lay behind cover of some thickets until they saw Noriyori's attack on the Taira right flank beginning to succeed near the shrine of the Ikuta Woods. Then they broke cover and rode hard down the steep slope, achieving complete surprise. They overran the Taira defenses and set fire to their camp, killing their commander in the melee. Noriyori maintained the pressure on the enemy's right, and the Taira with the sea behind them were unable to maneuver. Numbers were killed and captured and the remainder fled by sea, leaving the Minamoto in possession of the field.

After this Battle of Ichi-no-tani in March 1184, there ensued a lull of six months, in which the Taira were again able to recruit their forces. Subsequent Japanese accounts of the war (often highly colored, for it is the great source of drama and romance) tend to minimize the strength of the ultimate losers, the Taira; yet it is evident that even after Ichi-no-tani they presented a serious threat to the Minamoto. This is clearly seen in the difficulties that attended Noriyori when Yoritomo ordered him to proceed to the far west against the Taira in the autumn of 1184. The mission was dangerous but justified in the result. Noriyori had in front of him Taira Tomomori on an island at the west end of Honshu and Munemori with the boy-emperor on his flank at Yashima, the Taira base on Shikoku, whither Munemori had fled after Ichi-no-tani. The lords of central and western Japan were for the most part adherents of the Taira and in a position to deny to Noriyori both transportation and supplies. Noriyori nevertheless succeeded in reaching the west end of Honshu. He sent desperate appeals to Yoritomo, who was directing affairs from his headquarters at Kamakura far east of Kyoto and at the same time keeping an eye on affairs in the eastern part of the country. Yoritomo, however, could not send reinforcements rapidly or easily because of the Taira control of the Inland Sea route and of the central route to the west. It took six weeks even for a messenger to travel from Kyushu to Kamakura. In the end Noriyori received both food for his men and a fleet of small ships from certain lords in the west and transported his force over to Bungo in Kyushu.

The commanding general Yoritomo's political acumen and caution were very nearly his undoing, for these qualities were strongly mixed with suspicion and mistrust, directed particularly at his brilliant younger brother, Yoshitsune. At this juncture he overcame his jealousy sufficiently to give Yoshitsune an independent commission, and the latter set out about the month of March 1185 with characteristic speed, not to say impetuosity, to deal with the Taira force on Shikoku. A spring storm destroyed a number of the boats he had intended to use for the crossing, but he set out with a small force on the remainder. Taking advantage of the high winds, he made an unexpectedly rapid passage. Yoshitsune mustered his troops and descended on Yashima from the landward side. The Taira defenses were directed seaward, and Munemori gave up and fled to Kyushu—unnecessarily it seems, for he had the larger number of men. Yoshitsune followed at leisure, after securing Yashima as a base for his side and obtaining with considerable difficulty further ships for transport. His most valuable acquisition, however, was a member of a local clan who joined him and who was familiar with the treacherous currents running between the main island and Kyushu.

Events were now moving rapidly to a climax. Munemori and Tomomori joined forces and offered battle at sea. There has been speculation as to why they did this in view of the dangers to navigation in these narrow waters. Probably they expected to profit from the Minamoto lack of experience in naval warfare; and in any case they had to make some move, for they were caught between Noriyori on Kyushu and Yoshitsune's fresh advance on the mainland from the east.

The Taira took advantage of the flood tide to bear down on the Minamoto ships on the morning of April 25, 1185, near the village of Dan-no-ura on the main island. At first the Taira held their own, but in the afternoon they lost their advantage, for the tide had turned and the Minamoto now had both wind and tide with them. At the height of the battle a commander allied to the Taira deserted to the Minamoto side. Yoshitsune had given orders to all the soldiers on board the Minamoto ships to direct the fire of their arrows at the Taira steersmen in particular. The Taira ships were forced onto the Dan-no-ura shore or caught in the retreating tide, now roaring through the narrows at eight knots. It was a total disaster for the Taira. The boy-emperor Antoku and many of the Taira leaders were drowned. The Dan-no-ura defeat marked the end of effective Taira power.

Much could be written on the military assessment of the Gempei War. The Japanese romances speak of the transitory nature of human glory, and of the Taira pride and arrogance, which brought nemesis in its train. Personal factors in the characters of the leaders themselves undoubtedly played a large part in the outcome. The Taira showed a lack of skill and determination in exploiting their advantages, for there is no reason to think the quality of their fighting men was in any way inferior to that of the Minamoto. The prudent shift of sides made by Go-Shirakawa in 1183 gave the Minamoto claims a legitimacy that attracted allies to their side. But the greatest single factor was the combination of the political skill and rock-fast determination of Yoritomo with the élan and generalship of his brother, Yoshitsune.

The Minamoto victory marked the political triumph of the warrior class, a decisive event which had important social and cultural consequences. Where Taira Kiyomori, though of a warrior family, had attached himself to the court, Minamoto Yoritomo kept himself and his warriors aloof from court life and maintained his headquarters at Kamakura on his own ground in the east even after victory had made him master of Japan. There were political and personal reasons operating in each case; but the difference between the two men and the milieu in which each chose to exercise power is symptomatic of the cultural changes going on in twelfth-century Japan.

The cultural emphasis moved gradually from admiration of the gentleman, the scholar, and the aesthete to a code of fierce loyalty among fighting men and a worship of honor and the sword. As this martial spirit became more clearly defined it was known at first as *Kyuba-no-michi,* "the way of the horse and the bow," and later as *bushido,* "the way of the warrior." The actual swords themselves acquired a mystique of their own. In a man's sword resided his honor and he would sooner die than part with it. When a sword-smith embarked on the forging and tempering of a sword, he would prepare himself by religious rites of Shinto abstention and purification. Even at the work itself he would wear white clothes similar to those of a Shinto priest. The care put into the craftsmanship in medieval Japan produced swords of a quality and keenness scarcely ever excelled anywhere else at any time, not even by the great artificers of the Muslim world nor of Toledo in Spain.

Among the technical reasons for the high quality of the Japanese sword was the care taken to give a different temper to the edge and to the back of the blade. The metal was hammered and wrought to a close texture and density and the edge tempered many times to a great hardness. But each time it was tempered the broad back of the blade was carefully protected from the heating and cooling process by a layer of clay, making it more resilient and less brittle than the edge. The finished blade thus had both strength and keenness. The swordsmiths also took pride in the workmanship of the sword ornaments, the hilt guards in inlay and gold and silver damascene work, the scabbard ornaments of tiny animals, the handgrips of sharkskin, and so on. These have long been collectors' items both in Japan and the West (see cover and frontispiece).

The other traditional weapon of the Japanese warrior was the bow and arrow. Arrows were discharged by the warrior from on horseback, in the Mongol manner, as well as from the ground. Quivers on the warriors' backs, with the feathered ends of the arrows arranged in a narrow fan shape, figure prominently in contemporary pictures. The armor of a Japanese knight consisted of small, rectangular plates of steel or lacquered wood laced together with red silk or other cords. The armor was lighter in weight than the European suit of armor and gave more mobility to the wearer. The helmet usually consisted of a cap of iron segments skillfully curved to shape, with wide cheek pieces but less frontal protection than in the European helmet, and the whole surmounted by up-curving horns, reminiscent of the Viking headgear, and presenting a fierce aspect. The aristocratic warrior of Japan rode a horse into battle, was followed by a small company of foot soldiers, and often engaged in single combat with an opponent, as in the medieval West; but he was armed with sword and bow, not sword and lance.

A delight in finery and pride in the accoutrements of war can be seen in the romantic tale *Heike Monogatari*, where the appearance of Taira Shigehira is described:

He was attired . . . in a *hitatare* [ceremonial robe] of dark blue cloth on which a pattern of rocks and sea-birds was embroidered in light yellow silk, and armour with purple lacing deepening in its hue towards the skirts. On his head was a helmet with tall, golden horns, and his sword also was mounted in gold. His arrows were feathered with black and white falcon

[59]

plumes and in his hand he carried a "Shigeto" bow. He was mounted on a renowned war-horse called Doji-kage, whose trappings were resplendent with ornaments of gold.[2]

From this age of the clan wars comes the main source of those romances that have delighted generations of audiences in the popular *kabuki* theater as well as in the classical *No* plays, and have formed an ideal of bravery and loyalty for all Japanese. The effect of this ideal on Japanese thought and on later Japanese history has been very marked, extending right into the twentieth century. The modern situation in Japan is, of course, changing very rapidly under the full impact of technology. But at least until recently the famous names of medieval Japan have probably been more intimately present to the minds of their countrymen than the corresponding figures exactly contemporary with them would be to Western minds. These would include, among many others, twelfth-century figures such as Philip II of France, Frederick Barbarossa, Henry II of England, Eleanor of Aquitaine, Thomas à Becket, Richard I Coeur-de-Lion (King of England from 1189 to 1199, when the Gempei War was just over), Saladin (his opponent in the Third Crusade), and the minnesinger in Germany, Walther von der Vogelweide.

The best known of these stories of romance and adventure is the cycle relating to Minamoto Yoshitsune, the brilliant young leader in the wars against the Taira. When his father was killed, he was only an infant and was placed by his stepfather in a monastery. But as he grew up he felt the urge to avenge the humiliations of his family and made his way, for training and support, to Fujiwara Hidehira, a powerful lord in the north. At the age of seventeen he was in Kyoto. Crossing the Gojo Bridge he found his passage disputed by a stout and truculent monk, Benkei. The monk thought a few blows of his staff would put the impudent stripling to flight, but he soon found he was up against one of the most accomplished swordsmen in the country. Surrendering at length to his nimble opponent, Benkei swore he would follow Yoshitsune as his master wherever he went. This incident forms the theme of one of the favorite plays, "Benkei on the Bridge" (see Plate 17, center). It was Yoshitsune's daring attack that was the decisive factor in the victory of Ichi-no-tani. The highly colored account of the battle in *Heike Monogatari* makes evident even to non-Japanese eyes the popular appeal which these tales of bravery have had from the time they were written.

> Thereafter the battle became general and the various clans of the Gen and Hei surged over each other in mixed and furious combat. The men of the Miura, Kamakura, Chichibu, Ashikaga . . . charged against each other with a roar like thunder while the hills re-echoed to the sound of their war-cries, and the shafts they shot at each other fell like rain. Some were wounded

[2] Chomei Kamo, *The Ten-Foot Square Hut and Tales of the Heike*, selections from *Heike Monogatari*, tr. A. L. Sadler (Sydney: Angus and Robertson, 1928), p. 154.

slightly and fought on, some grappled and stabbed each other to death, while others bore down their adversaries and cut off their heads; everywhere the fight rolled forward and backward, so that none could tell who were victors and vanquished.

[At this point the launching of Yoshitsune's attack from the ridge above the Taira left flank at Ichi-no-tani is described.] The descent was of sand and pebbles, and their horses slid straight down and landed on a level place. From thence there were great mossy boulders for fifty yards to the bottom. Soldiers were recoiling in horror thinking that their end had come when Miura-no-Sahara Juro Yoshitsura sprang forward and shouted: "In my part we ride down places like this any day to catch a bird; the Miura would make a race-course of this"; and down he went, followed by all the rest.

So steep was the descent that the stirrups of the hinder man struck against the helmet or armor of the one in front of him, and so dangerous did it look that they averted their eyes as they went down. "Ei! Ei!" they ejaculated under their breath as they steadied their horses, and their daring seemed rather that of demons than of men. So they reached the bottom . . . They fired the houses and huts of the Heike so that they went up in smoke in a few moments.[3]

Yoshitsune was the main architect of the final Minamoto victory, but the gratitude of his envious and powerful half-brother Yoritomo was not forthcoming. Even when Yoshitsune came to report the victory, Yoritomo would not receive him, and Yoshitsune in the end was forced to flee at times in the guise of an itinerant monk, still accompanied by the faithful Benkei and by Shizuka, his loyal mistress. On the run for over a year, he finally made his way back to Fujiwara Hidehira in the north, where he had stayed as a boy. But the old man was already ninety, and when his son succeeded him, Yoritomo, ruthless to the last, brought such pressure to bear that Yoshitsune was betrayed and attacked. Rather than surrender he committed formal suicide. He was only thirty years old.

It is this last incident of betrayal which brings the emotion and the catharsis to its height for the Japanese who see the historical drama. For loyalty has become the supreme virtue and the highest duty of the warrior caste. The virtue is also a Confucian one and is represented by the character "center" over "heart," "heart central," or "without deviation"—"his heart is in the right place." But, though prized in China, this virtue is held in very special esteem by the Japanese, whose society exhibits to this day a network of obligations and loyalties that serve as an intangible but strong binding force.

Among the fighting men of the feudal period, the Zen form of Buddhism was the most popular religious belief. Zen (Ch'an in Chinese) is based on the early Indian Buddhist practice of seeking release through meditation; but in China this was amalgamated with a Taoist emphasis on individualism, independence, and a strong identification with nature and the natural order,

[3] *Ibid.*, pp. 147 ff.

to form the Ch'an sect. The doctrine was introduced into Japan by the monk Eisai, who brought the Rinzai sect of Zen to Kamakura, Yoritomo's headquarters, in 1191, while Yoritomo himself was still alive (see Plate 17). Eisai's disciple, Dogen, introduced another form of Zen, the Soto sect, a little later in 1227, but wishing to avoid the distractions of the town and the encumbrances of patronage however advantageous, he went to settle on the remote west coast. Both sects flourished and continue active at the present day.

It is at first surprising that any form of the Buddhist religion, with its gentleness, reverence for all forms of life, and shunning of desire and hate, would be practiced at all by warriors. But Buddhism was so well established and Shinto had so little to offer in the way of a coherent philosophy, that those who were in any way religiously inclined had little alternative to some form of Buddhism. And such is the power of human rationalization that they probably were scarcely conscious of any contradiction between faith and conduct.

Why Zen in particular? The original Nara sects and the foundations on Mount Hiei and Mount Koya demanded the study of abstruse doctrines and scriptures, while the more popular devotional sects, such as the Jodo (Pure Land) worship of Amida Buddha (see Plate 15), tended to pietism, if not to sentimentality. Zen, on the other hand, was more likely to appeal to men of action, for its practitioners were offered a direct road to enlightenment and release through discipline and inner control. The aspirants were given a rigorous training in *zazen*, "sitting in meditation." During long periods of concentration the Zen master would seek to jolt their bodies by a kick or a cuff on the head, or to jolt their minds by a series of *koan*, nonsense puzzles, such as, "How do you make a noise by clapping with one hand?" or "A monk asked Yun-men, 'Who is the Buddha?' 'The dried-up dirt-cleaner.'" The disciple might then, by these means or independently, achieve a sudden, intuitional breakthrough, and reach enlightenment. A certain austerity, challenge, and mystery about this approach, and especially its independence of ritual and complicated book learning, intrigued and captivated the warrior mind.

There is another feature of Buddhism in general that may have had a peculiar appeal to men accustomed to take risks and to stake all on the outcome of a battle or an individual combat, and that is the Buddhist sense of the transitory nature of human life and glory. Many *samurai* (the word means "one who serves" but is used in a proud sense of those in military service as vassals to a lord) were far from being crude, unthinking fighters. Glory and honor were of great importance to them, but they were intelligent and subtle enough to realize that these things were transitory. They welcomed a rationale which would account on a universal scale for the known and experienced fact, *sic transit gloria mundi*—"thus passes the glory of the world." That tinge of Buddhist melancholy which pervades the aesthetic pleasures of the *Tale of Genji* in the early Heian age—"Beauty fades, beauty passes, However rare, rare it be"—is felt again in a different way amid the pawing of horses and the clatter of arms which close the period. For all the *samurai* optimism and confidence, they know that swift defeat and then oblivion can overtake the bravest. Buddhism knows this too, faces it, and seeks to transcend it. The warrior, whose native Shinto is too shadowy and thin to provide an integrated view of the world, is prepared to embrace Buddhism because this faith allows a qualified value to a man's station and duty in life, but points him on beyond the vanity of this world to the Buddha whose Law has universal validity. Many warriors who survived the wars took the tonsure and went into a monastery not from convenience, as in the case of some emperors and nobles, but from a conviction that thus they might atone for the sins of their years of battle in the world.

The way of the warrior in Japan is sometimes linked, if only by implication, to the knightly code of honor in the medieval West. There are many genuine similarities, the paramount need for bravery and loyalty being the most important. These similarities arose, it seems, from parallel social circumstances that produced in each case a feudal system in which land was held in return for military service to an overlord who granted protection to all in his domain. The circumstances were genuinely parallel in that a strong lord-vassal relationship was a necessity in both Japan and Europe as the only available barrier to the anarchy and chaos that threatened society after the breakdown of an earlier, stable order. In the West the breakdown was that of the Roman Empire under pressure of the barbarian invasions, while in Japan it was the less spectacular but equally fatal breakdown of the T'ang government system borrowed from China.

The physical circumstances of combat also yield minor parallels, such as the terms "chivalry" from the French *cheval* (horse) and the "way of the horse and the bow," both expressions with important ethical overtones but both derived originally from the fact that the knights went mounted into battle. But here there is one important difference between Japan and the West.

As G. B. Sansom has pointed out, the quality of chivalry as consideration for women and weaker persons is entirely lacking in the Oriental code. And the very idea of tilting for a woman's favor would be shocking to a Japanese. Courtly love and the worship of womanhood were unknown. The motivation for deeds of incredible bravery and endurance came only from two sources: from personal pride and honor, and from loyalty to one's lord, which took precedence over loyalty to the emperor or to religion. The link with the Homeric hero is closer than with the medieval knight, for as he enters battle the Japanese warrior shouts out his name and ancestry as the gage of honor he will do everything to preserve. His strength is in his pride, and he is fighting loyally for his lord; but he is less apt than the medieval knight to speak of fighting for a cause idealistically conceived. Like the

[63]

Homeric hero, or Arjuna in the *Bhagavad-Gita,* he is fighting because that is what he has to do. Yet still in the midst of blind Destiny there is an inexplicable depth and a certain magnificence in his disregard of death.

Rising high in his stirrups he cried with a loud voice: "Kiso-no-Kanjai you have often heard of; now you see him before your eyes! Lord of Iyo and Captain of the Guard, Bright Sun General, Minamoto Yoshinaka am I! Come! Kai-no-Ichijo Jiro! Take my head and show it to Hyoye-no-Suke Yoritomo!" [4]

[4] *Ibid.,* pp. 139–140.

7

GOVERNMENT
BY The MILITARY shoGUN

Kamakura Period: 1185–1336

After the victory of Dan-no-ura in 1185 Minamoto Yoritomo was the virtual master of Japan. He had reached this position by long and thoughtful planning and by being careful always to consolidate his position politically, while delegating the military operations to those, such as Yoshitsune, even better able than himself to carry them out. Yet his position of leadership was still potential rather than actual. He proceeded to make himself un-assailable, mainly by administrative measures of a bold and simple design, accompanied by certain judicious assassinations.

Immediately after the Dan-no-ura triumph, whose suddenness apparently took him by surprise, Yoritomo ordered Noriyori to stay in Kyushu and take over the properties of the defeated Taira lords in that area. This was obviously with a view to rewarding his own successful warriors. At the same time he ordered Yoshitsune to bring the imperial regalia and the chief prisoners back to Kyoto. Yoshitsune complied, but had to report that the sacred sword had been lost from the regalia during the sea battle. When Yoshitsune came on from Kyoto to report his victory to Yoritomo himself, Yoritomo, as we have seen, refused to grant him an audience and was soon chasing him for his life. Yoritomo's attitude to Yoshitsune is hard to explain. Personal jealousy played its part. Yoshitsune was popular at court and had received a number of honors and rewards from Go-Shirakawa, whereas it was Yoritomo's policy to forbid all his followers to have anything to do with the court, or to receive any rewards or appointments other than from himself. In addition a rather disreputable spy appointed by Yoritomo began reporting that Yoshitsune was planning a revolt. It is not likely that this was so, but Yoritomo found it profitable to believe the report. It was an excellent excuse to assert to Go-Shirakawa that the country was in danger from Yoshitsune's activities, and that the safety of the realm could be guaranteed only if Yoritomo himself were put in control and allowed to levy a special military tax and to send his own retainers as officials into every part of the country.

Meanwhile, Yoshitsune was unable to raise any sizable force of men to defend himself against his brother, and fled in disguise to the north where he met his end. But it did not profit Fujiwara Yasuhira, son of the old man Hidehira, to have carried out Yoritomo's orders and harried Yoshitsune to his death in 1189. Yasuhira himself was the last great land-owner not yet under Yoritomo's control, so in a matter of months Yoritomo attacked him with three large armies, defeated and killed him, acquiring thereby a great addition to the wealth he had available for the granting of rewards. It is evident that Yoritomo was completely merciless, and to this both personal and policy reasons must have contributed. In 1186 his remaining uncle, Yukiiye, was assassinated, and in 1193 Noriyori, his other brother, was arrested on a fabricated charge of conspiracy and executed.

Yoritomo's power was based on the new warrior class. He was careful to establish and maintain it as a privileged order. The status of the *samurai* as a fighting man was defined and regulated, and none could claim this status without permission of Yoritomo. The *samurai* was generally a mounted warrior, with full armor and a flag bearing his insignia. There were, of course, other fighting men of various types who were not of *samurai* status. They fought on foot and had lighter armor.

A smaller and more privileged class was that of the *go-kenin* or "honorable house men," the vassals of Yoritomo. *Samurai* status was necessary to qualify for becoming a member of the *go-kenin*, but actually the two categories were different in origin, *samurai* denoting military rank and *go-kenin* feudal relationship. The "house men," who became a kind of minor nobility, were at first only Yoritomo's own retainers of Minamoto connection, but soon he began to invite allies and finally former enemies into this exclusive group. In the end half of his total number of vassals were of Taira descent.

Much of the time that Yoritomo spent at his Kamakura headquarters before, during, and after the Gempei War was devoted to constructing this system of political and military alliances. He was building for the future by gaining control first in the Kanto. The Kanto Plain is the largest single agricultural area in Japan, situated around the modern Tokyo. It is well to the east of the earlier political and cultural center of Kyoto. The foundation of the Kamakura Shogunate marks a shift eastwards in political power which had begun earlier in the economic and military spheres. Yoritomo also increased his control by attaching warriors to himself. Always careful to see to their economic status, he rewarded the loyal with estates and income-bearing offices. Then, at the conclusion of the war, he was able gradually to gain authority over all Japan, including the north, center, and west, by a double process, sending out his own vassals into key positions and securing the loyalty of allies and former foes by making them vassals, always with suitable emoluments. This policy, which seems to have been thought out by Yoritomo in his early years of exile at Izu after his father's downfall, was carried out cautiously and thoroughly. It made for a stability never achieved by his Taira predecessor in power, Kiyomori, and resulted in the establishment of the first stage of feudalism in Japan. The necessity of attaching warriors to himself and his house meant that he alone had to be the fount of all honors and appointments; hence the ban on warriors forming links with the court or receiving favors at the hands of the emperor.

Thus Yoritomo's vassals were soon in positions of authority all over the country, and the system he set up to regulate and reward his own retainers and those under them became the effective government of Japan. This system was superimposed upon and not substituted for the earlier imperial structure set up by the Taika Reform and the latter continued to function, but in an increasingly feeble and nominal manner.

The essence of Yoritomo's system was that one of his own retainers was named as manager of each estate. This manager (*jito*, "steward") was supported by a share of the yield of the estate assigned to him, and in addition he was supervisor of the proper distribution of the other shares of the crop, including those belonging to the owner. He was responsible for keeping the peace, and thus came to act as a local magistrate. He was also in charge of collecting and forwarding to Kamakura the "commissariat rice" or special military tax. This was the tax which Yoritomo had represented to Go-Shirakawa as being necessary in order to finance the suppression of Yoshitsune's "rebellion." It was not burdensome, being only about 2 percent of the crop, but no exceptions were permitted and it was levied on public and private land, regardless of whether the land had received exemption from the earlier imperial taxes. Officers known as constables (*tsuibushi*) or protectors (*shugo*) were appointed to provinces. Their duties were to oversee the stewards, assign the vassals in general to guard service, and keep law and order in their domains. They were often given the title of governor in the parallel imperial structure, but this was more a matter of honor than of substantive power. Both these offices, of steward and constable, became hereditary, and both tended to become lucrative posts, combining both civil and military authority.

The central organs of the Kamakura government were of the same simple and practical kind as the local arrangements just mentioned. The first to be set up, as early as 1180, the beginning of the Gempei War, was the Samurai-dokoro ("service room" or "orderly room"), sometimes translated as the Board of Retainers. This office dealt with the assignment of military duties and the rewards and punishments meted out to the warriors. But its commands extended over wider areas than would be considered proper in the West, and covered many concerns in the private lives of the soldiers, their marriages and families, friends and recreation, anything, in fact, which might have a bearing on their ultimate loyalty to their superior. In wartime the Samurai-dokoro assumed the functions of a headquarters staff.

The second organ of Yoritomo's government was the Mandokoro, or Council, analogous to the secretariat set up earlier to manage the affairs of a great family such as the Fujiwara. The name emphasized the personal character of Yoritomo's rule, but the function of the Mandokoro was that of a policy-making body at the highest level. The Mandokoro was headed by a *shikken*, or director, and after 1203, when Hojo Tokimasa was appointed to this post, it became hereditary in his family.

The third body was known as the Monchujo or Board of Inquiry. This judicial body was the final court of appeal, administering the Minamoto house law which had gradually grown up. Strictly speaking this law applied only to the Minamoto and their retainers at first; but since this was the only effective law whose writ ran throughout the land, litigants from all over Japan, even nobles from the capital, began to come to Kamakura for justice. The Board of Inquiry took careful note of documentary evidence and won the reputation of dispensing even-handed judgments. The fairness of this court in a time of postwar confusion without doubt enhanced the reputation of the Kamakura regime. The customary law administered on the basis of Minamoto house law was later collected and reduced to order as the Joei Code in 1232. These Kamakura boards do not appear to have been dominated by single men for whom they acted as mere mouthpieces. They functioned as committees, giving unanimous public decisions, and bearing the responsibility collectively. It has been noted that the Japanese as a people prefer anonymity of this kind and are skilled at reaching collective decisions.

The setting up of the Monchujo provided a link between Kamakura and the court in Kyoto, for certain experienced nobles and legal experts were invited from Kyoto by Yoritomo to assist in drawing up the regulations under which the Monchujo would function. In ways such as this the intentional barrier that Yoritomo erected between the luxurious and corrupt court and his own stern and frugal warriors began to be broken down. It is evident at the beginning that there was a considerable social gap between the two, for the nobles scorned the military for their uncouth ways, while the warriors despised the nobles for their sheltered lives and their effete manners, and inclined to say, like Hotspur of the courtier,

> . . . he made me mad
> To see him shine so brisk, and smell so sweet,
> And talk so like a waiting gentlewoman
> Of guns and drums and wounds—God save the mark!
> —(*Henry IV*, Pt. I, I, ii)

But it must be placed to the credit of the soldiers that they were always aware of the values of records, books, and the art of literature.

The arranging of these and other administrative matters kept Yoritomo at Kamakura for a full year after his conquest of the domains of Fujiwara Yasuhira in the north. Only when he felt secure through the distribution of rewards, the disciplining of offenders, and the consolidation of his rule did he proceed to the capital, in 1190. In that year he was granted the highest honorific title of Nairan. The position he really coveted was that of Shogun, or Supreme Military Commander, commanding all military forces on behalf of the emperor. This could only be given by the emperor, and the most powerful figure in the imperial house, Go-Shirakawa, was not willing to grant it to Yoritomo. Finally in 1192 Go-Shirakawa died and Fujiwara Kanezane, a powerful minister faithful to the imperial interests but ready to cooperate with the new military regime, persuaded the new retired emperor, Go-Toba, to grant Yoritomo the title. Such was the prestige of the imperial house that Yoritomo, the most powerful figure in the country, felt he had to wait until the emperor bestowed the title on him.

The title of Shogun had a history dating from the early wars of conquest against the Ainu. The emperor had then conferred the office on a particular general for a limited period. Yoritomo, however, regarded the title as a permanent mark of his and his descendants' right to rule Japan in the name of the emperor. His government and that of his successors was known as the *bakufu* ("tent government" or military rule).

After shunning Kyoto for so long, Yoritomo made some extended visits, taking up residence in the Rokuhara mansion, which had been the Taira headquarters. He contributed munificently to the rebuilding of the Todaiji temple and was present at its rededication, for throughout his life he was a devout Buddhist. He died in 1199, without having long enjoyed the fruits of his achievement, yet with his main work essentially done. The portrait of Yoritomo in the British Museum painted by Fujiwara Takanobu shows him in the pose and dress of an official, seated and in black robes. He has a small head and narrow, precise features. The eyes are penetrating, the mouth full and sensual. The whole expression is poised and aloof but with a hint of inner tension. The portrait does not show Yoritomo's iron will and determination, but only their potential presence behind the calm and rather strained expression of the face. Yet the historical record reveals resolute purpose and organizational power of an uncommon order, making him one of the greatest men in the history of Japan. Enough has been said of his cruelty in the struggle for power, a characteristic he shared with others of his age in the West as well as in the East. He was not an attractive personality but he was extremely successful, an innovator and a combination of thinker and man of action.

After the death of Yoritomo the shogunal power did not long remain in his family line. During a series of sordid struggles his two sons were killed, one after the other, and authority passed to Hojo Tokimasa, Yoritomo's father-in-law and early guardian, and then successively to Tokimasa's son, Yoshitoki, and to his grandson, Yasutoki. In contrast to Yoritomo's Minamoto relatives, who all died young and usually by violent means, the

Hojo family were well suited to consolidate the Kamakura Shogunate, for none down to Yasutoki died before the age of fifty-nine and Tokimasa lived to the age of seventy-seven. This consolidation they faithfully carried out, despite the violence with which they began, and gave Japan in the process nearly a century of comparative tranquillity. They did not themselves become the shoguns, but exercised the real power as the Hojo regents by retaining in their own hands the post of *shikken*, or head of the Council, first acquired by Hojo Tokimasa in 1203. Ten more members of the Hojo family held the post in succession after him. After a time the position of Shogun, now itself a nominal one, was usually held by a prince of the imperial blood.

An extraordinary anomaly thus emerged in the government of Japan, a complicated system of indirect rule probably without parallel anywhere else. In Kyoto a titular emperor had handed over power to a Fujiwara regent, who in turn had yielded to the authority of a retired or cloistered emperor. But even he did not exercise the realities of power, which belonged first to a powerful military shogun, and then were exercised on behalf of the shogun by a regent of the Hojo family in Kamakura.

Relations between the *bakufu* and the court were on the whole amicable. They were seriously disturbed only once during the height of Kamakura power, and that near the beginning of the long period of peace referred to as characteristic of the Hojo Regency. The Emperor Go-Toba succeeded Go-Shirakawa in 1192, ruling first as titular and then as cloistered emperor until 1221. A man of ambition and charm, Go-Toba flattered and made friends with members of the Kamakura government stationed in Kyoto in a calculated attempt to undermine the shogunate and restore a measure of imperial independence. He gradually determined, against the strong advice of his advisers, to make a strong bid to overthrow the *bakufu* by force. Go-Toba had allies among some of the clans in the north and west who had never become reconciled to the Minamoto dominance. Moreover he showed great skill in his treatment of the monasteries. Ecclesiastical quarrels had broken out again, and in the course of their intrigues the monks had once more tried to blackmail and force the court into supporting one side or the other. Go-Toba, however, was less affected by superstitious dread than his predecessor, Go-Shirakawa, and dispatched guards to scatter the ill-organized troops of the monasteries. But he followed this firmness with conciliation, pointing out to the abbots that they had much to gain by uniting with each other and with himself. And indeed the monasteries had no love for the Minamoto, who had treated them harshly on numerous occasions. There was also a new factor in the church situation. The rise of Amidist and Zen sects in the eastern region was offering serious competition to the older sects in and around the capital. For several reasons, therefore, the abbots of the older monasteries were ready to listen to Go-Toba.

With the support of certain clans and the leading monasteries Go-Toba made his move in 1221, and summoned all the eastern warriors to a great festival in Kyoto, in order to draw them away from their base. He declared Hojo Yoshitoki an outlaw in June, and gave notice that all the eastern region was officially in a state of rebellion. The *bakufu* received a last-minute warning of the state of affairs. They gathered three armies and marched on the capital by different routes. There was considerable sympathy for Go-Toba's cause, and, given better leadership in the field, he might have made a sufficiently good showing to have reached a compromise arrangement with Kamakura. But neither his generals nor his troops were up to the standard of the experienced Kamakura fighting men, and his side was defeated. Go-Toba failed to get help from the Mount Hiei monastery when he needed it, and he resolved to make a last stand on the river between Seta and Uji, scene of earlier battles. After inflicting heavy losses on the Kamakura forces, who had to contend with the difficulties of the river crossing, Go-Toba's men were surrounded and vanquished. A few of the leaders were executed, but in general the *bakufu* had the good sense not to press the matter of punishment for this revolt too far. Go-Toba and the titular emperor were sent into exile in remote parts of Japan, and their estates and those of many court nobles were confiscated. This incident was known as the Jokyu Disturbance. Thereafter the *bakufu* watched the court much more closely, even determining the succession to the positions of titular and cloistered emperor; but they were always correct and careful in respecting the sacred prerogatives of the Throne. The distribution of the confiscated estates proved very useful in allaying discontent among the vassals of the *bakufu*.

During the remainder of the thirteenth century the Hojo regents maintained domestic peace. They themselves showed an example of frugal living and faithfulness to duty. The structure set up by Yoritomo proved a durable one, and the vassals were assured reasonable justice and security in their holdings. But in the last quarter of the century a serious threat developed from abroad. The Koreans had not been strong enough and the Chinese not ambitious enough to attack Japan. But the Mongols were a different matter; their restless zeal for conquest knew no bounds. The Yüan or Mongol Dynasty came into full control of China in 1280, after the defeat of the Southern Sung Dynasty, and thus the dates of the Yüan Dynasty are usually given as 1280–1368. But the Mongols were already in control in North China from about 1230 and Khubilai, the Great Khan of the Mongols, established his capital at Peking in 1264. Korea proved quite incapable of resisting and succumbed to the conqueror. In 1268 Khubilai sent an embassy to Japan demanding submission. The court would probably have compromised, but Hojo Tokimune and his Council of State decided to resist and sent the envoys back without an answer or even an acknowledgment. Hojo Masamura, an experienced general of sixty, was put in charge of the defense. The Mongol preparations had been delayed but were sufficiently advanced by 1272 to cause Masamura to order all Kyushu vassals who were residing elsewhere to return to their estates. He commanded that they and the Kyushu constables see to the manning of the western defenses.

Another Mongol envoy was expelled from Japan in 1272, which amounted to a declaration of war. The attack came in 1274 by a force of some 25,000 Mongols and Koreans, who made a landing at Hakata Bay in North Kyushu. The Mongols were a terrifying enemy and had the advantage of skill in the use of massed cavalry and heavy catapults flinging explosive bombs. But they had little room to maneuver, and the Japanese, fired by desperate zeal to defend their homeland, used their swords and bows to such good effect that they were able to hold off the Mongol attack at least partially on the first encounter.

When night fell the Japanese retreated a few miles inland and lay behind dikes erected as defenses in earlier times. Bad weather was brewing and the Korean pilots advised urgent reembarkation lest the ships be caught on a lee shore in a storm. For some reason the Mongol commanders feared a night attack by the Japanese in wind and rain, though in fact the exhausted Japanese were in no position to deliver one. Fortunately for the Japanese defenders, the Mongols did decide to retreat after just one day's fighting. A number of ships were lost in the ensuing storm and many soldiers drowned.

The Japanese had gained a respite. They took full advantage of it by beginning immediate construction of a stone defensive wall all the way round the Hakata Bay, by calling up troops for garrison duty on a regular roster, and by making arrangements for the drilling and movement of reinforcements in the event of a second attack, which they felt sure would follow. It was to be five years before Khubilai was ready with a much larger force. Japanese vigilance did not slacken and preparations went on unabated, with a dedication and united sense of patriotism which the country had scarcely known hitherto. One of the items that proved most important among the defense preparations was the building of a large number of small warships. Envoys sent again from Peking were this time summarily executed in defiance. The court led in offering prayers to the deities, especially the Shinto gods. Special measures were taken to encourage loyalty and efficiency among the vassals.

In 1281 the Mongols made their second and more determined attempt. They had gathered an immense force of 140,000, but it should be noted that some 100,000 of these were Chinese from South China, a region only recently conquered by the Mongols. These men had little stomach for a fight on behalf of their Mongol masters. The invaders made several landings along the Kyushu coast, but Hakata Bay was the most strategic location and there the Japanese wall was effective in preventing the deployment of cavalry. The Japanese warriors in a heroic defense held the Mongols at bay for two months from June to August and denied them any significant expansion of their beachheads. Meanwhile the smaller and more maneuverable Japanese warships inflicted serious damage on the Mongol war junks in the narrow waters of the bay. On August 15 and 16 deliverance came. A tremendous typhoon blew up and wrought havoc with the Mongol fleet. In such tropical storms winds of 120 miles per hour are not uncommon, and the fleet of the Chinese contingent received the worst damage. They were in a bay farther down the coast to the west and caught the full force of the on-shore hurricane. Ships were jammed together in the narrows and the loss of life was appalling. The large number of Mongol and Chinese soldiers left on shore fell prey to the swords of the exultant Japanese. The typhoon was hailed as an answer to prayer, the "wind of the gods," *kamikaze*. The *bakufu* maintained their Kyushu defenses for twenty years more, but the Mongols never returned.

From the Mongol point of view this failure was not important. There was little incentive for the Mongols to press the matter of the conquest of Japan to a conclusion. The Chinese emperors heretofore had never viewed these offshore islands as either a threat or a valuable prize. For the Mongols the reduction of Japan was a matter of prestige, an attempt to round off their conquest of East Asia, not a matter of economics or necessity. They already had all the land they could exploit or administer, right down to South China and into Indo-China. But for the Japanese the victory was a miraculous deliverance. This was the first attempted invasion of the sacred soil of Japan in historic times, and the last until the end of World War II. It is little wonder that the experience made a lasting impression and that the memory of *kamikaze* was reinvoked in World War II as the name for suicide pilot attacks. In view of Japan's later achievements the defeat of the Mongols must be considered one of the decisive battles of world history.

The religious aspect of this deliverance from the Mongols was emphasized in the enthusiasm generated by a priest, Nichiren (1222–1282). He claimed that he had prophetically foretold the foreign attack as a punishment for the country's leaders, and the eventual triumph of Japan. His doctrine was a combination of Buddhist beliefs with fervent nationalism, and his fiery personality seems to have inspired in his followers a fanaticism in keeping with the crisis of the times. Nichiren exalted the Lotus Sutra as containing all the truth needed for salvation. He summarized this in the phrase, *Namu myoho rengekyo*, "Hail to the Wonderful Law of the Lotus Sutra!" which his followers would chant to the beat of a drum, "dondon dondoko dondon." He showed more intolerance of other sects than any Buddhist leader hitherto, and criticized the authorities for supporting false teachers. He was sentenced to death for open censure of the Hojo regents, but escaped, according to his disciples, by a miracle when a bolt of lightning struck the executioner's sword. "Banished then to a lonely island in the Sea of Japan, Nichiren wrote, 'Birds cry but shed no tears. Nichiren does not cry, but his tears are never dry.'" [1]

[1] Ryusaku Tsunoda, William De Bary, and Donald Keene, *Sources of the Japanese Tradition* (New York: Columbia University Press, 1958), Vol. I, p. 215.

1 *Haniwa* figure representing a man with a miter-shaped hat. Ibaraki Prefecture; burial figure, late Tomb period, sixth to seventh century. Reddish buff earthenware. Ht., 56 in. The hilt of a sword that hung from his waist marks his elite profession. (*The Asia Society, New York: Mr. and Mrs. John D. Rockefeller 3rd Collection. Photography by Otto E. Nelson*)

2 Ainu Festival, Island of Hokkaido. The ancestors of these Ainu, Caucasian by race, lived in Japan before the Japanese and have always engaged in hunting and fishing. Note non-Japanese patterns on their robes. (*Japan National Tourist Organization*)

3   Shikoku Island, Ehime Prefecture. The islands and tree-covered headlands of the
Inland Sea form some of the most beautiful scenery in the world. Fishing boats and
rice fields provide the two main staples of Japanese diet. Rice fields must be level to
retain the standing water required. The dikes and terracing seen here need hard
work to maintain. (*Japan National Tourist Organization*)

4   Farm at Ohara, near Kyoto. The farm and the farmer's family look much the
same now as in medieval Japan; but technology has brought improvements in
production and convenience. (*Japan National Tourist Organization*)

5 Peasants winnowing rice in the presence of officials (left), an instance of the strict control of agriculture. Scroll painting of the Ashikaga (or Muromachi) period (1392–1573). (*Fogg Art Museum, Harvard University; gift of Dr. Denman W. Ross*)

6 Picking and collecting tea. The cultivation of both tea and rice are highly labor-intensive. Tea requires moisture but not standing water, and hence can be grown on hillsides with less terracing than rice. (*Japan National Tourist Organization*)

7 Taking a lunch break. Much of the field work in Japan is done by women. Protection from suntan is considered desirable. (*Japan National Tourist Organization*)

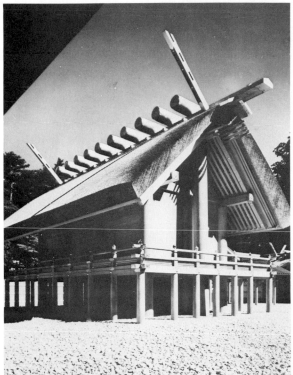

8 Shrine at Ise, early and most revered center of the national religion of Shinto. This, the inner shrine, in archaic Japanese style, is dedicated to Amaterasu, the Sun Goddess. (*Japan Information Center*)

9 The Phoenix Hall of the Byodo-in, a Buddhist temple dating from 1053, at Uji near Kyoto, and associated with the powerful Fujiwara family. The two wings of the building and the delicate roofs are said to be reminiscent of a phoenix bird alighting. (*Japan Information Center*)

10 Wooden statue of a Buddhist guardian god, or Deva King, at an inner gateway of the Horyuji Temple, Nara (see Plate 11). (*Japan National Tourist Organization*)

11 Yumedono (The Hall of Dreams), in the Horyuji Temple, Nara, built by Prince Shotoku in 607 for use as a chapel. The Horyuji is the oldest complete Buddhist monastery complex in Japan. (*Japan National Tourist Organization*)

12 Pagoda of the Daigoji Temple, Kyoto, dating back to 951 and restored in the sixteenth century by Toyotomi Hideyoshi. Daigoji is a temple of the Shingon, "True Word," sect. All pagodas have an odd number of stories, and do not as a rule contain images. (*Japan Information Center*)

13 Buddhist *Sutra* (scripture) of the Heian period, c. twelfth century. The frontispiece and first part of the text, gold ink on deep blue paper. (*Fogg Art Museum, Harvard University; Wetzel Bequest*)

14 *Gigaku* mask. This dramatic mask of the head of an old man is composed of lacquer on a cloth base and dates from the Heian period, tenth century. The drama of this time was forerunner of the classical *No* drama. (*Fogg Art Museum, Harvard University; gift of Miss Mildred Ellis*)

15   Buddha, probably Amida, Kamakura period, c. thirteenth century,
(wood, *yosegi* or joined block tech-
nique, with polychrome and *kiri-
kane*, cut gold leaf decoration). Ht.,
47 in. Amida's disciples in the Jodo
(Pure Land) sect believe they are
saved and received into the Western
Paradise by faith alone. (*The Asia
Society, New York: Mr. and Mrs. John
D. Rockefeller 3rd Collection. Photography by Otto E. Nelson*)

16   Ginkakuji (Silver Pavilion Temple), in Kyoto,
was the retreat of the eighth Ashikaga Shogun,
Yoshimasa, the great art patron in the fifteenth
century. (*Japan Information Center*)

17   Garden of the Tenryuji Temple, Kyoto, designed in the fourteenth century by a famous monk, Muso Soseki. The simplicity of rocks, pond, and raked sand is an aid to meditation in this temple of the Rinzai sect of Zen Buddhism. (*Japan Information Center*)

18   *No* play, principal actor (*shite*). The voluminous kimono is of rich silk brocade and the mask that of a woman, although the actor is male. (*Japan Air Lines*)

19 *The Tale of Genji*, Lady Murasaki's famous novel, dates from the eleventh century and has been frequently illustrated. This painting of a scene from the Yugao chapter is of the Tosa school and dates from the eighteenth–nineteenth century. (*Fogg Art Museum, Harvard University; gift of Charles Parker*)

With no lack of self-confidence he saw his own mission in terms of two saints mentioned in the Lotus Sutra, the Bodhisattva of Superb Action, a pioneer in propagating the Perfect Truth, and the Bodhisattva Ever-Abused. "How much more, then, should this be the case with Nichiren, a man born in the family of an outcast fisherman, so lowly and degraded and poor!" [2] Completely convinced of his mission, he could say:

> I, Nichiren, am the master and lord of the sovereign, as well as of all the Buddhists of other schools. Notwithstanding this, the rulers and the people treat us thus maliciously. How should the sun and the moon bless them by giving them light? Why should the earth not refuse to let them abide upon it? . . . Therefore, also, the Mongols are coming to chastise them. . . . It is decreed that all the inhabitants of Japan shall suffer from the invaders. Whether this comes to pass or not will prove whether or not Nichiren is the real propagator of the Lotus of Truth.[3]

The name which the prophet adopted symbolized his love of Buddhism and of Japan, for *nichi* (sun) standsa for both the Light of Truth and the Land of the Rising Sun, while *ren* means lotus. He sees Japan as the center from which Buddhism will spread to the whole world.

> Then the golden age, such as were the ages under the reign of the sage kings of old, will be realized in these days of degeneration and corruption, in the time of the Latter Law. . . . The Holy See in Japan will then be the seat where all men of the three countries India, China and Japan and the whole Jambudvipa world will be initiated into the mysteries of confession and expiation; and even the great deities, Brahma and Indra, will come down into the sanctuary and participate in the initiation.[4]

Nichiren was by no means the only prominent Buddhist teacher active in this era, for there was a considerable revival of Buddhism during the Kamakura Period. The coming of the Zen sects to Kamakura has already been mentioned, but it was in the Pure Land sects that two of the most influential priests, Honen (1133–1212) and Shinran (1173–1262), were to be found. Trust in the mercy of Amida Buddha for entry after death to the Pure Land had been a feature of other sects of Buddhism for some time. But Honen laid exclusive emphasis on this Way and on the repetition of Buddha's name in faith as the supreme means of salvation, thus for the first time marking off the Pure Land as a distinct and separate sect. He was extremely successful in winning converts, especially among the common people. It is said that the ex-Emperor Go-Toba was annoyed at the fact that two of his maids of honor were among those who were converted and became nuns, and that this was a contributory reason for the exile of Honen in his old age. An extract from his famous *One Page Testament*, written two days before his death, will give an idea of the essence of his teaching:

[2] *Ibid.*, p. 221.
[3] *Ibid.*, pp. 219–20.
[4] *Ibid.*, p. 224.

The method of final salvation that I have propounded is neither a sort of meditation, such as has been practiced by many scholars in China and Japan, nor is it a repetition of the Buddha's name by those who have understood the deep meaning of it. It is nothing but the mere repetition of the *"Namu Amida Butsu"* without a doubt of His mercy, whereby one may be born into the Land of Perfect Bliss. The mere repetition with firm faith includes all the practical details. . . . Those who believe this, though they clearly understand all the teachings Shaka taught throughout his whole life, should behave themselves like simple-minded folk, who know not a single letter, or like ignorant nuns or monks whose faith is implicitly simple. Thus without pedantic airs, they should fervently practice the repetition of the name of Amida, and that alone.[5]

Shinran was banished, at about the same time as Honen, for taking a wife in violation of the vow of celibacy. This action, his followers claimed, was part of his identification with the common man and demonstrated the belief Shinran held that monastic discipline was not essential to salvation and that family and home formed the right setting for the religious life.

He [Shinran] was, he admitted, a lost soul, unsure of himself and of all else in this life except the abiding grace of Amida. His only aim was to bring this faith in Amida to those like himself who needed it most, to those ignorant and illiterate souls who could not distinguish good from bad, to "bad people" rather than "good people." Shinran even went so far as to say that wicked men might be more acceptable to Amida than good men, since the former threw themselves entirely on the mercy of the Buddha, while the latter might be tempted to think that their chances of salvation were improved by their own meritorious conduct. "If even good people can be reborn in the Pure Land, how much more the wicked man!"[6]

The parallel in this last passage to the parable of the Pharisee and the tax gatherer in the New Testament (Luke 18: 9–14) is striking. Successors of Shinran organized the scattered groups of converts into a solid body called the True Pure Land sect. Under the name Ikko, "the Single-Minded," they later formed communities and fought fanatically in the wars of the sixteenth century. This True Pure Land sect, known in Japanese as Shinshu, is now the largest Buddhist sect in Japan.

Many features of popular Buddhism in this era exhibited close similarities to religious developments in Reformation Europe, notably married clergy, the use of scriptures in the vernacular, emphasis on salvation through faith in divine grace, and even the religious divisions and intolerance. These divisions in Japan were now more over points of doctrine and less over questions of prestige and politics than had been the case with the intermonastic quarrels of the earlier sects.

The Mongol War had proved a severe strain on the finances of the Hojo Regency, and after about 1284 their power began to decline. Always

[5] *Ibid.*, p. 202.
[6] *Ibid.*, pp. 203–4.

uncertain as to whether the Mongols might return to the attack, the Hojo had had to maintain the Kyushu defenses for twenty years, and this had been a very costly burden. Moreover they had not acquired in this war any fresh captured territories with which to reward their fighting men, such as those Yoritomo had been able to dispose of after the defeat of the Taira. Discontent was slowly growing, particularly since the monasteries had had first chance at what rewards were available in return for their prayers for victory, and there was then little left for the soldiers. As time passed, warriors who had felt a close personal tie with Yoritomo came to feel much less intimately attached to a succession of Shoguns who were mere figure-heads. Justice in the Kamakura courts began to be administered less promptly, fairly, and efficiently than in the early days. Finally quarrels among the Hojo themselves weakened their position. The Hojo regents, in fact, had compiled a remarkable record of good administration and an example of high personal character; but inevitably there were exceptions. It did not enhance the reputation of the *bakufu* when one of the regents, though a monk, kept forty concubines and was passionately addicted to dogfights, making the populace bow down to the champion dog when it was paraded in the streets of Kamakura.

The country as a whole had an expanding economy; but many individual retainers were in financial distress. There was no law of primogeniture, which would have retained estates intact in the hands of the eldest son, and as the warrior class increased in this time of peace, the holdings of each member tended to decrease by constant division. In 1297 the *bakufu* tried the somewhat desperate expedient of passing a law of "virtuous administration," which was in effect a cancellation of debts owed by the retainers to those outside their class. This proved to be no help, for they still needed money, and new loan contracts began to carry a clause specifically excluding cancellation by future acts of "virtuous administration." The result was that money became tighter and loans harder to obtain. The rich became richer, and the poor poorer. The stewards throughout the country tended to fall lower in the property scale, and the higher officials, such as the constables, to rise. This social change presaged the rise later on of the great territorial lords known as *daimyo*, or "great names."

These general causes of decline in the power of the Hojo regents came to a head in certain specific events which occurred when the Emperor Go-Daigo came to the throne in 1318, not as a child but as a grown man of thirty. He planned neither to abdicate nor to remain as a mere titular emperor, but to rule as the reigning emperor. A considerable measure of power might have been his, since the Hojo Regency was no longer strong; but he incited their opposition and in a sense compelled them to take a stand because of a succession dispute. In the mid-thirteenth century the ex-Emperor Go-Saga had left a will that was bound to cause future trouble for the *bakufu*. Each of his two sons had been titular emperor in turn, and the will carefully divided his property between them but was silent on the

[86]

question of the succession, in effect leaving the choice to the *bakufu*. In the intervening period up to Go-Daigo's time the lines descending from these two sons had provided emperors in turn; but Do-Daigo, in his newfound resolution, planned to keep the succession in his line only. He was opposed, somewhat naturally, by the *bakufu*.

This dispute began the Genko War in 1331. Repeating the earlier pattern of Go-Toba, Go-Daigo enlisted the help of some of the monasteries around the capital and of certain clan leaders who had become disillusioned with the Hojo regime. Go-Daigo himself was soon captured and sent into exile; but one of his supporters, a famous and unselfish warrior, Kusunoki Masashige, held out in a mountain fortress near Nara and kept the cause alive.

Then events took an odd turn. Go-Daigo escaped from his place of exile in 1333. The general sent by the *bakufu* to recapture him, Ashikaga Takauji, head of a distinguished branch of the Minamoto, changed sides and seized Kyoto in the name of Go-Daigo. The Hojo regents were becoming increasingly unpopular, and Takauji's success in taking the capital was the signal for others to join him. Most of the Kanto region rose in revolt and found a leader in Nitta Yoshisada, who marched upon Kamakura, suddenly defeated the last of the Hojo regents, and consigned the city to the flames.

Go-Daigo was triumphant. He made a thorough-going attempt, in what is known as the Kemmu Restoration, to put the old imperial system of government back into operation, reviving all the former ministries and official positions. But the attempt was an anachronism. The power still lay with the wielders of the sword and the holders of land, and the Emperor had neither. The resolution of the situation came through a further twist in the warrior struggle for power. Ashikaga Takauji and Nitta Yoshisada each had too much ambition to brook the presence of the other, and they became involved in conflict in the Kanto region in 1335. Go-Daigo sided with Nitta Yoshisada, but he had made the wrong guess. Ashikaga Takauji suppressed his rival during the next year, removed Go-Daigo, and installed an emperor of the rival branch. Go-Daigo, however, once more escaped and proceeded to a place called Yoshino, in the mountains south of Kyoto, where his supporters established him as emperor of a southern line. For the next fifty-six years, from 1336 to 1392, there were thus two imperial lines claiming legitimacy, the southern at Yoshino and the northern at Kyoto. The war of the two dynasties was the outward form of the struggle; the real issue was which warrior group would dominate the court and control the country as had the Hojo regents. Ashikaga Takauji was the victor and this ushered in the Ashikaga Shogunate, the first part of which, up to 1392, was called after a period in Chinese history, the Nambokucho, the South and North Period, when a similar situation had prevailed.

8

The ASHIKAGA ShOGUNATE

Nambokucho: 1336–1392
Muromachi: 1392–1573

The devious shifts and complicated power struggles through which Ashikaga Takauji rose to the summit of authority in the early fourteenth century continued to characterize the political scene throughout the Ashikaga Shogunate. The Ashikaga, in contrast to Yoritomo, never controlled all of Japan. They maintained a grip on eight eastern provinces, but could not hold down the rest of the country by placing their own retainers in key positions, as Yoritomo had done. They had rather to resort to bargaining with powerful landowners and warlords for support. The age was therefore one of constant war, with alliances dissolving and re-forming, and the center of gravity in the nation shifting away from the capital to the great landed estates and feudal domains of a new type. This shift incidentally distributed to other parts of Japan many of the benefits hitherto enjoyed exclusively by the dwellers in the capital region. There was no strong, central, feudal court of justice, such as had given cohesion to Yoritomo's rule, and the diminishing authority of the emperor was further weakened by the split between the factions of the northern and southern courts.

The distribution of the *shiki*, rights or shares in the produce of estates, was no longer carried out, for the stewards had become outright owners, or, in many cases, lost their land to a superior. The feudal pattern had therefore altered to a direct overlord-vassal relationship, operating locally, with no strong central authority. The income from estates was not remitted to absentee owners, with the result that the emperors and court nobles were seriously impoverished. In 1500, for example, the funeral of an emperor had to be delayed for six weeks until enough money could be collected to pay the funeral expenses. Emperors were actually reduced to selling their autographs. Anyone could leave a written request and a small amount of money and the emperor would be willing to copy out in his own hand a verse from one of the poets or a section from one of the warrior romances. There was no recourse for those thus deprived of customary income, for the Shogun was not strong enough to compel his followers or allies to give up any of their wealth.

Fortunes rose and declined within short periods of time. The Yamana family, for instance, originally allies of Takauji, became dissatisfied and changed their allegiance to support the southern court. After a while they withdrew from the fighting to consolidate their family position, and came to an agreement with the second Ashikaga Shogun, who made the head of the Yamana clan constable of no fewer than six provinces. By 1390 the family controlled eleven provinces, but they broke their oath to the Ashikaga two years later and in overweening confidence attacked the Shogun. They were defeated and deprived of all but their own original two provinces.

The Yamana, though outstanding, were but one among many families whose fortunes fluctuated wildly. The romances spoke of loyalty to the death, but opportunism and treachery seem to have been equally common. One leader, however, Kitabatake Chikafusa, proved unswervingly loyal to Go-Daigo and the southern court. Learned and a man of many parts, he felt Go-Daigo to be the legitimate emperor and devoted his life to the cause of his master. Kitabatake's bravery and brilliant planning kept the southern cause going long after Go-Daigo's death in 1339. He gathered intelligence from all over Japan and kept dividing and confusing the forces of Takauji and the northern court by guerrilla tactics. The cause was maintained successfully even after his own death in 1354 by his stratagem of having sons of Go-Daigo stationed in various parts of the country to form rallying points of loyalty to the southern line.

The confusion of the period may be seen from the fact that Kyoto changed hands four times between 1353 and 1355. The Ashikaga would have been able to maintain firmer control had Takauji and his brother not fallen out. When Takauji died in 1358, the dire results of their dispute continued, for their quarrel weakened the cause of the northern court. Lords in various parts of the country continued to keep the struggle between the northern and southern courts alive, supporting one side or the other. They did this not so much out of conviction as from the hope that fighting would bring them improved fortune in the form of booty or land.

In accordance with Kitabatake's policy for the southern court, Prince Kanenaga had gone to Kyushu and by 1365 had gained control of the whole of that island. He was opposed by a talented general of the Ashikaga side, Imagawa Sadayo, who was a scholar-poet as well as a soldier, and similar to Kitabatake in that he took an overall view and planned carefully every detail of his campaign. Both in this respect showed an advance in generalship and strategic grasp over the commanders of the Gempei War era, who were courageous and dashing, with an eye to tactical advantage, but less able to plan thoughtfully for the effective use of numbers in a whole campaign. Imagawa won back the northern part of Kyushu by 1372, but the southern loyalists held out for nearly twelve years more and surrendered only upon the death of Prince Kanenaga. Finally the third Shogun, Yoshimitsu, prevailed on the southern court to give up the struggle and return to Kyoto in 1392. The regalia were to be brought back by the southern court, a division of property was agreed to, and the succession was to alternate between the two lines. The regalia were duly surrendered, but the Shogun broke his promise about the succession; the line of Go-Daigo was excluded and supplied no future emperors. The reunion of the courts in 1392 marked the beginning of the political sub-period known as the Muromachi, which was named after a district in Kyoto and which continued until the end of the Ashikaga period in 1573.

After the union of the courts the first half of the fifteenth century was a period when no major wars were fought between territorial lords. But it could not be described as a time of peace, for it was marked by serious agrarian unrest. The peasants were becoming more conscious of their strength and less satisfied with the conditions of their life. They found leadership among those warriors who had taken to farming or who had, by some accident of fortune, lost their place in the territorial power structure. Since the weak *bakufu* could give them no redress for their grievances, they formed leagues, *ikki*, for self-protection. The word *ikki*, from meaning "league," underwent a transformation to mean "a revolt promoted by a league." There was a famine in 1420, another famine followed by plague in 1425, and the first armed peasant rising on a large scale near the capital in 1428. Thereafter such risings became extremely frequent. Mobs broke into buildings owned by sake brewers, pawnbrokers, and monasteries, all of whom were engaged in moneylending, in order to destroy evidence of their debts. The *bakufu* tried the expedient of cancellation of debts on more than one occasion, but with little effect, and its authority became minimal after 1441. Two years later the capital itself was attacked by rioters.

The ultimate in tragic futility was reached in the Onin War of 1467–77. Yoshimasa, the eighth Ashikaga Shogun, was overwhelmed by problems of government he could not solve and was in any case more interested in the enjoyment of art than in the exercise of power. He wished to retire at the age of thirty, and the two most powerful families, the Hosokawa and the Yamana, became involved with rival claimants to his vacant seat. In the course of the maneuvering the Yamana chieftain requested permission to punish Hosokawa Katsumoto for interfering in a matter concerning the Shogun's deputy. He was refused, but Katsumoto saw which way the wind was blowing and began to mobilize troops. The rivals were content to glare at one another for a time, since neither wished to be officially branded as a rebel and thus to offer his enemies a chance to annex his property without penalty. In May 1467 fighting broke out in the city of Kyoto itself.

This was no longer single combat between mounted knights but fierce slaughter in streets and alleys, arson and looting by a new type of soldier, the *ashigaru* or light infantry. These men, often absconding peasants, were armed with one weapon, a spear, halberd, or sword, and were expert in the art of street fighting. The results of months of battle and burning in the civilized and beautiful capital of Kyoto were disastrous. The temple of Shokokuji was burned down during intense fighting in the northeast quarter, whole sections of the city were gutted by fire, and the slaughter at close quarters was fearful. After one engagement eight cartloads of heads were collected, and this represented only some of those killed. The fighting was not continuous. Forces were withdrawn from the capital to fight elsewhere. Lulls occurred in the struggle, during some of which poetry contests were held to relieve the tedium of waiting under arms.

In 1473 the original opponents, chieftains of the Hosokawa and Yamana, both died. The spark went out of the useless struggle, and Ouchi, now leader on the Yamana side, at length withdrew from Kyoto in 1477 and submitted to the Shogun. One result of the Onin War was to make men sick of civil strife; but there was still to be a century of disunity before the rise of any power strong enough to provide unquestioned central authority. The Ashikaga ceased altogether to be effective after the end of the Onin War. Such government as there was came from their deputies in the Hosokawa family, who were left as dubious victors when the Yamana retreated.

The period of decentralized feudalism under the Ashikaga, which forms the second stage of feudalism in Japan, coincided with and in part caused a considerable economic expansion. The earlier feudalism of the Kamakura period under Yoritomo and then the Hojo regents in their days of strength had already seen a movement of goods and people much greater than in the early times of Nara in the eighth century and the beginning of Heian in the ninth. Technological skills such as those required for making pottery and paper and casting iron had spread during the Kamakura period. Taira Tadamori and Kiyomori slightly before that time were interested in trade with China and did a good deal to promote it by improving harbor facilities in the Inland Sea. But an increase in wealth and a rise in the standard of living become much more marked during the Ashikaga Period. This is sufficiently proved by one fact alone: Agricultural production per acre increased two- or even three-fold in many parts of the country due to better farming methods and to larger economic units in the new type of feudal estate.

In spite of disturbed conditions, there was economic advance during this period, both domestically and in the foreign trade with China. The wars of the fourteenth and fifteenth centuries created demand in remote parts of the country and also rendered better transportation a necessity, both by land and sea. Handicraft industry expanded to meet the requirements of war, in arms and armor, and of peace, in agricultural implements and in the creation of those luxuries—textiles, lacquer, and numerous other goods—which the territorial lords could now better afford. At the same time the disturbed conditions of the country made it advisable for merchants and craftsmen to band together for mutual protection. There was a system to hand for this purpose in the *za*, or guilds, which had existed since the twelfth century but were now strongly developed. The word *za* means a seat or pitch at a marketplace, usually associated with a temple fair and under the protection of a powerful religious institution. This symbiotic arrangement between monks and merchants was mutually profitable, for it was well worthwhile for the merchants to pay fees to the temple for their stalls in the nearby market area in return for the support of the temple in cases where the merchants had to complain to court or *bakufu* concerning some invasion of their rights. It is even said that temple support was of aid in the collection of debts.

Businesses and trades associated with a particular region would turn to a prominent shrine in that region for protection. Thus in the course of time the guild dealing in cotton clothes became associated with the Gion shrine, the brewers of yeast with the Kitano shrine, and so on. The warehouse keepers were also the pawnbrokers, and they, too, were connected with a religious institution: the Enryakuji on Mount Hiei, one of the most powerful monasteries in Japan. Great families played a similar role as patrons, the Bojo associated with the papermakers, the Konoe with the craftsmen in gold leaf, and the Kuga with the guild of courtesans.

The proliferation of independent estates resulted, exactly as in Europe, in the multiplication of tolls and customs dues collected at barrier points between different regions of jurisdiction. One main reason for the rise of the *za* was to facilitate the movement of goods by the purchase for a fee of exemption from tolls. Armed with this exemption from their powerful patron, individual merchants in a guild could move their products more freely from the place of manufacture to distant places of sale. The securing of local monopoly in the sale of certain articles is a well-known feature of medieval European guilds, and this factor also operated in Japan.

The shrine patrons mentioned above are in the Kyoto area, but guilds were to be found in other parts of the country. There is evidence of interconnection between the guilds of one craft in different places, though such alliances were not nearly so tightly knit nor so powerful as the great combination of the Hanseatic League in northern Europe. The presence of guilds outside the capital, however, indicates the rise of provincial and castle towns, a feature of this period in Japan. Only one of these new towns, Sakai (the modern Osaka) at the head of the Inland Sea, developed such privileges and immunities as to make it a "free city," able to bargain as a corporate body with the *bakufu*. Sakai had its origins in a salt-producing manor, and went on to become a port for the capital area. During the wars of the Kamakura and Ashikaga periods it gained in importance by providing military supplies, and also became a port for the China trade rivaling the nearby Hyogo (the modern Kobe), whose early leadership in commerce with China can be traced to Taira influence. The *bakufu* borrowed money from the Sakai merchants in 1543 and secured their loan by pledging the tax returns from the Ashikaga domains. Sakai must have proved attractive to merchants seeking security for their operations, for it obtained certain freedoms in administering its own laws, and it drew to itself a number of *ronin*, or masterless *samurai*, a class of fighting men who could defend the city, and who were to become an important factor in later Japanese history.

One of the main imports from China was copper cash in response to new demands for money in place of barter as a medium for internal exchange. Japan had minted coins earlier, but had ceased to do so in the tenth century, and did not resume until the sixteenth. During this time of expanding trade she therefore depended on Sung and Ming coins from China. Other imports were iron, textiles, drugs, and items to satisfy a growing luxury trade: books, pictures, and embroideries. Japan, in turn, exported to China copper and sulphur as raw materials, luxury goods in whose manufacture she excelled, such as fans, lacquerware, and weapons, particularly swords and halberds. In 1483 the astonishing total of 37,000 swords were exported to China. The export trade was very profitable, Japanese goods selling in China for four, five, and even ten times their value in the home market.

The trade with China was opened up by merchants who doubled as pirates: the line between the two professions was never very clearly drawn in any part of the ancient world. China always attempted to keep government control over foreign trade, and she was suffering from the activities of the Japanese "pirates," sometimes violent, sometimes no doubt merely extralegal, along most of her coastline in the fourteenth century. Yung-lo, the emperor of the Ming Dynasty under whom China's own overseas trade was vastly expanded, then came to an agreement with Ashikaga Yoshimitsu, the third Shogun, concerning Japanese privileges for a limited, regulated trade in return for suppression of piracy by the Shogun and the acknowledgment by the "king of Japan" of the usual "tributary" status under which China recognized her neighbor countries. This agreement in 1404 provided for two Japanese ships to trade with China every ten years, but in fact, with Chinese connivance, the number of ships was larger. They carried "tallies" to establish their identity and authenticate the exchange of goods. After 1469 a virtual monopoly of the China trade was obtained by a family, the Ouchi, prominent in the western part of the main island, and it continued in their hands until they were overthrown by one of their own vassals in 1557.

Although the Shogun made the trade agreement noted above, the *bakufu* was not involved in the actual commercial transactions. Much of this was carried on under the aegis of certain Buddhist temples—one more instance of the important role of the Buddhist Church in Japanese society. A famous statesman-monk, Muso Kokushi, of the Zen sect, organized the sending of a ship to China as far back as 1342, with the backing of the first Shogun, Ashikaga Takauji, and from the profits of this voyage he was able to build the Tenryuji temple. "Tenryuji ships," as temple ships were thereafter called, continued to make successful voyages, and other monasteries followed this example (see Plate 17). Among the reasons for the involvement of the monasteries in the trade were their knowledge of China and the Chinese language through Japanese monks trained in China, the amount of surplus capital from endowments and other sources which they had to invest, their political power derived from religious immunities and from their access as trusted advisers to those in power in both court and *bakufu*, and finally, no doubt, their education and experience in planning and decision making. In the changing fortunes of the period, the monasteries benefited from the stability and comparative freedom from interference accorded them through their sacred character. Thus monasteries not only financed trading ventures but also developed port facilities. The Sumiyoshi shrine, for instance, had a controlling interest in the port of Sakai, and the ancient Kofukuji monastery of Nara in the port of Hyogo.

The collapse of central authority, which began before the Onin War but was more marked after it, did not mean the advent of total chaos. Local law and order was maintained by the house laws of the territorial lords, often rigorously administered. Economic gains and a new self-realization among the warrior-farmer class brought about changes in the structure of society and a certain degree of social mobility. One example of such a change took place in 1485 in the restless province of Yamashiro where peasant rebellions had already occurred. The farmers were incensed at the damage caused by war and arson on the part of two groups fighting in their province. They themselves raised an armed force under reliable leaders and denied all supplies to both sides in the fighting. On receiving an ultimatum backed by force, the intruders withdrew and a provisional government of the province was chosen, with a clause requiring a monthly rotation of executive officials. This interesting semi-democratic experiment lasted for eight years.

The foregoing pattern of warfare and shifting alliances marked the whole of the sixteenth century. In the absence of acknowledged authority, the character of war itself changed and gave rise to an increased emphasis on fortified castles and methods of siege warfare to capture them. The period from 1534 to 1615 is known as the Sengoku-Jidai, or Period of the Country at War. Meanwhile in the midst of the inconclusive fighting and widespread unrest of the Ashikaga Period, a limited circle of scholars and aesthetes around the Shogun's court was producing new art forms and evolving canons of taste that were to be definitive for the future.

9

The GOLDEN AGE OF JAPANESE ART

1378-1490

The Ashikaga Shogunate wore a very different complexion from the shogunate of Yoritomo and the Hojo regents, and this was partly due to the location of each. Yoritomo had selected Kamakura in the eastern region as his base because it was a center of his own feudal power and far from the distractions and intrigues of the court at Kyoto. Military power and feudal justice were his interests and in the main those of his successors, the Hojo regents. But when Ashikaga Takauji rose to prominence, the center of gravity in national affairs was once more of necessity in the Kyoto region. The long dynastic struggle between the northern and southern courts, and the Ashikaga attempts to build up their power and oppose the sourthern court in all parts of the country, meant that Kyoto as a center became the key to control.

The literary and artistic life which had always centered around the court would have held little attraction for the first Shogun, Takauji, even if he had had time and leisure for such pursuits. But the third in the Ashikaga line, Yoshimitsu, who became Shogun in 1368, and the eighth Shogun, Yoshimasa, who succeeded in 1443 and died in 1490, were both devoted to the arts and generous in their patronage. Yoshimitsu was lavish in his expenditures on building to the point of exhausting the treasury, but Yoshimasa was much more able and creative as a critic and discerning patron of architecture, painting, and drama. Yoshimasa carried on these activities and gathered round him a remarkable group of scholars and artists at the very time when the horrors of the Onin War were at their height. He did this no doubt partly as an escape from a military and political situation which had gone far beyond his control, but Japan since his time has reason to be grateful, for he was instrumental in forming what is acknowledged to be the greatest age in Japanese art.

After Takauji, his generals, and his immediate successor, Yoshiakira, had painfully disposed, for the time being, of all effective opposition, the century of Ashikaga rule was ushered in by the accession of Yoshimitsu. The headquarters of the Ashikaga were located in the Muromachi district of Kyoto, and there, in 1378, ten years after he became Shogun, Yoshimitsu built the Hana-no-Gosho, Palace of Flowers, with its magnificent gardens. This marks the beginning of the art period known as the Muromachi.[1] He went on to build a sumptuous villa for religious retreat at Kitayama, erecting in its grounds the famous Kinkaku or Golden Pavilion, which was destroyed by fire in 1952, but restored in exact replica of the original.

The Silver Pavilion, Ginkaku, on the other side of Kyoto, was commissioned by the later Shogun, Yoshimasa, as part of his retreat, the Higashiyama. These grounds and gardens were the scene of the contemplation and creative activity of men celebrated in several fields of art and drama, Noami, Geiami, Soami, Kanze, and the great painter, Sesshu, in the last decades of the fifteenth century, and as such merit a brief description.

The Silver Pavilion itself, delicate and simple, is two stories high and contains a shrine and rooms for rest and recreation with views over the garden (see Plate 16). The word "silver" refers to some of the planned decoration which was never carried out. This quiet and restrained pavilion was built on the edge of a miniature lake, whose steppingstones, islets, and bridges consist of stones contributed by lords from all over Japan. There is a temple in the grounds and near it a mound of white sand piled up in a regular, conical form to make a "moon-viewing platform." And just beyond the temple is the small building of four and a half mats[2] which claims the distinction of being the first tea-ceremony room in Japan. Its outlook well illustrates the quiet, understated, almost severe canon of taste which ruled at this time and which came to form the highest standard in all subsequent Japanese aesthetics. The view from the teahouse reveals no flowers, no bright colors, not even a glimpse of water, but only pine trees and underneath them undulating stretches of moss on the ground. Observing more closely one notices that these moss beds differ subtly in hue, some green, some brown, other parts russet or almost red—and this is all that meets the eye (see Plate 22). This quiet taste the Japanese call *shibui*. The word means "astringent," puckering the mouth, as persimmons do when they are barely ripe. It is the direct opposite of the taste of the succeeding era, the Momoyama. Momoyama was all strawberries and cream, preceding slightly in time the baroque era in Europe, a style which it distantly resembles.

[1] The points of division between Japanese periods, and indeed the whole subject of Japanese chronology, is a confused and controversial one. The political beginning of Muromachi was marked by the reunion of the northern and southern courts (see. p. 90), but the building of the Hana-no-Gosho was a decisive point in art history and as such is selected as the beginning of the art period known as Muromachi. (The name Muromachi is sometimes used as an equivalent to Ashikaga for the whole period 1336–1573.)

[2] Rooms in Japan have their floor area measured in terms of the standard six by three foot (Japanese measure) *tatami* or woven grass, padded mats.

The quiet, modest nature of the prospect from the teahouse was exactly suited to the attitude of mind cultivated in the tea ceremony itself. The pomp and circumstance of the world must be left behind when one enters the teahouse, for its low door will only permit entry on hands and knees in an attitude of humility, and without the projecting sword and dirk which the samurai were accustomed to wear. Having entered, the participants behave in a formal and reserved but inwardly relaxed manner as they inspect and comment upon the ancient kettles, pots, and bowls (see Plate 25) used in the ceremony or admire the simple flower arrangement or single hanging scroll. It is less customary to comment upon the kimono and the skill of the hostess, *simplex munditiis*, "simple in her neatness." But they note the play of her hands and all her gestures as she carries out the anciently prescribed movements of preparing and offering the green tea, whisked to a froth, to each guest in turn (see Plate 23). These movements are like a progression and sway of an antique ritual dance. The whole experience, though strange and rather flat to a Westerner, is charged with significance to a Japanese. The combination of withdrawal from the cares of the world, artistic appreciation, intellectual conversation, and observance of a restful and loved pattern or ritual—and all of this in the atmosphere of Buddhist contemplation—gives to the Japanese soul a sense of refreshment and well-being. Perhaps it is that very formalism antipathetic to a Westerner which enhances the ceremony in Japanese eyes, for the Japanese, more than most, find security in prescribed patterns of behavior. Seen in this setting a moss garden is precisely what is required in front of the teahouse. Overstatement in color or line makes its appeal to the eye. But Buddhists are trying to get beyond the senses altogether, and understatement speaks more directly to the mind.

The Muromachi Period is remarkable because so many arts flowered at once. Some of them were very minor, such as incense-judging competitions. Even the burglar alarms of medieval Japan were given a poetic art form. The corridors leading to the monks' dormitory in some temples were called nightingale walks, the heavy floorbeams being set on supports in such a manner as to give out thin musical notes or chirrups when trodden, thus compelling night intruders to give audible warning of their approach.

At the center of all this intense artistic activity was a succession of three remarkable men, Naomi (1397–1476), a monk and companion of the Shogun Yoshimasa; his son, Geiami, and his grandson, Soami. All were versed in Chinese learning, were practicing artists themselves, and acted as arbiters of taste at the court of the Shogun.

Two earlier men, Kanami (1333–1384), a Shinto priest, and his son Zeami (1363–1444), of common origin but dramatic genius, were favored by the third Shogun, Yoshimitsu, and encouraged to develop the *No* drama as a classical form, using earlier materials of dance, music, and poetry and combining them in a new and distinctive manner. The character *no* is the same as the Chinese *neng,* meaning "to be able," "ability," hence "the skill of a virtuoso." *No* plays are virtuoso performances combining poetic chant, mime, and slow posture-dance with accompanying music and elaborate costumes and masks. The subjects treated come from the realms of legend, history, and magic, and all the atmosphere and action is impregnated with Buddhist thought. The origins of *No* go back much earlier than the times of Kanami and Zeami to sacred dances or mimes performed on an open-air stage raised up so that the performers were visible both to the notables and the populace. Parts of the performance were known as *sarugaku*, "monkey plays," indicating an element of ribald buffoonery probably associated with fertility rites. At a later point in the development the comic element is preserved separately in the *kyogen* plays put on in the intervals between the serious *No* performances. This feature is a parallel to the double development of tragedy and comedy in Greece, both having their origin in the religious Dionysiac festival. In each case an artistic purpose is served, that of providing light relief long after the religious function of comedy as promoting fertility and warding off evil influences has been forgotten.

Some pointers to the meaning of the *No* plays may be derived from a brief description of the traditional stage on which the performances take place. A rather small, square platform some three feet high is connected by a sloping bridge at the left (as the audience faces the stage) rear corner to the green room from which the actors emerge through a curtained doorway. The principal actor (*shite*) makes a slow and impressive entrance down this bridge and performs for the most part near the pillar at the left front, one of four pillars supporting a roof over the stage area. The right front pillar is associated with the *waki* or second actor. Supporting characters (see Plate 18), two or three in number, usually attendants, may be seated in a line on the right, while the musicians occupy the rear. The whole arrangement gives varied and open views to the audience, who are seated on two sides of the stage, the front and the left-hand side leading up to the green room doorway and the bridge. The effect is a good example of the Japanese preference for asymmetry.

There is no scenery save a pine branch painted on the rear wall, and there are almost no props. The gorgeous antique costumes, wigs, and masks give the required interest and color. The effect of the intoned chanting and the slow, controlled, occasionally violent gestures and postures is immensely heightened by the small orchestra at the rear, consisting of flutes and drums. The percussion effects and gradually accelerating rhythms can create an almost unbearable tension at moments of crisis in the action.

The use of masks—masterpieces of artistry in lacquer; impressive, oval features for a young girl or contorted, wrinkled, or exaggerated features for an old man (see Plate 14) or a demon—raises interesting dramatic and psychological considerations which might apply to both Japanese and Greek tragedy. In both instances the audience is perfectly familiar with the plot and already knows the dénouement. There is no need to have surprise reflected on the faces of the actors. The element of the dance, originally of paramount religious importance, acts as the channel for the highly charged emotions of actors and audience. It is better *not* to see the faces of the actors. Costume and mask lift the actor onto another plane, heroic and larger than life. The force of word and gesture is heightened by the mask, remote and unmoved in its antique beauty, while the person who wears it goes through exalting or crushing experiences of hope and love, of despair and death. He is anonymous and he goes through these experiences for all of us.

In both Greece and Japan classical tragedy shows man struggling with his destiny and involved in the great realm of the gods, shot through with sunlight and shadow from beyond this world. One great difference, however, between Greek and Japanese drama lies in the use of the chorus. The classical Greek actor declaims his part in the story but the chorus dances it out, expressing in the poetry both of motion and words their feelings and those of the audience. But in the intimate theater of *No* the chorus has a much smaller part, provided as it is by only a few supporting actors. The main actors themselves fulfill the exacting role of intoning the words over a wide range of pitch and tone, at the same time executing elaborate dance postures while robed in stiff and often fantastic costumes. Even in Japan, however, *No* is an entertainment for the sophisticated. The average man prefers the more direct "blood and thunder" statement of *Kabuki* theater (see Plate 28).

In Japan and especially in the Muromachi Period the ambience of all these quiet but rich developments in art was the Buddhist world-view, for Buddhism influenced Japanese art profoundly. This was evident from the very beginning in the sophisticated combination of artistic force and spiritual tenderness seen in the sculpture of the Tempyo era, when Buddhism was first introduced. Now in the Muromachi Period the Buddhist philosophical concepts of nature and man were more thoroughly mastered, and they affected directly the most highly regarded art form, that of landscape painting.

One of the best-known artists of Japan, Sesshu, has already been mentioned as belonging to this period. Leaning heavily on Zen training and inspiration, his work has an impressionistic character. With hard, decisive, angular brush strokes and superb balance, Sesshu captured not only the form but the essence of a landscape and a mood, and so his work becomes a channel for the great insight of Buddhism. This insight is notoriously hard to trap in words. It has to do with the fact that this world has value, but only relative value, while the abiding essence that gives meaning to all things is to be found only in the Buddha and his all-pervading Law.

Buddhist influence went behind Japanese art to its origins in China. The famed landscape painting of the Sung Dynasty (907–1260) had an exciting effect on the Japanese artists of the important Kano School (see Plates 20 and 21). Examination of a Sung or other classical landscape painting usually reveals a small focus or two of human interest, a man with a donkey crossing a bridge, or a scholar reading in a mountain pavilion. But the persons are dwarfed by the grandeur of the scenery of mountain or river. Humanity is subordinated to nature. Man is present, but only as part of a greater whole.

This attitude to man and his place in the scheme of things shows a marked difference from the Hebrew view, where man is represented as having a dominion over all other creatures given him specifically by God. Adam and Eve in the Genesis account *name* all the creatures, and to know the name of something is to have power over it. Man is supreme in creation. A contrasting Buddhist story, in quite a different vein, appears in the *Hsi Yu Chi* ("Record of the Western Pilgrimage"), a favorite tale known to all Chinese (translated by Arthur Waley as "Monkey"). The hero, a monkey who is always up to mischief but is potentially worthy of being changed at last into a man, has been bragging to Buddha in his usual fashion. He says that by his magic jumping somersault he can reach the end of the world; in fact, he says he has been there. Buddha smilingly shakes his head in disbelief and reproof, so Monkey says he will do it again. He makes his fantastic leap and when he comes down signs his name on the great Pillar at the End of the World. He comes back, stands on Buddha's hand, and says that, if Buddha does not believe him, he can look at his signature. Buddha in reply merely holds up his middle finger and shows Monkey the signature written there. For all his vaunted leap he had never been out of the hand of God; for the whole world is God's hand. Man has a place in the universe, but to the Buddhist any exaggerated idea of his role is absurd.

The second influence of Buddhist thought on Chinese and hence on Japanese painting was the creative use of space. In the subtle changes which overtook Chinese Buddhism in its passage from the earlier Indian form, Taoist nature-mysticism played a part. The Taoist classic, the *Tao Te Ching,* speaks of space as a positive, a creative factor in Chapter 11:

> We put thirty spokes together and call it a wheel;
> But it is on the space where there is nothing that the usefulness of the wheel depends.
> We turn clay to make a vessel:
> But it is on the space where there is nothing that the usefulness of the vessel depends.
> We pierce doors and windows to make a house;
> And it is on these spaces where there is nothing that the usefulness of the house depends.
> Therefore just as we take advantage of what is, we should recognize the usefulness of what is not.[3]

Painters steeped in Taoist and Buddhist thought "recognized the usefulness of what is not." With an elevated perspective, as though looking at a view

[3] *The Way and Its Power: A Study of the Tao Te Ching and Its Place in Chinese Thought,* by Arthur Waley (London: George Allen and Unwin, 1949), p. 155.

from the slopes of an opposing mountain, they eliminated teasing and unnecessary detail and presented the essentials in a serene and pleasing simplicity. In a landscape by Tung Yüan (active ca. A.D. 1000) a boat is floating alone on a vast expanse of river. Water merges with sky, and a hill in the background is faintly sketched in. The skiff and the lonely figures just discernible in it carry a nostalgic significance, a Buddhist tinge of melancholy, they could never have in a crowded picture. The same effect is found on a smaller scale in a picture of two birds on a bough by Mu Ch'i (1181–1239), also of the Sung Dynasty. A plum branch thrusts up in uneven naturalness and upon it is a pair of small birds huddled very close together. They are viewed as they are in nature, without the obtrusion of man's feelings. Yet they seem to nestle more closely together, to need each other more, to be more true to their bird nature, because they are surrounded by ample space. The temperate use of line and emphasis, the large amount of space "left over," deliberately unfilled, even in a narrow hanging scroll, represent a profound and philosophical reflection by the artist, a reverence for life as it is in itself, not life as dominated by egotistical man. It was qualities such as these in the great Chinese tradition of painting that appealed to the Japanese. The tea ceremony, and still more Zen Buddhist meditation, were further examples of space created in the crowded press of life. And these qualities, interpreted by Buddhist masters such as Noami and his successors, captivated by their restrained and astringent discipline the minds of the Muromachi Period and set a standard of artistic taste which Japan has never lost.

10

The UNIFICATION OF JAPAN

Sengoku-Jidai, The Period
of the Country at War: 1534–1615

Some unity of emotion and loyalty had always existed in Japan, fostered by the national legends and later promoted by Confucian ideals. Developments of literature and thought during the Heian period must have given birth to a sense of cultural unity. A degree of political unity had been forged by the powerful Minamoto Yoritomo after the clan wars of the twelfth century. But a period of constant war and frustrating rivalry between innumerable grasping warlords had intervened and had lasted for about 250 years. At length, at the end of the sixteenth century Japan became unified and pacified in a much more definite and complete sense. This period in Japan [1] happened to coincide roughly in chronology with the solidifying of the nation-states in Europe, and particularly with the centralizing power and skill of the Tudor monarchs in England. However in Japan it was not the monarchs but the generals who were the architects of unity. This unification ushered in the most peaceful and homogeneous period in Japanese history, the Tokugawa Shogunate, lasting also for 250 years. It must be recognized, nevertheless, that this internal peace was characterized by some of the rigidity of a police state and was purchased at the cost of free development and unhampered intercourse with other nations. Japan went into an isolation that was almost but not quite total.

Although the civil wars of the Ashikaga Period and the Onin War (1467–77) in particular were bloody and wasteful, there were also factors leading to positive growth and development which were, as so often in history, operative at the same time. A notable increase in domestic and

---

[1] The dates for this period of unification begin before the end of the Ashikaga line of Shoguns, who became steadily weaker and ceased altogether in 1573. The Sengoku-Jidai dates run from the birth of Oda Nobunaga to the final establishment of the Tokugawa Shogunate. The year of the decisive battle of Sekigahara, 1600, is sometimes substituted for 1615.

foreign trade, the rise of commercial towns, and improvements in agriculture began to cause far-reaching changes in the framework of society. Class lines between aristocratic warriors on the one hand and the common people, merchants, and peasants on the other, were becoming much less distinct. All this led to the decline of feudalism, with its self-sufficient and mutually hostile enclaves, and rendered both possible and desirable a move toward unification of the country. It is significant that after the end of the Onin War there were only about twenty major *daimyo* (territorial lords) left. Many of these were newcomers who had supplanted the older noble and feudal families.

In three distinct ways the commoners were beginning to acquire a power and influence they had never known before. First, battles were being decided by large bodies of foot soldiers and no longer by mounted knights of the warrior aristocracy. Second, some *daimyo* found it to their profit to encourage rather than suppress the activities of merchants in the new commercial towns. And third, fanatical Buddhist sects, such as those founded by Nichiren and the Ikko or "Single-minded" sects of the Shinshu persuasion, whose strength was drawn from the common people, asserted themselves successfully against some of the *daimyo* and even acquired territory of their own. An Ikko group conquered the province of Kaga in 1488 and held it for a century. These factors in social change corresponded closely to similar factors in Europe at about the same time. In one important respect, however, Japanese history took a different course; unification was accomplished not by abolishing feudalism but by "freezing" it, using certain elements in it, and at the same time isolating the country from outside influences making for further change.[2]

Those who practice the art of history are only beginning to discover how sweeping are the changes brought about by advances in technology. The startling and swift changes that took place in the Japan of the late sixteenth century would not have been possible had it not been for the advent of the smooth-bore musket. In one of the ironies of history its arrival in Japan coincided with the coming of Christianity. A Portuguese sailing ship bound for the China coast was wrecked on the shores of Kyushu in 1542, and the muskets on board were soon expertly copied by the Japanese. Just seven years later, in 1549, Francis Xavier, the pioneer Jesuit missionary, also landed in Kyushu, and began his work, which soon met with great success. Not for the first nor the last time did the West bring to a non-Western land the powerful and explosive forces of its inventions and its ideas, so often in contradiction to one another. Yet the contradictions were usually not felt either in the West or in the East of the sixteenth century to the extent that we feel them in the twentieth.

The Roman Catholic Jesuit order was of such immense importance in the early history of the contacts between Europe and East Asia that it is necessary to glance briefly at its origins and ideas. The Jesuits were not the

[2] For an interesting discussion of the similarities and differences between Japanese and European feudalism, see Reischauer and Fairbank, *East Asia, The Great Tradition*, pp. 579–81.

first Christian missionaries to reach East Asia. The Nestorian form of Christianity had been successfully propagated in T'ang China, but then had died out completely, though it was later reintroduced among the Mongols. Franciscan friars arrived in China just prior to the time when Marco Polo spent his seventeen years of service at the court of the Mongol emperor, Khubilai Khan. But in length of stay and depth of influence in both China[3] and Japan the Jesuits were by far the most effective of the early representatives of Christianity.

One possible reason for this effectiveness was that they were a modern order, only just founded, with strong emphasis on academic, scientific, and practical knowledge, and a high degree of discipline. The founder, Ignatius Loyola, was a Spanish nobleman who had an experience of identification with the sufferings of Christ as he lay in his castle recovering from a wound. The spiritual exercises he practiced at that time and later wrote out for his followers have been a formative influence in the order up to the present. Aware of his need for intellectual training, Loyola became a student at the University of Paris and there gathered round him a group of men of outstanding ability. After the Pope had accepted their offer of special service for the Church anywhere in the world, they were constituted the Society of Jesus. One of the original Paris band, Francis Xavier, became a missionary to the Far East. When he discovered that the Japanese derived much of their culture from China, he set out with incredible daring and that sense of strategy which has always distinguished the order, to make an entry into China, but died on an island off the coast.

The advance of Christianity in Japan, which Francis Xavier initiated, was favored by one or two special features in the Japanese situation at the time. Good feeling existed between Japan and Portugal, particularly in the early days. The Portuguese liked the Japanese better than any other Asian nation, perhaps because they sympathized with the Japanese code of honor. The Japanese, on their side, admired the Jesuits because they exhibited a discipline reminiscent of the best Zen monks. Many converted *daimyo* were sincere and loyal Christians; others had more mixed motives, concerned with trade and technological advantages. They found the Jesuits had considerable influence with the Portuguese merchants, and were also possessed of scientific and technical knowledge which could give them an edge over their rivals in the interclan struggles that were still going on. Once a *daimyo* embraced the faith, all his retainers tended to follow suit. Thus where Christianity gained an entrance at all, its advance was rapid; and this seems particularly to have been the case in Kyoto.

Francis Xavier had gone to Kyoto in 1550, but found in the midst of war

[3] The most noted Jesuit pioneer in China was Matteo Ricci. After infinite pains he reached the court at Peking in 1600 and became so expert in Chinese that he was accepted as a scholar colleague by many of the literati. He was succeeded by Father Adam Schall, the astronomer, and other Jesuits, who continued to be an influence at the Chinese court for nearly 200 years.

and destruction no effective authority to whom he could make an appeal. He was invited by a *daimyo* of Bungo in Kyushu, Otomo by name, to visit him, and there the work prospered. A Father Vilela went later to Kyoto and in 1560 secured a guarantee of good treatment and tax exemption from the Shogun. He was reinforced by the arrival of Father Frois, who made friends with several leading figures in the capital. Both priests operated not only in Kyoto but in Sakai, Nara, and other places in the environs.

So successful was the work of the Jesuits that the Buddhist authorities became alarmed and brought sufficient pressure to bear on the government to have the priests ousted from the capital. They withdrew to Sakai, the independent city, and, although safe there, found little response among the merchant class. Father Frois succeeded in returning to the capital in 1569 after four years' absence. He had interviews with Oda Nobunaga and secured a license to preach. There is no doubt that his message had the more appeal in that Buddhism at this time had sunk to a very low point in public esteem.

The Jesuit Visitor-General Valignano reported to the Society in Rome in 1582 that there were 150,000 Christians and 200 churches in Japan. The vast majority of these were to be found in the western part of the country. It is no wonder that Valignano was encouraged with the situation, for Nobunaga had been gracious and invited him to spend several weeks at the new and splendid castle of Azuchi on Lake Biwa. It appears that Nobunaga was much intrigued by Valignano's Negro servant.

A good many *samurai* and some *daimyo* were among the Christian converts. They adopted Christian names, such as Simeon and Francisco, the latter being the name chosen at baptism by Xavier's host, Otomo. They wore the cross on their helmets and even used to go into battle with war cries such as "Jesu" and "Santa Maria." Four Japanese youths of noble lineage were sent as a delegation to visit the Pope and the king of Spain. The common people also had an opportunity to hear the doctrine in church and Christian schools. As has been found to be the case in other parts of the world, they derived both comfort and a new sense of dignity and personal worth from their Christian belief. Many remained faithful to their vows through the severe persecution that was to follow.

There were thus a number of factors both internal and external, concerned with trade, firearms, and foreign ideas, which combined with profound weariness of civil war, to make Japan ready for certain fundamental changes. The country was in a sense ripe for unification, but the task was not easily accomplished. Three strong men, Oda Nobunaga (1534–1582), Toyotomi Hideyoshi (1536–1598), and Tokugawa Ieyasu (1543–1616) accomplished it, the last two building upon foundations laid by their respective predecessors. Their common task and personality differences are symbolized in two anecdotes. In the first Nobunaga is said to have quarried the stones, for the imaginary castle of a unified Japan, Hideyoshi to have shaped them, and Ieyasu to have laid them in place. In the second the three discuss what to do about a songbird in a cage who will not sing. Nobunaga says, "I'll make it sing"; Hideyoshi, "I'll kill it if it doesn't"; but Ieyasu, "I'll wait until it does sing." The three worked together in spite of serious differences and rivalries; but fundamentally they had the same aim, the pacification and unification of the country. It was well for Japan that they did, for one man alone in the span of a lifetime could scarcely have accomplished the task. And without a long period of security and quiet after so much turmoil, it is doubtful whether Japan would have been ready for her sudden and dramatic entry into the competitive world of the late nineteenth and twentieth centuries.

Oda Nobunaga's family was minor in rank and importance but began a rise to power by becoming deputy constables for the lords of Shiba in the province of Owari. Nobunaga's father increased the family estates and on his death the youthful Nobunaga gathered a force of fighting men to secure a strong position in the province. At this point a powerful neighbor, Imagawa, began a drive on Kyoto with some 25,000 men and had to pass through Nobunaga's province. One of Imagawa's lieutenants, later to take the name of Tokugawa Ieyasu, captured the fortress of Marune and Nobunaga's advisers became despondent. But Nobunaga himself resolved on a bold attack, even though he could command a force of only about 3,000 men. The Imagawa forces were relaxing and drinking in an ill-chosen campsite situated in a narrow defile. After a heavy rainstorm Nobunaga executed a brilliant surprise attack, routed the enemy, and killed Imagawa himself. This battle of Okehazama in 1560 proved decisive. Nobunaga felt the time was ripe for him to begin a gradual and calculated move on the capital.

He secured his rear somewhat by a pact with Tokugawa Ieyasu, his former opponent, and disarmed the opposition of neighboring *daimyo* by alliances and suitable marriages. Strong resistance was offered by Saito Dosan and his son in Mino province, which lay on the route to Kyoto. This was a parvenu but powerful clan who had made money in vegetable oil. Their castle at Inabayama was at length reduced in 1567 in maneuvers directed by Toyotomi Hideyoshi, who had risen rapidly from a common foot soldier in Nobunaga's service.

There was still some resistance to Nobunaga's ambitions in Ise and Omi, but the fall of the castle of Mizukuri meant that by 1568 the way was open to the capital and in that year Nobunaga was welcomed there and lauded by the emperor. The advance of Nobunaga demonstrated that the reduction of fortresses was now the key to successful warfare.

Nobunaga had Yoshiaki appointed the fifteenth Ashikaga Shogun, but when he proved intractable drove him out in 1573 and did not trouble to choose a successor, thus bringing to an end the Ashikaga line. Neither Nobunaga nor Hideyoshi after him attempted to acquire the title of shogun for themselves but preferred to support and protect the imperial line and use such court titles as seemed suitable for themselves, knowing that their real power lay in military control. They did, however, restore moderate incomes to the court and relieve emperor and nobles from the abject poverty they had suffered under the Ashikaga.

Oda Nobunaga was now established in Kyoto and had clearly won the first round in the struggle. He was a warrior first and foremost and determined to rule by military force. But there was still a large part of the country not by any means under his control. With some difficulty he subdued two *daimyo* threatening him in provinces north of the city. He then ensured for himself greater security at the center by a ruthless destruction and burning of the large Enryakuji complex of monasteries on the hills outside Kyoto, which had for so long been a thorn in the side of the government. Next he turned his attention to another branch of Buddhism, the fanatic Ikko sect, whose strongholds at the mouth of the Kiso River, east of Lake Biwa, had given him constant trouble. He besieged the last two of their fortresses there, refused an offer of surrender, and put the crowded forts to the flames with enormous loss of life. He was moving to the north against other Ikko adherents when he had to turn back to help Tokugawa Ieyasu hold off the powerful Takeda chieftain in the east. Together they defeated Takeda in the battle of Nagashino in 1575. This battle marked an important new departure in the fact that it was the intelligent use of firearms which decided the issue. The mounted enemy force were brought up short by a high stockade and then shot down by musketeers sheltered behind it. Since loading and firing were such clumsy processes, the troops were divided into three sections, who fired volleys in succession while the others reloaded. But even so the results among the enemy were devastating, while Nobunaga's losses were minimal.

Nobunaga had little time between campaigns to devote to civil affairs but he put in force some economic measures, notably provisions for free markets and free trade, currency regulations, and arrangements for the erection of bridges and repair of roads. He devoted special attention to attracting merchants to the new town built round his strong headquarters castle of Azuchi, completed in 1579.

The west was not yet brought under control. Hideyoshi was entrusted with this task, and he undertook it on behalf of Nobunaga with characteristic skill and thoroughness. Again fortresses were the key, and one of them Hideyoshi reduced by diverting the course of a river and flooding the place. But Nobunaga's time was running out. He had taken the sword and he was to perish by it. In 1582 one of his generals, Akechi Mitsuhide, turned on him and took him completely by surprise in a temple in Kyoto when Nobunaga was passing through on his way to take a short holiday. Nobunaga committed suicide to avoid capture and his body was destroyed in the flames of the burning temple. On hearing the news, Hideyoshi brought compromise negotiations with the powerful Mori in the west to a quick conclusion, rode for the capital at breakneck speed, and utterly defeated the rebellious Akechi.

The vengeance exacted by Hideyoshi for the treachery of Akechi might appear to be one more personal conflict in the dreary record of ambition, rivalry, and blood. It is true that all three of the great leaders of this period, Nobunaga, Hideyoshi, and Ieyasu, were determined to rise to the top. Yet they differ from the adventurers of the Ashikaga Period in a number of important ways. They showed some continuity of plan, much good sense, political as well as military ability, evidence of economic planning, and, above all, intelligent application of principles of law and order.

Hideyoshi acted with his customary decisiveness immediately upon the death of Oda Nobunaga. The provinces which Nobunaga had held were divided up among a few loyal generals, Hideyoshi retaining a goodly share for himself. He called a council of the four leading commanders, but it soon became clear that he would be the dominant member. The sons of Nobunaga and one of the four commanders, Shibata, each made bids for independent power, but were defeated within a year of Nobunaga's death. Hideyoshi reached the site of the culminating battle at Shizugatake in one of his swift night rides, covering about fifty miles in six hours. He rallied his hesitant officers and made a prompt end to Shibata's threat.

Hideyoshi now had control, directly or indirectly, of thirty provinces out of a total of some sixty in the country, and including the twenty it had taken Nobunaga so long to dominate. A further important factor in his strength was that the provinces not under his control were at a distance from the center and did not pose any immediate threat. Tokugawa Ieyasu, his powerful ally in the east, however, was something of a problem. Ieyasu had not been present at the first council of four commanders, and was now sufficiently jealous and alarmed at the extent of Hideyoshi's power to take up arms against him. Ieyasu in fact gained a small advantage in two battles; but both were men of sense and decided they could profit more by co-operation than by rivalry, a pregnant decision by which neither lost and the country gained immeasurably.

When matters were settled between them, Hideyoshi proceeded to consolidate his position and evolve a peacetime policy. He felt that Osaka on the Inland Sea near the capital would be the best center for control and built a strong castle there, a move which was feasible now that the Ikko monastery fortress of Honganji at Osaka had been destroyed. He had already ordered a land survey, a step that may be compared in significance to the Domesday Book of William the Conqueror. The survey began in 1583 and continued until Hideyoshi's death in 1598, by which time all the provinces in Japan had been covered. The size and yield of every rice field in the country was set down (though in practice some areas were inevitably left out), and the permanent tenancy of a plot guaranteed to the actual cultivator, who was then entirely responsible for the tax. This move of simplification did away with the jungle of *shiki*, rights, dues, and proportions of the crop owing to various officials and owners. The rate of tax was high, as much as 50 percent of the crop, but there were no further dues or obligations. The land was divided into two types, wet and dry fields, and each of these into three categories by yield. The calculated yield of the lowest category was 28 percent less than that of the highest.

The fiefs which Hideyoshi thus had at his disposal were granted, along with their accompanying taxes, to his vassals, and varied in value of yield (irrespective of acreage) from 10,000 koku to over 1,000,000 koku. (The koku measure is equivalent to five bushels and was supposed to feed one man for one year.) In return the vassal pledged fealty to Hideyoshi and promised to supply military aid on demand, usually up to two-thirds of his income. The land survey was conducted by Hideyoshi's own officials and was ruthlessly enforced. In an attempt to correct decades of self-protective evasions of tax he even threatened to crucify the inhabitants, including women and children, of villages which falsified their returns.

Although Hideyoshi's central position was secure, he could neither rest nor feel safe until the outlying parts of the country were also under his control. In 1587 he himself commanded an expedition against Shimazu, the *daimyo* of Satsuma at the extreme south of Kyushu. After a leisurely advance in enormous force, Hideyoshi won a decisive battle near the Sendai River. One of his contingents was at the same time coming in by sea, and Shimazu was completely at his mercy. With a wise combination of firmness and clemency he did not press matters to a conclusion, but allowed Shimazu to keep his own territory and a part of what he had won in previous fighting. The rest of Kyushu was secured by being granted to loyal commanders and allies. After returning to his base he enacted a pacification measure known by Hideyoshi's title as the "Taiko's Sword Hunt," the object of which was twofold. The confiscation of swords from all except *samurai* deprived peasants, gentlemen-farmers, and soldier-monks of the means of raising armed rebellion, and it also served to make a clear distinction between the *samurai* and the farmer classes.

There remained the Kanto Plain and the far north to be brought into subjection. The refusal of a proud Hojo chieftain to come to Kyoto and offer submission gave Hideyoshi the needed excuse to mount an expedition to the Kanto region. Since he now had ample resources, he was able almost to guarantee the outcome by assembling a force estimated at 200,000 men, and planned to reduce the central Hojo citadel of Odawara by a siege conducted for as long as was necessary. To keep up the morale of his troops he allowed them to bring their wives on the expedition, and himself provided musicians, dancers, and other forms of entertainment. Odawara was surrounded by May 16, 1590, and what followed was almost an anticlimax. There was treachery within the gates, and the fortress surrendered by August 4 of the same year. The major *daimyo* in the north were summoned and made their submission. By the end of 1590 Hideyoshi was supreme in all Japan. The eight rich Kanto and surrounding provinces were offered to and accepted by Tokugawa Ieyasu in exchange for his own family territory and subsequent acquisitions. This was an advantage for Hideyoshi in that it moved the powerful Tokugawa farther away from the capital and detached them from the old family ground where they could count on traditional loyalties if they should attempt revolt. On the other hand the Kanto was of great value to Ieyasu because it had been well developed both agriculturally and industrially.

There is a story concerning the grant of the Kanto land which deserves to be true—*si non e vero, e ben trovato*. Hideyoshi one day dismissed his followers and rode out alone with Ieyasu. Without a word, in the taciturn spirit of *bushido,* Hideyoshi drew out from his sash his sword and scabbard and handed them over to Ieyasu, indicating that he trusted him completely. The two men discussed the future of Japan and then Hideyoshi, waving his arm toward the head of Edo Bay, said, "Make your capital there." The significance of this advice lay in the fact that the center of gravity of the country had been moving eastward over the past centuries, and Edo (the modern Tokyo), surrounded by the largest single stretch of agricultural land in the country, and geographically near the center, could in the future become the best point of control. Whether Hideyoshi entirely trusted Ieyasu or not, he probably reflected that the Kanto was better placed in his hands than in those of any other. In any event Ieyasu moved into the castle of Edo well content.

As the edict concerning the sword hunt followed the Kyushu campaign, so in 1590 following the Kanto campaign an expulsion edict was promulgated. The land survey had uncovered the existence of a number of *ronin* or vagrant warriors. A list of houses and occupants was to be prepared under this new edict and all who entered a village from another village or an outside province were to be expelled.

Hideyoshi's organization of government consisted in general of the feudal system of vassals under strict discipline with Hideyoshi at their head as suzerain. The ultimate authority, as always, was that of the emperor in the background; but he had almost no freedom of action or independent initiative. When affairs had been sufficiently settled by military action, Hideyoshi appointed a Commission of Five to govern the capital and home provinces, but he himself issued orders and edicts in both civil and military matters for the country as a whole. A body with more of a policy-making character was that known as the Five Elders (Go-Tairo), but it was only appointed toward the end of Hideyoshi's life and for the purpose of guarding the status quo and preventing changes that would threaten Hideyoshi's family after his death. The Elders were assisted by the Junior Advisers, but the task of these latter, to settle differences arising among their seniors, was an impossible one. Lower but important officials were the *daikan*. These were deputies for Hideyoshi in the extensive territories directly owned by him. They were as often as not rich merchants who acted as managers, but were also appointed to watch the activities of nearby *daimyo*.

Christianity, meanwhile, continued to prosper under Hideyoshi's rule as it had under that of Nobunaga. Takayama Ukon, one of Hideyoshi's leading generals, was a Christian and helped Father Organtino secure a site for a church and a house near the great Osaka Castle. Nagasaki city was practically run by the Jesuits and Portuguese trade was increasing. In 1587 the vice-provincial, Coelho, came from Nagasaki to pay a state call on Hideyoshi and the talk was amiable. There was further friendly contact the next year after Hideyoshi's successful Kyushu campaign, and the Japanese leader paid a visit on board a Portuguese ship. But the very next morning the missionaries learned to their dismay that an edict banning Christianity had been published, and that they were ordered to leave the country within twenty days. Two of the reasons given in the edict were that Buddhist shrines had been damaged and that Japanese were being sold abroad as slaves. Some enthusiastic converts had smashed images and certain Portuguese traders were known to have purchased and exported slaves. But the real reasons behind Hideyoshi's decision are not known. He may have regarded the slave trade, though small, and the independence of Nagasaki as defiance of his authority, and he may have considered the success of Christianity a possible source of disunity in the country, particularly in view of the attack on Korea which he was contemplating.

This was a severe setback but the missionaries kept their heads. They gave every appearance of complying with the order and gathered their whole body at the port of Hirado. Some sailed away, but possibly as many as 100 stayed behind, went underground, and carried on their work in secret, aided by loyal converts. They found in course of time that the ban was only sporadically enforced. The number of converts continued to increase, until by 1596 the total was reckoned to be 300,000. These included some in high places, such as Gracia Hosokawa, daughter of that Akechi who had killed Nobunaga, and Maria, sister of Hideyoshi's favorite consort, Yodogimi. There cannot have been any extensive alarm at associating with Portuguese, for the gilded youth of the capital began to copy Portuguese fashions and even to carry rosaries and crucifixes. A number of Portuguese words were adopted into the Japanese language, such as *pan* for bread, *karuto* from *carto* for playing cards, and, more farfetched than these, *tempura*, for shrimp fried in batter, derived from the fact that on the Ember Days, *quattuor tempora,* the Jesuit fathers ate seafood. But another reversal of policy occurred in 1597, the year before Hideyoshi's death. In a fit of rage he ordered the torture and death of twenty-six Christians, six Spanish Franciscans, three Portuguese Jesuits, and seventeen Japanese believers. They were mutilated and paraded through a number of cities and then crucified in an upside down position at a site near Nagasaki.

The last great event in the long, arduous, and successful career of Hideyoshi was the invasion of Korea. Counting the reserves at the campaign headquarters at Nagoya, over a quarter of a million men were involved. The logistics of supplying such an army would have been unthinkable in earlier days, but the army staff had gained experience in decades of warfare and more recently in the ambitious campaigns in Kyushu and Kanto. The invasion was launched in April 1592, and a landing successfully made. The

Japanese naval convoy was unaccountably late in arriving, but the Korean Navy did nothing to stop the invasion because their admiral had received no orders. Pusan was captured and the Japanese columns moved swiftly north. They encountered little resistance and captured Seoul, the capital, without much difficulty. Having advanced to the Manchurian border, they spread over most of Korea. They tried to conciliate the populace and persuade them to throw in their lot with Japan. They even began a land survey.

But the Koreans, recovering from the first surprise, began to offer some serious resistance. They organized guerrilla bands and would have been even more successful if their government had not been so weak and confused. Sickness and the severe winter took their toll of the Japanese forces, until by 1593, the second year of the campaign, perhaps one third of the Japanese in Korea had succumbed.

China claimed suzerainty over Korea, and at this point an army dispatched by the Ming emperor entered the struggle. The Japanese were compelled to fall back. A war party and a peace party developed within the ranks of the Japanese commanders. Ming envoys came to Kyoto in 1596 to arrange terms of peace and to invest Hideyoshi with the title "king of Japan" from the emperor of China. But Hideyoshi, incensed by the condescending tone of the emperor's letter, lost his temper with the envoys and made preparations to launch a new campaign in 1597. The Chinese sent in a fresh army and the Japanese, though reinforced, were compelled to retreat all the way to the south coast. The majority were evacuated, but a rearguard of picked troops, mostly from Satsuma, held positions around Pusan, and inflicted severe casualties on the Chinese and Koreans. The long war was reaching a stalemate, and the death of Hideyoshi in 1598 gave the Japanese a reason to make a final evacuation and end the war.

Measured by standards of achievement, power, and wisdom, Toyotomi Hideyoshi was probably the greatest individual in the history of Japan. He was capable of swift decision and action, as at the time of the unexpected death of Oda Nobunaga. But he was not rash or impetuous. He would not waste lives making frontal attacks on fortresses when he could reduce them by siege or stratagem. His origins among the common people gave him an understanding of character and a certain sympathy which tempered his ruthlessness. He knew better than his predecessor, Nobunaga, when to follow firmness with mercy, as when he spared the Satsuma house at the conclusion of the war in Kyushu. His combination of thoughtful planning and abounding self-confidence carried him to the summit of affairs. At the end, when he attacked Korea and suffered from the delusion that he could take on China as well, this confidence turned into megalomania. He loved pomp and display, was overly fond of women, and was subject to fits of rage; but by any count he was a great man.

There is a portrait in the Itsuo Art Museum in Osaka, painted within a year of Hideyoshi's death by an unknown artist. It shows a face almost emaciated, with hollows beneath the high cheekbones, as of one who has been ill. Since it is not a complimentary likeness, it may well be true to life. The head is bent slightly forward, and this, with the keen and glittering eyes, gives an impression of great concentration and nervous energy. The chin is pointed and the wide mouth set in a determined line. The man radiates an air of decision and capacity, above all capacity. Voluminous black court robes give, as they are intended to, an air of great calm; but in Hideyoshi's case this attitude is entirely belied by the head and eyes, trying to stare into the future. He died at sixty-two after an illness of two or three years. In his last weeks he had spent much time in lucid intervals having Ieyasu and all the great vassals sign oaths vowing to support the Toyotomi family and his son Hideyori when he came of age. As events turned out, what Hideyoshi had built on Nobunaga's foundations did remain; but it was under the firm hand of Tokugawa Ieyasu and not that of Hideyori; as Hideyoshi probably guessed that it would be.

Tokugawa Ieyasu had been born in 1543 into a small *daimyo* family, Matsudaira, situated between the more powerful families of Imagawa and Oda. He had spent no less than thirteen years of his youth as a hostage with one or the other of these houses, and it may not be fanciful to suppose this was a source of his caution and close attention in later life to political methods of control of his *daimyo* rivals. He had benefited from his association with both Oda Nobunaga and Toyotomi Hideyoshi and gained an immense amount of battle experience. On several occasions he lay low instead of rising to challenge Hideyoshi; but all the while he was consolidating and adding to his own domains in the east. At the death of Hideyoshi he was by far the most powerful of the Council of Regency, holding estates worth 2,500,000 koku in revenue, or more than double the wealth of any of the other four members. Incidentally, the five members of the Council together held fiefs of one third of the value of all fiefs in the country.

Ieyasu had as his main object to preserve the unity of Japan. From this unity he naturally stood to benefit; but also his outstanding position made him the object of envy and intrigue. His most dangerous enemy was Ishida Mitsunari, who did everything possible to cause bad blood between Ieyasu and his colleagues, and even made two attempts on Ieyasu's life. In 1600 another opponent, Uesugi, raised a rebellion in the north, and Ieyasu marched against him. But Uesugi was held in check by two *daimyo* loyal to Ieyasu, and Ieyasu's own advance was in the nature of a feint. He was watching Mitsunari, who now gathered allies and made an advance from the west. Battle was joined on October 21, 1600, at the pass of Sekigahara, a strategic defile between the plain east of Lake Biwa and the plain surrounding Nagoya. Each side had mustered approximately 80,000 men, but Mitsunari did not succeed in bringing all his forces into action, and the loyalty of some was doubtful. At the beginning of the fight at dawn the advantage went to Mitsunari. At a crucial moment one of his commanders, Kobayakawa, was supposed to charge down a hill onto Ieyasu's rear; but he remained inactive and then changed sides and attacked other regiments of Mitsunari's. Although the commanders of these regiments were veterans of the Korean War and had large numbers of men at their disposal, the element of surprise and shock must have been great, and they were pushed back. There was considerable slaughter and Ieyasu emerged with an overwhelming victory. This was the final battle in the long and exhausting series of civil wars, and the last major engagement fought on Japanese soil to the present day.

Ieyasu at once set about the matter of punishments and rewards. By confiscating ninety fiefs and reducing the size of many others of his recent enemies, he had land worth 6,500,000 koku to dispose of. A good part of this he kept in the Tokugawa family, but rewarded his retainers and allies generously. He was careful to assign estates near the main routes in the center of the country to those whom he considered absolutely reliable. He was cautious in actions affecting certain powerful feudatories, most of them distant from the center, in order not to drive into the arms of his enemies those faithful to Hideyoshi's memory and to his young son, Hideyori. He then spent the next years strengthening his castle at Edo, whose inner ramparts now enclose the emperor's palace in Tokyo, in protecting Edo by erecting a series of fortresses around it, in building the Nijo Castle as headquarters for his deputy at the capital in Kyoto, and in providing for the growth of industry and foreign trade.

By 1611 the old supporters of the youthful Hideyori had been removed by death, and by 1614 Ieyasu had decided, in spite of his repeated oaths to Hideyoshi, not to permit the continued existence of the house of Toyotomi in case it might still become a rallying point for the disaffected. No *daimyo* were prepared to come out in the open to Hideyori's aid, but *ronin*—masterless *samurai* -rallied to him. This increased the garrison available to Hideyori in the castle of Osaka to 90,000. Hidetada, appointed by his father, Ieyasu, to conduct the attack, could not breach the defenses of this famous stronghold, so, after a period of siege in the winter of 1614, he induced Hideyori's advisers to sign a compromise peace, whereby Hideyori would keep his domains and castle, while Hidetada would demolish the outer works of the castle. Hidetada did not keep to his part of the bargain, had his men fill in the inner moat as well, and attacked again without any justification in the summer. The defenders sallied out and were overwhelmed. Hideyori committed suicide and Yodogimi, his mother, was killed by a retainer to forestall capture. The whole episode was the more disreputable as Hideyori's wife was Hidetada's own daughter and had sent a last appeal for the lives of her husband and Yodogimi. The message was totally ignored.

Ieyasu was now the unchallenged leader of the country. He had already revived the institution of the *bakufu* and been made Shogun by the emperor in 1603. He retained the office for only two years and then handed it over to Hidetada, his son. He thus signalized the fact that the office was to continue in the Tokugawa family and at the same time set himself free to devote time to a system that would preserve his house from overthrow. The details will be considered in the next chapter, but in essence the plan consisted in treating the powerful *daimyo* with firmness and respect, and placing his own family members and close allies in estates in key positions to keep an eye on them. His greatest weapon was his wealth, which was constantly increasing through the operation of gold and silver mines, through foreign trade, and through taking the main cities of Japan under his direct jurisdiction.

The system mentioned above was a system of control, but not an administrative pattern of government. Of that there was very little. Ieyasu governed by giving direct orders, as one would govern a fief. His subordinates then carried out the orders as circumstances seemed to dictate. In the early period Ieyasu had no involved scheme of boards or government offices. At a later stage in the Tokugawa rule a more detailed and quite unbending organization was worked out. Ieyasu laid down general principles, especially for the control of the "outside lords," the great feudatories, in the *buke sho-hatto* of 1615, the "ordinances for military houses." This document forbade these lords to marry without approval of the Shogun, did not allow them to repair or enlarge their castles without a permit, and ordered them to denounce subversive activity. The details of administration were in any case handled locally by the *daimyo* in each fief, so there was little need for an elaborate central structure of government.

Ieyasu was a shrewd judge of men but had a curiously casual way of employing some persons. He used talent wherever he saw it. Thus he employed a falconer on diplomatic missions and an actor as director of his mining operations because they had a flair for these things. It was by a strange accident that he found one of his most valuable experts, a shipbuilder, Will Adams, pilot-major of a small Dutch flotilla, who was one of a few survivors of a typhoon which severely damaged the flagship, the *Liefde*. The little group of foreign sailors landed in Kyushu and in due course Ieyasu came to hear of Will Adams. He was a native of Kent in England and had served a thorough apprenticeship as a shipwright. He built several small ships for Ieyasu and explained Western methods of navigation. He arranged for the salvaged guns and ammunition of the *Liefde* to be used in the siege of Osaka Castle. Ieyasu admired Adams' determination and native shrewdness and held frequent conversations with him. In the course of their discussions Adams persuaded Ieyasu to grant the English trade privileges, a move which commended itself to Ieyasu, who was anxious for competition to offset the Portuguese monopoly. Adams warned him against the potential dangers of relations with Spain and Portugal and pointed out that there were other European nations, England among them, who did not insist on propagating their faith but were content with trading privileges alone. The Dutch received permission to trade in 1609. The British East India Company was at this point offered a gilt-edged opportunity to acquire a favored trading position. But the company official in charge, possibly jealous of Will Adams, selected an unsuitable site for his trading station against Adams' advice. The British "factory" never really prospered and was closed down after some years, leaving the Dutch the only gainers from the whole affair. Will Adams acquired a considerable estate and married a Japanese wife. He ultimately died in Japan, somewhat homesick for England but full of honors, and is commemorated by a monument that looks out over the sea which was his livelihood and his sorrow.

From his own observations as well as Adams' advice, Ieyasu was well aware of the rivalries among European nations in securing trade openings. He thought he could profit from these rivalries and treated all nations impartially. He hoped to gain technical aid, and was in correspondence with the Spanish governor of the Philippines, to whom he suggested trade arrangements and from whom he requested the help of mining and ship-building experts. The governor was slow to respond, and when he sent a ship, the personnel proved to be more missionaries than either traders or experts. This annoyed Ieyasu. He welcomed Dutch and English trade and felt less dependent on the ships of Portugal and Spain. He had long been tolerant of Christianity, but toward the end of his life he became more suspicious. He seems to have felt that Christian allegiance might make some *daimyo* less loyal to his regime, in view of the fact that foreign policy was becoming a more complicated matter with more European nations involved. In 1614 he had an edict issued suppressing Christianity. Churches were destroyed in the capital at Kyoto, prominent Japanese Christians exiled and foreign missionaries placed under arrest. No missionaries were killed at this time.

In the winter of 1614–15 he took the most difficult step to secure the future, namely the attack on Osaka Castle and the elimination of Hideyori and the house of Hideyoshi. He must have long considered this move and been reluctant to make it, at least until he was quite sure he could do it with impunity and without risking revolt. He was just in time. The year following, 1616, he died, aged seventy-five. His life was the most fitting to close the work of the three men who had succeeded in unifying Japan, for he was as strong in politics as he was in military affairs. He had the patience and determination for the one as well as the physical stamina and strategic brilliance for the other. He fought over forty-five battles in his time. In his case the portrait appearance is deceptive. He was small in stature and rather stout. His face looks like that of a *petit fonctionnaire*, round and rather ordinary, except for the eyes. But in fact he liked riding and swimming and was accustomed to fatigue and hard exercise, enjoying excellent health right up to the time of his last illness.

The artistic climate during the sixteenth century, the Period of the Country at War, shows a contrast almost as great as can be imagined to the earlier Muromachi Period under the Ashikaga Shoguns. The pendulum of taste has swung from restraint to exuberance, from chaste and cultivated simplicity to the florid use of gold and color. Inside the buildings the screens have larger, bolder designs and much gilt background, while outside the roof lines have been altered to the rounder, swelling, and somewhat ostentatious forms connected with the art period of Momoyama (1573–1615). The very name Momoyama, "Peach Mountain," taken from the site of Hideyoshi's villa, suggests a lush opulence quite different from the understatement of the earlier period.

This marked artistic shift had at least something to do with the tastes of the political leaders themselves. Hideyoshi once gave a tea ceremony party to which everyone, from the greatest to the humblest, was invited. The affair went on for ten days, with art exhibits, concerts, plays, and dance performances. Every device of ostentation was employed to enhance the public image of the leading military figure who was aiming to unite Japan under his personal banner. Hideyoshi enjoyed entertaining and took pride in showing visitors around his Osaka castle, where the bowls, tea kettles, and other vessels, and even the hardware on the doors, were all of pure gold. No greater contrast could be found than that between this magnificent rococo display and the deliberately quiet and spare character of the tea ceremony in the original small room in the grounds of the Silver Pavilion.

The Western world also exhibited a change in the favored style of art from the classic and restrained to the extravagant and theatrical at about the same time, the latter half of the sixteenth century and the beginning of the seventeenth, when the painting and architecture of the Renaissance gave way to those of the Baroque era. Yoshimitsu, the third Ashikaga Shogun, who governed latterly from his retreat at the Golden Pavilion and died in 1408, falls in time just before the active period of the Early Renaissance painters, Fra Angelico, Masaccio, and Fra Filippo Lippi. Yoshimasa, builder of the Silver Pavilion and patron of the great monk-artist and connoisseur, Noami, corresponds roughly with the age of Giovanni Bellini, Sandro Botticelli, and Leonardo da Vinci. But by the time the swashbuckling Hideyoshi gave his gigantic tea party, Rubens as a young man was forming his style of glorious exuberance; and the elaborate allegorical ceiling paintings of overblown Baroque in the Italian mansions and churches, such as Pietro da Cortona's "Triumph of Divine Providence" (between 1633 and 1639) in the Palazzo Barberini, coincided with the final consolidation of the Tokugawa regime.

The progress of elaboration in Europe was more gradual and steady, and transition from the simple to the magnificent in Japan more sudden and more marked. The severity of Giotto in the fourteenth century and the simple dignity of Masaccio in the fifteenth yielded by gradations to the magnificence of Leonardo, Raphael, and Michelangelo in the High Renaissance of the sixteenth century, before the mannered painting of the Baroque came to fill the center of the stage. The period of restraint, even of severity, in Japan owed its origin to the artists of the Sung Dynasty in China (960–

1280), but its most famous Japanese practitioners came much later. They were Josetsu (c. 1410), Shubun (active from 1414 to 1465), and Sesshu (1420–1506), most renowned of them all. All three were deeply influenced by the philosophy of Zen. (The name of the first, Josetsu, means "as if unskillful," reflecting a Zen notion of direct spontaneity.) Sesshu, with his strong, severe style, was still active at the beginning of the sixteenth century; but by the second half of the century the painter Kano Eitoku (1543–90) was at work on such commissions as screens for Nobunaga's new castle at Azuchi. One of these, with the title Karashishi, "Chinese Lions," offered both in theme and execution a marked contrast to the earlier simplicity. Painted on a background of gold, it is full of flamboyant curves and mock fierceness. In an exaggerated Chinese convention the animals' tails are so bushy they could be mistaken for flames of fire or waves of the sea.

Although the shifts in style took place in East and West at about the same time, the two movements seem to be quite independent of one another. The parallel changes in artistic taste do not show any evidence of a causal connection. The Portuguese visitors, as curiosities, were made the subjects of a few Japanese paintings. There was for a time a superficial fashion, already noted, for things Portuguese. But the influence of the Jesuit missionaries and a handful of merchants, Portuguese and Dutch, was too marginal to have had any real effect on the course of Japanese art.

In one field, however, that of architecture, the influence of European technology is clearly to be seen, though the outcome is distinctively Japanese in style. The advent of firearms made necessary an entirely new form of fortification, and Oda Nobunaga made a characteristically thoroughgoing response to the problem. In 1576 he erected the castle at Azuchi on Lake Biwa which dominated central Japan. Hideyoshi followed with the great stronghold of the castle of Osaka in 1583–85, and Tokugawa Ieyasu with the rebuilding and enlargement of the castle of Edo. In these and subsequent castle buildings an immense square with sloping sides formed of large stone blocks gave an unbroken foundation extending up to fifty or sixty feet in height. Upon this was erected the castle proper, constructed of wood and plaster with wall faces and gables between layers of small projecting roofs. The towering structure of five or six stories gradually diminishes in size as it rises. The gables and projecting roofs are designed to give advantageous lines of fire to the defenders but to provide no horizontal valleys in the roofs in which incendiary materials could easily lodge (see Plate 24). The castle at Azuchi is aptly named "The White Heron," for the massive stone base surmounted by white walls and gray roof tiles, visible from far away, gives an impression of surprising lightness and airiness considering the functional strength and power of the structure. The interiors of the castles were sumptuously furnished with screens and decoration in the ornate Momoyama style. (The full name often given to this period in art is Azuchi-Momoyama, to include Nobunaga's castle at Azuchi as well as Hideyoshi's villa at Momoyama.) The considerable sums spent on these fortified dwellings were a calculated expense incurred to help the leaders establish their dominant position among the *daimyo*. The exterior would overawe the visiting lords with its impregnability and the interior impress them with the owner's vast reserve of wealth.

II

JAPAN IN ISOLATION

The Tokugawa Shogunate:
Part I, 1615–1715

Japan in the seventeenth century was at length peaceful and prosperous. The *Tokaido*, "the eastern road by the sea," between the old capital at Kyoto and the new one at Edo, was thronged with people, some traveling on business, some on pilgrimages combined with pleasure and sightseeing. If they noted the procession of a great lord moving up to Edo, they would scatter and kneel prostrate on either side of the road till the lord had passed. First came the *samurai* warriors, wearing the traditional long sword and short dirk, the first group of them a bodyguard surrounding one of the important officials of the lord's estate, mounted on horseback. Then followed servants carrying boxes and baskets of treasure and supplies, more *samurai* with banners, then the *daimyo* himself, borne in a palanquin, with whole regiments of *samurai* and servants forming the rear of the procession. The entire equipage might amount to hundreds or even thousands of men. It went ill with any bystander of the common people who did not show proper respect, for the *samurai* had the legal right of *kirisute*, "to cut down and leave," the right to kill with impunity, without questions asked or explanations offered.

Constant processions of this kind to and from Edo were the most characteristic part of the contemporary scene. They were occasioned by the practice of *sankin-kotai*, "alternate attendance," first a custom then a requirement of the Shogunate, whereby the *daimyo* spent four months of each year, or sometimes of every second year, in attendance at the Shogun's court, and the remainder of the year on their estates. But when they returned to their estates, they had to leave their wives and families in Edo as hostages for their good behavior. The word "alternate" referred to the fact that each category of *daimyo* was divided into two groups, one of which was in attendance while the other was in the country. In this way the Shogun was able to prevent the lords from plotting those uprisings which had disturbed the peace for so long in the past. He was also able to divert the spending of the lords' finances from military purposes into peaceful, if wasteful, channels by forcing each lord to keep up two establishments in a style befitting his rank.

The *daimyo* were divided into three categories, the *shimpan*, related fiefs, belonging to collateral branches of the Tokugawa family itself, the chief of these being the *go-sanke*, "three houses," the estates of three of Ieyasu's sons in Owari, Kii, and Mito provinces respectively; the *fudai*, or hereditary vassals, who had been allied with the Tokugawa house before the battle of Sekigahara; and the *tozama*, "outside lords," who had sworn fealty to Ieyasu only after Sekigahara and the fall of Osaka.

The Tokugawa family took full advantage of the prestige and position given by the title of Shogun, which was secured by Ieyasu as a member of a branch of the famous Minamoto, to which Minamoto Yoritomo, the first Shogun of the new, permanent style, had belonged. The title had never been claimed by Nobunaga or Hideyoshi. The importance of the *go-sanke* lay in the fact that they were eligible to supply a member for the office of Shogun if a son failed to the direct line. The *fudai daimyo* were located for the most part in central Japan and held fiefs averaging about 50,000 koku, though a few were much larger. Although holding the privileged place of loyal vassals, they had often to undergo the hardship of being moved from one estate to another, for the Shogunate used them to keep watch over outside lords of doubtful fidelity. The outside lords themselves were originally the equals of the Tokugawa, and some of them held very large fiefs. The Maeda held estates worth over 1,000,000 koku, and Mori of Choshu at one time controlled thirteen of the sixty-six provinces in the country. They could do little outside their fiefs but were largely autonomous within them. They had to be handled tactfully by Ieyasu at the beginning, but subsequent Shoguns found the methods of control evolved by the *bakufu* to be increasingly effective.

These methods of control included not only the alternate attendance, hostage system, and encouragement of heavy financial expenditure on the part of the lords, but also a ban on any repairs, strengthening, or enlargement of fortresses by any *daimyo* without express permission, and the device of compelling the outside lords in particular to undertake public works, including the rebuilding of Tokugawa fortresses. Two further measures were in the nature of police control, namely the upper and lower ranks of *metsuke*, or censors, who supplied secret intelligence to the *bakufu* concerning *daimyo* and lesser ranks of landholders, and the institution of *gonin-gumi*, "five-man groups" among the farmers. The five-man groups were mutually responsible for keeping the peace and seeing that taxes were paid and obligations discharged within their own group. Another precaution, drawn from the lessons of the civil wars, was to forbid any *daimyo* to enter into direct communication with the emperor; everything had to be done through the Shogun's deputy in Kyoto.

The lesser vassals who held land under 10,000 koku in value were called *hatamoto*, "bannermen" (originally the bodyguard of a general). Many held land worth only 500 koku or less. It became customary to withdraw such men from the land altogether and pay them a fixed stipend instead. The *bakufu* was anxious to dissociate the warrior class as much as possible from the peasants, so as to avoid the agrarian revolts under *samurai* gentleman-farmer leadership which had presented such a problem in the recent past. But the presence of idle warriors in the castle towns, living on an income that fluctuated with the price of rice, began before long to cause embarrassment of another kind to the regime.

The organization of the Tokugawa government, minimal under Ieyasu, became gradually more elaborate and formalized under his successors, until it attained the following form under Iemitsu, the third Shogun (1623–51):

The Tairo, "Great Elders," advised the Shogun on important matters of policy and ruled as regents during the minority of a child. At first there were three Tairo, but later only one.

The Roju, "Council of Elders," originally two and finally four in number, served on a rotation system for one month each. In addition to some advisory duties they were responsible for the direction of the bureaucratic machine. Their administrative supervision covered a wide range, the affairs of the *daimyo* and of the monasteries, relations with the emperor's court, the affairs of the Shogun's own vast domains, public works, and coinage.

The Hyojosho, "Judicial Council," was formed by the addition of certain commissioners to the Roju councillors. These commissioners were in charge of various government departments and had both executive and judicial functions in areas such as city government, reporting on *daimyo* activity (the commissioners known as *metsuke*, mentioned above), control of the bannermen and of religious organizations, and responsibility for the finances of the Tokugawa domains.

It was not necessary for the central government of the Shogun to provide manpower or funds for local government, since this was decentralized in the hands of the various *daimyo*. But commissioners for the large cities were always appointed by the Shogunate from among the *fudai daimyo*, their own vassals. The resultant whole was quite evidently a police state with tight supervision, organized to preserve as closely as possible the status quo.

This strong impulse to preserve the country exactly as it was explains in part the mounting persecution of the Christian church in Japan, viewed with ever-increasing suspicion as the agent of foreign powers. During the rule of Hidetada (1616–23), Ieyasu's son and successor, some 700 Christians were executed. An English merchant reported seeing children burned alive in their mothers' arms, while the women prayed to Jesus to receive the children's souls. Many more than the number killed must have had to leave their homes and have been reduced to abject poverty. Those enforcing the edicts against Christianity tried to induce their victims to place their feet on a sacred picture or image—*fumi-e*, "treading picture"—and so to renounce their faith. A remarkable number refused.

The climax of persecution came in the years 1637–38, during the reign of Iemitsu, third Shogun, when 37,000 peasants, the majority of them Christians, were joined in armed rebellion by *ronin* and others driven to desperation by bad local government and poor economic conditions. All made a stand in an old fort on the Shimabara Peninsula, an area near Nagasaki which had for long been a Christian center. The *bakufu* could not fail to take strong action in face of this threat to the peace of the realm; but it took the authorities three months, 100,000 troops, and the help of Dutch naval bombardment from the sea to reduce the rebels. The slaughter was hideous and only a handful escaped with their lives.

The failure of the Shimabara Rebellion was decisive. Christianity in Japan was compelled to go underground and in many areas was rooted out altogether. The Roman Catholic Church officially lists 3,125 individual instances of martyrdom (the unrecorded deaths at Shimabara being omitted) between 1597 and 1660. And yet, when the country was opened to foreigners after 1868, Christian families were discovered who had handed down the faith in secret from father to son. The savage suppression of Christianity was not unrelated to the internal political situation in Japan. Foreign and Christian influence had always been strong in Kyushu and the western end of Honshu, and it was precisely here that some of the greatest *tozama* (outside lords) had their seats. There can be no doubt that the *bakufu* feared that these lords might at any time offer trade privileges to Portugal or Spain in return for foreign weapons and even military reinforcements of troops and naval vessels to overthrow the regime. Following the Shimabara Rebellion, therefore, the *bakufu* took the final steps of expelling all Portuguese merchants and missionaries, imposing the death penalty on all Japanese attempting either to go abroad or return, and placing a limit of 2,500 bushels capacity on the construction of new ships, a size suitable only for coastal and not overseas trade. The Chinese merchants were kept under strict supervision and the only Europeans admitted were the Dutch. The Dutch traders were granted limited privileges only, being confined from 1641 onward to a small, artificial island called Deshima in Nagasaki Bay. There they lived in cramped conditions and without their families for the long months between the annual trading exchanges. Their massive and well-armed vessels were slow but for their day reliable and able to carry a large amount of cargo. The round trip could be made only once a year, and the risks from pirates and from tropical storms were great. But if the voyage was successful, the profits were very high. In the corresponding trade of the British East India Company with Canton a captain could sometimes retire comfortably on the gains secured from three or four voyages, if his luck held. The parallel is not an exact one and the height of the British trade occurred at a later date, in the second half of the eighteenth century. But the low-bulk, high-value cargoes from Asia were generally a profitable venture. The profits of the Dutch seem to have made their endurance of the hardships of Deshima worthwhile. In any event it was soon evident that the *bakufu* meant business by their new regulations, for all the members of a Portuguese diplomatic group which came in 1640 to negotiate the resumption of trade were summarily executed.

Thus Japan decided neither to admit foreigners to free and open trading nor to continue the overseas trade ventures to Southeast Asia which she herself had undertaken with considerable success in the sixteenth century. By this decision for retreat and isolation she gained stability and internal solidarity at a time when these factors were urgently needed in her society. But there was a certain irony in the fact that this closing down and sealing off took place just when the rest of the world was being opened up to an interchange of goods and ideas incomparably more thorough and extensive than had ever been known before. The rate of social and technological change in the West became rapid in the two centuries following 1640, whereas in Japan the rate of change was deliberately slowed down by Tokugawa policy. Thus when Japan reopened her doors she had much lost ground to make up; but she was in a stronger position to do so when the time came.

The main roots of the strength which Japan exhibited in the crucial period of modernization in the latter half of the nineteenth century lay in the *samurai*. This class provided a manpower source with a strong sense of duty, courage both physical and moral, and a thorough, if narrow, experience in handling public business in the various fiefs. These valuable qualities were developed by generations of training in the hard school of war; but they derived also from the Confucian ethic which had been introduced when Chinese culture was first acclimated to Japanese soil in the sixth century.

Ieyasu had issued in 1615 his *buke sho-hatto*, "ordinances for the Military Houses," in which the *samurai* were bidden to give themselves equally to the practice of arms and the pursuit of polite learning. Polite learning in actual fact meant Confucianism. Buddhism, earlier a main factor in cultural advance, was now declining. Shinto played its part as an ally of Confucianism against the power of Buddhism. But Confucianism, with its conservative qualities and its stress on loyalty, was ideally suited to the static pattern of Tokugawa rule. The pattern was further reinforced by the form which Confucianism had already assumed in China, namely the Neo-Confucianism of Chu Hsi (1130–1200), a state orthodoxy that became increasingly rigid with the passage of time. Neo-Confucianism had been the subject of discussion in Japan at the court of the Emperor Go-Daigo as early as 1333; but it came into its own in Tokugawa times.

One of the great proponents of the Neo-Confucian philosophy was Hayashi Razan (1583–1657), a scholar who acted as secretary to Ieyasu and helped with the drafting of laws at the beginning of the Tokugawa Shogunate. It was due to him in the first instance that Neo-Confucianism became almost equivalent to a state orthodoxy in Japan. He encouraged the Shogunate to become independent of the West, and to lay stress, in the traditional Confucian manner, upon farming, not trade, as the foundation of the state. There was, however, a change of emphasis. In the Confucian ethics of the *samurai* loyalty to one's lord took precedence over all other considerations, even over the family loyalty and filial piety which were such a feature of the Confucianism of China. Hayashi Razan was immensely learned and a prolific writer in the fields of history, literature, and Shinto studies, as well as Confucian philosophy. A drawing of his face shows deep lines of concentration on the brow and around the eyes, while a small, pursed mouth suggests a legal mind of rigid precision. His house in Edo became a center of Confucian studies, and the tradition was carried on by his son and grandson. The latter, with the enthusiastic support of the fifth Shogun, Tsunayoshi, became the president of the Shohei Academy, a Confucian university providing for instruction in philosophy and the performance of a ritual cult centered on Confucius.

The Tokugawa government preserved a firm social stability in Japan, but it was always plagued by an inner contradiction, namely the need to maintain peace and at the same time preserve in the *samurai* a stance of military preparedness and an attitude of pride, not to say of bellicosity. The *samurai* could find no avenue for military action outside Japan, for the country was insulated from almost all contact, positive or negative, with other powers. The warning of Hideyoshi's misadventure in Korea had been heeded. Those *samurai* not employed in administration could find little outlet for their energies inside Japan, for a social freeze between peasant and warrior and between warrior and merchant had occurred. Class distinctions were intentionally fostered by the government, and had been ever since Hideyoshi's sword hunt. Upward social mobility was very difficult, in part owing to lack of money among the lower grades of *samurai*. Indeed fluctuations of the rice market, in which their stipends, paid in rice, were converted to cash, made any social movement for the *samurai* likely to be a downward one. The classic means for a warrior to enrich himself by fighting to gain possession of the lands of others was totally denied to him by the overwhelming power of the Tokugawa police state. It is no wonder there was a deep sense of frustration in the *samurai* ranks.

Some enterprising *samurai* founded military academies where the practice of arms and the theory of strategy were taught. These schools naturally became social centers where many of the warrior class congregated and discussed all manner of topics, not excluding politics. It was at one of these academies in Edo that a *ronin* conspiracy was planned. The objective was to set off an explosion in a government powder magazine on a night when a strong wind would start a large fire. In the ensuing confusion the conspirators proposed to break into the Shogun's castle and kill the highest officials. Simultaneous arson and violence was to take place in Osaka and Kyoto. The plot took a long time in preparation during the last years of Iemitsu, and was not ready for execution until 1651, the first year of the rule of Ietsuna, the fourth Shogun. Even then there was a further postponement due to the illness of one of the leaders. He was heard to mutter details of the plot during a bout of fever and the authorities were forewarned. The rising proved abortive. The leaders committed suicide or were punished by crucifixion and their relatives by decapitation.

Some change in the attitude of the government had, however, already taken place. The young Ietsuna (in office 1651–80) was fortunate in having good advisers. The regime felt secure, and a change from the military government of the first three Shoguns was now initiated. Policy began to be directed from this time on into civilian channels. Enlightened attempts were made to find openings for *ronin* in constructive work. Many of them were not eager to assume clerical tasks, and others had not sufficient education to enable them to do so. But better education and the gradual growth of a central government bureaucracy enabled most *ronin*, with the exception of the most restless and the least reputable, to be taken up into useful employment by the early 1700's.

The fifth Shogun, Tsunayoshi (1680–1709), who succeeded his brother, Ietsuna, was a curious character. He supported Confucianism, as his patronage of the Shohei Academy showed, and was himself a scholar of some ability. But he was all his life under the influence of his mother, a strong and ambitious woman, who was a fanatical believer in Buddhism. She persuaded him to issue in 1687 an edict protecting all living things, especially dogs, since he had been born in the Year of the Dog in the traditional calendar. Those mistreating dogs were punished and the city officials ended by building shelters outside Edo which housed 50,000 of these animals. The ultimate absurdity was reached when citizens were required to address dogs as O Inu Sama, "Honorable Dog."

The years of Tsunayoshi's rule coincided with the important cultural period known as the Genroku Era (1688–1704). This period was associated with a new urban culture and the flowering of a new type of art and literature whose patrons were no longer the court nobles, great monasteries, or powerful *daimyo*, but the merchants, the *samurai*, and the townspeople.

The peaceful years and expanding economy of the Tokugawa Period had led to a remarkable urban growth. Although the financial distress of the *samurai* was real, the economy as a whole was prosperous and more diversified. Cash crops such as sesame oil, mulberry, indigo, sugar cane, and tobacco supplemented the staple, rice. Cotton accounted for 25 percent of the produce of four provinces by the first quarter of the eighteenth century. Large ancestral farms were breaking up into smaller units which could be run by single families, whose members, in the current shortage of labor, were able to increase their earnings by work in village and town industries. Some small businesses burgeoned into large merchant enterprises.

The house of Mitsui, for example, started by brewing *sake* in Ise. They opened a pawnshop and then began dealing in rice. A member of the family founded a retail textile store in Edo in 1673, which proved so successful that branches were opened in Kyoto and Osaka. The Mitsui house then conducted the banking business required both by the Shogun and the emperor. The Mitsui firm adapted itself more successfully than some other merchant houses to the changes that came later with the Meiji era and went on to become one of the great industrial companies of modern Japan.

In the course of this urban growth the three great cities were Kyoto, the old capital, Edo, the new capital, and the combination of four towns which formed the city of Osaka—"the kitchen of the world," as it was called. There the Dojima Rice Exchange was set up in 1697, though trade in rice had been a feature of the city previously. By 1710 the exchange was operating with warehouse notes in place of actual grain and was dealing in futures. Numerous towns, some of considerable size, grew up in the centers of the various fiefs, towns such as Nagoya, Sendai, Kumamoto, Kagoshima, Kanazawa, Hiroshima, Hakone, and Kofu, as well as over 100 other towns of smaller size. Road transportation improved under the Tokugawa, but the mountains and headlands of Japan make road construction peculiarly difficult. The cheapest and most efficient form of transport was by sea. An eastern circuit and a western circuit were developed for coastal trade by sea on a regular basis. Without sea-borne traffic it would scarcely have been possible to deliver to Osaka the four million bales of rice which were reaching that port annually by the time of the Genroku Era.

The merchants, until now despised as a class, began to assume an altogether new importance. The surplus wealth in the hands of these new merchants and their servants was sufficient to support a type of urban living almost unknown hitherto except possibly around the fringes of the court in Kyoto. A life of leisure, particularly evening leisure, now became available at a price to the city dweller. There were tea houses and taverns, many of which also served as places of assignation for lovers. The pleasure quarters of Edo and Osaka became famous and provided for the enjoyments of unrestrained good company as well as for those of sex. The theaters and public baths were more frequented and tourism, travel for pleasure and sightseeing, became more common.

The popular Kabuki theater in its early phases had a bad moral reputation with the result that the *bakufu* forbade women to be associated with the theater as actresses (see Plate 28). The challenge of having men present female parts helped to form a highly stylized dramatic art. This fully developed *Kabuki* theater satisfied the common people's love of gaudy and bright costumes, violent action, and strong emotional tension. The parallel art of Bunraku, the popular puppet plays, also affected Kabuki in the exaggerated and sometimes jerky gestures adopted by the actors.

Chikamatsu Monzaemon (1653–1724), one of the most notable figures of the Genroku Era, wrote both for the Bunraku puppet stage and for the

Kabuki popular theater. His plays were of two types, those depending on historical events for their themes and those dealing with contemporary and domestic affairs. In both cases the dramatic tension emerges from the conflict of duty and affection, of the social code and the impulses of the heart. There are records of discussions which Chikamatsu had with his friends concerning the difficulty of writing for the puppet stage. He said in effect that the dialogues and descriptions had to be more than usually vivid and alive to compensate for the fact that the actors were inanimate creatures. The best-known of his Kabuki plays is *Chushingura*, the tale of the forty-seven *ronin*. Their lord had been unbearably provoked by the deliberate taunts of another *daimyo* and had drawn his sword to kill the man while both were within the confines of the Shogun's court. For this crime against the Shogun's majesty he was condemned to death. His forty-seven loyal followers vowed they would avenge him. To divert suspicion they scattered and took up employment in different places, biding their time. At an agreed moment they gathered, marched through a snowy night, caught their enemy off-guard, and killed him. They then gave themselves up to the authorities. They should have been executed, but in view of the faithfulness to *giri*, duty and obligation, they were allowed to commit suicide, the lesser punishment of a more honorable death.

The most famous novelist of the Genroku Era was Ihara Saikaku, who died in 1693. The theme of his tales, one of which was entitled *Five Women Who Loved Love,* was bourgeois life, with all its materialism and love of pleasure realistically and amusingly portrayed. His stories are filled with idle young men about town, miserly merchants, ladies of easy virtue, simple folk, and priests with dubious past histories. The style is light but the characterizations masterly. There are touches of poetry sufficient to give charm and a feeling of continuity with the past to what was at the time a very modern genre in literature. A complete contrast is to be found in the work of a later Tokugawa novelist, Takizawa Bakin (1767–1848), whose father was a *ronin* and whose many popular books reflect the traditional virtues of the *samurai* class.

Undoubtedly the most beloved and most quoted literary figure of the period was the poet Matsuo Basho (1644–94). He was chiefly renowned for the short poetic form known as *haiku*, in which he had many successors but few equals. The traditional *tanka* lyrics, found as early as the seventh century in the Manyoshu collection, were short enough, thirty-one syllables only, arranged in lines of 5-7-5-7-7. But the *haiku* made its point in only seventeen syllables, 5-7-5. This extreme brevity demanded a bright wit and was the invention of the "cockney" city society of the sixteenth and seventeenth centuries. The form began as the opening section of a chain type of poem known as *haikai*, but soon became established in its own right. It has remained popular down to the present day and now enjoys a considerable vogue in the West as well as in Japan. It depends for its impact on a vignette, the fragment of a scene, usually from nature, and then a sudden subjective turn indicating the effect upon the poet. The literary force which the form generated at the time of its invention was considerable, for its gaiety and impudence offered an implied challenge to staid aristocratic art and feudal society. The *haiku* is deliberately open-ended; it begins in the middle of a scene and ends, perforce, immediately the contrast has been pointed up or the turn of thought indicted. The artist depends upon the imagination of the reader to apply the image the poem brings and complete its effect in his own mind. This unfinished nature of the *haiku* may be said to correspond to the creative use of space in the best landscape painting, for it too is a positive use of what is *not* there.

One or two actual examples may make these points clear.

> On the moor: from things
> detached completely—
> how the skylark sings!
>> —Matsuo Basho,
>> tr. Harold G. Henderson

> My hut, in spring:
> true, there is nothing in it—
> there is Everything!
>> —Yamaguchi Sodo (1642–1716),
>> tr. Harold G. Henderson

The poem is miniature; so, often, is the subject.

> In its eye
> the far-off hills are mirrored—
> dragon-fly!
>> —Kobayashi Issa (1763–1828),
>> tr. Harold G. Henderson

> A one-foot waterfall
> it too makes noises, and at night
> the coolness of it all!
>> —Kobayashi Issa,
>> tr. Harold G. Henderson

The small serves to illustrate beauty as well as, perhaps better than, the great; and the poet takes a cultivated delight in simplicity.

In suggesting moods *haiku* offer an Oriental alternative to the pathetic fallacy so common in Western literature. Instead of the Western habit of transferring the poet's feelings to Nature—"the angry waves," "the sullen clouds"—man's mood and nature's face are kept separate but linked. Basho, in his prose poem "The Unreal Dwelling," says:

> Mountain wisteria hung on the pines. Cuckoos frequently flew past, and there were visits from the swallows. Not a peck from a woodpecker disturbed me, and in my joy I called to the wood dove, "Come, bird of solitude,

and make me melancholy!" I could not but be happy—the view would not have blushed before the loveliest scenes of China.

—tr. Donald Keene

The state of solitude is natural for the bird; the feelings of happiness and melancholy may be induced by surrounding nature, but they take place in the spirit of the man. In one of Basho's most famous *haiku* no feeling whatever is attributed to the grasses; but they are a symbol powerful in their simplicity.

> The summer grasses—
> of brave warriors' dreams
> all that remains.
>
> —tr. author

Or again:

> The place where I was born:
> all I come to—all I touch—
> blossoms of the thorn!
>
> —Kobayashi Issa,
> tr. Harold G. Henderson

The increased wealth of the merchant class and their pleasures, in which many of the *samurai* also took part, are all reflected with great clarity in the popular art of the time, the woodblock prints. These prints, brought to the Western world by ship captains and traders, became collectors' items in Europe and America. They had a marked effect on the work of Toulouse-Lautrec and other artists of his time in France. Although popular in Japan, they were despised as inferior and vulgar in their subject matter by Japanese connoisseurs of traditional painting in the Chinese style. Collectively these prints are known as *ukiyo-e*, "pictures of the floating world," a Buddhist term denoting the impermanence and fleeting nature of human pleasures. Hishikawa Moronobu (1638–1714) is accounted one of the founders of the *ukiyo-e* style, but the form continued to develop and flourish throughout the eighteenth century and some of its greatest artists were still alive in the middle of the nineteenth.

The possibility of reproducing many copies from one set of blocks enabled the prints to be sold at a very reasonable price and they found a ready market. The prints have a peculiar charm and show great technical skill, not only on the part of the original artist, but also in the work of the wood-block carver and the printer, who applied the colors to the blocks by hand. The blocks required—one for each color used in addition to the master block with the black outlines of the drawing—range in number from three or four to as many as fifteen. In all cases the registration of one block printing over another is perfect. The favorite subjects are pictures of the pin-up type, well-known actors in their celebrated roles, famous courtesans and their attendant maids, geisha entertainers, and celebrated landscape scenes, such as "Thirty-six Views of Mt. Fuji" by Hokusai or "The Fifty-three Halting-places on the Tokaido" by Hiroshige. Prints depicting the various activities of women give an insight into the processes of home industries such as silk culture and dyeing. In addition to such social scenes many artists also drew for their publishers erotic scenes which were circulated as "spring books."

The variety of colors, the flow of line, a high standard of taste, and the natural human appeal of the subject matter all combine in the great age of the Japanese color print in the second half of the eighteenth century and first half of the nineteenth to form a body of popular art almost unrivaled in the world. The individual artists and their schools are too numerous to mention; but some of the greatest names are Hokusai and Hiroshige for landscape, Sharaku and Toyokuni I for pictures of actors, and Utamaro, Harunobu, and Shigenobu for the charm of their delineation of women.

The art of printing from wooden blocks was, of course, not new in Tokugawa times. The Chinese had used it for centuries, both for reproducing written characters and pictures of human and landscape subjects. The rapid mass production of Buddhist charms was made possible in ancient Japan by the wood-block process. Characters and a frontispiece of gods and saints were combined in some of the earliest printings of Buddhist sutras. A complete sutra was printed from blocks, one block for each page, in A.D. 868. Even after the introduction of movable type in China about the year 1030 (four centuries before Gutenberg), the method of using a wood block for an entire page was continued, especially in the printing of sacred books.

Many examples exist of Chinese landscape prints with very fine lines in black and white. What was distinctive of the great age of Japanese wood blocks was the masterly use of color, subtle effects being obtained by the mixing of colors and by gradation and the wiping away of color already applied. Groups of subscribers would combine to commission sets of New Year greeting cards, and these would often incorporate elaborate effects obtained by sprinklings of gold, silver, and mica dust. Certain artists became famous for the skill with which they could represent images extremely difficult to portray through the medium of woodcutting. Hiroshige (1797–1858), for instance, was celebrated for his showers of rain, and Utamaro (1754–1806) for his figures seen behind a bamboo screen or through a diaphanous gauze, as in a print where women are depicted drying dyestuffs.

No artist excelled Hokusai as a colorful personality, and anecdotes from his life are numerous. He is said to have provided himself on one occasion with a barrel of ink and a broom and to have rushed around to complete an enormous painting in a few moments. The spectators could make nothing of it until some went up to the roof of a temple and saw that the design was the face of the Buddhist saint Daruma. The mouth was as large as a gate and each eye had room in the center for a man to sit down. To show his command of the other extreme, Hokusai painted a picture of two sparrows on a grain of rice. Summoned to an artists' competition before the Shogun Ienari, Hokusai asked for a paper screen door, laid it down, and painted a broad, waving stripe of blue upon it. He then produced a cock, dipped its feet in scarlet color, and made it walk down the blue band. That was his picture—the title, "Maple Leaves Floating Down the Tatsuta River." Hokusai had risen by constant struggle from a life of poverty, but by the end he was in great demand. He was chosen to illustrate the *Life of the Hundred Heroes*, one of the works of the famous author Bakin. The two fell out; but when the matter came to the ears of the publisher, he dispensed with Bakin and found another author to finish the text rather than lose Hokusai.

12

The WINDS OF CHANGE

The Tokugawa Shogunate:
Part II, 1716–1867

The eighth Shogun Yoshimune sat up late one night in 1719 talking animatedly to a man called Nishikawa Joken, an interpreter for the Dutch traders near Nagasaki. He was asking for an explanation of a terrestrial globe Nishikawa had constructed, and pressing for more details of the celestial wonders revealed by a Dutch telescope his guest had used. And, like all responsible rulers in China and Japan, he was anxious for religious reasons to have the calendar made as accurate as possible. Only thus could the proper time for sowing and reaping be observed and the true harmony between Heaven and earth maintained. That was why the Shogun sent to Nagasaki for a copy of an astronomical work which Father Adam Schall had compiled for the court of Peking a century before. As a result of these scientific interests and his sense of the value of Western knowledge, Yoshimune lifted the ban on the importation of foreign books, provided they did not teach Christianity. Thus a movement for acquiring Western or "Dutch" learning, *rangaku*,[1] which already existed in a clandestine manner, came out into the open and made considerable progress.

The Japanese had derived from the Portuguese some acquaintance with Western practice in firearms and cannon, maps, navigation, and naval affairs generally, and, perhaps most important of all, the existence and nature of the European world. But the West had made vast strides between the first arrival of the Portuguese at the end of the sixteenth century and the shogunate of Yoshimune (1716–45) at the beginning of the eighteenth. In between lay the achievements of Galileo, the polite but ultimately earth-shaking conversations in the Royal Society (founded 1662) and the Académie des Sciences (founded 1666), the chemical experiments of Robert Boyle, and

---

[1] *Ran* is the middle syllable of *Ho-ran-da* for Holland, and *gaku* means "study" or a "branch of learning."

the solid theoretical work of Sir Isaac Newton. His *Philosophiae Naturalis Principia Mathematica* was published in 1687 and did more than any other single treatise to form the scientific world-view of the West. Once this world-view was established in the physical sciences, it was not long before it was applied to the social sciences. After the Enlightenment the world would never look, nor be, the same again.

The earlier Japanese scholars who had suffered imprisonment and death to gain a knowledge of Western technology and those who were at this time taking advantage of the new freedom permitted by Yoshimune were pragmatic in their approach. They were not at first primarily interested in theory. They studied, through the medium of the Dutch language, such practical subjects as botany, medicine, gunnery, Western drill, and tactics, but included also some theoretical subjects such as mathematics and astronomy. The last, as we have seen, had a useful application to the calendar. The Japanese had little means of knowing the theories that lay behind the improved technology of the West; but they sensed that the new discoveries were significant for Japan and that it would be perilous to neglect them. They were intensely curious and faced with determination obstacles which might have been thought insurmountable. Pioneer physicians with great difficulty obtained Dutch works on medicine and in 1771 dissected the body of a criminal by reference to the illustrations in one of these books. They then slowly and painfully translated the text of the work at the rate of ten lines a day.[2]

One such scholar, Aoki Konyo, helped Yoshimune, who was concerned with improving the food supply, by introducing the sweet potato to Japan. He thus earned the nickname Doctor Potato. Yoshimune commissioned him to work on a Dutch-Japanese dictionary which was published in 1758. The majority of these scholars worked in one or two specific areas; but one of the most famous, Hiraga Gennai (1728–79), made contributions in such varied fields as botany, iron ore, electricity, and European-style oil painting. He was interested in improving the economy overall, both in agriculture and in industry, and coined a Japanese word, *bussangaku*, the "science of production" to express his aim. By the close of the eighteenth century books on astronomy, medicine, botany, and mathematics which were considered standard works in Europe had been translated and published in Japan. In 1811 an official translation office was instituted by the government and came to be known later by the title Institute for the Investigation of Barbarian Books. Some twelve years before the arrival of Commodore Perry and his American squadron a demonstration was given in Edo of Western gunnery and drill using Dutch words of command. Japan thus reacted much more promptly and thoroughly to incoming Western knowledge than did China, although China had the incomparable advantage of the presence of the Jesuits, most of them highly trained scientists or technical experts. Japan

[2] G. B. Sansom, *The Western World and Japan* (London: Cresset Press, 1950), p. 217.

had thrown out the Jesuits for political reasons but made use of every other available source of information, however meager. It was to the credit of Yoshimune and his advisers that they saw, however dimly, the shape of things to come and made it possible for the trickle of scientific and other Western books to become a flow, and thus to lay the foundation of Japan's present greatness.

Yoshimune was the most noteworthy and successful of the Shoguns after Ieyasu. By a combined policy of retrenchment in expenditure and the opening up of new land, he strengthened the shaky economy. Better irrigation, more efficient farming, and the introduction of mechanical devices to aid in threshing and in raising water from a lower level to flood the fields, all helped to increase the agricultural yield. But an attack of insect pests ruined much of the rice crop in 1732, and this was followed by alarming fluctuations in rice prices, which in turn led to riots.

Following Yoshimune the effectiveness of the *bakufu* declined. Neither the ninth nor the tenth Shogun was strong enough to cope adequately with affairs. A liberal statesman, Tanuma Okitsugu, held office under the tenth. He did much to encourage foreign trade and, in contrast to the conservative Yoshimune, stressed the industrial and mercantile sector of the economy. He promoted mining and state monopolies to strengthen the government's fiscal position, and had the vision to attempt the development of Hokkaido, the northern island. But he was a controversial figure and was attacked by the conservatives on the grounds of dishonest administration. Another conservative reaction set in under the eleventh Shogun, Ienari (1787–1837). Matsudaira Sadanobu was the Elder responsible for this reactionary policy, known as the Kansei Reforms. Sabanobu cut back on foreign trade and had strict sumptuary laws enacted severely limiting expenditure on luxuries, even to the extent of forbidding the use of barbers and hairdressers. He arranged for the cancellation of the debts of the poor among the warrior class, and restored emphasis on farming as the mainstay of the state. His measures were effective at first and brought back some confidence in the government. In the long run, however, they were economically stultifying, being based on traditional Confucian theory and not on empirical economic results.

The Kansei Reforms were followed by ten years of acute famines. Peasant uprisings became frequent and the violence spread to the towns. The *bakufu* reacted with a certain desperation in a third series of reforms, those of the Elder Mizuno Tadanari, in 1841 and 1843. To the standard procedures of government economy and cancellation of debts were added measures such as price regulation and orders to absconding peasants to return to their farms. These orders proved ineffective.

The rural economy of Japan from the seventeenth to the middle of the nineteenth century showed both positive and negative features. On the one hand, the total crop yield increased in the seventeenth century alone from 18 million koku to 25 million. Better irrigation, more intensive farming, and an increase in cash crops other than rice made possible a rising standard of living. But the government's financial difficulties led to increased taxation. Where peasants were harshly treated, many absconded to the towns, while those who were left had to bear the same total tax as before, but divided among fewer workers. Three major famines, or famine series, beginning in 1732, 1783, and 1832 respectively, caused intense and prolonged suffering. In the famine which began in 1783 and continued for five years there were reports of cannibalism and thousands of deaths by starvation in the north. In good years many landowners and even small farmers did well. But the farm laborers suffered a great deal of hardship. The *bakufu* professed to regard the farming class as the foundation of the state; but they treated its members with little mercy nonetheless. The theory was to allow the farmer just enough to live on and to set aside as seed for the next spring, and to take the rest of his produce from him in tax. In a sententious edict of 1649 the peasant was bidden to save leaves for fuel or to serve as food in time of famine; he was forbidden to drink tea or sake, and if his wife went sight-seeing or even walking on the hillsides and neglected her household tasks, she was to be divorced. In 1652 the headman of a village appealed strongly for a reduction of tax on the village. The reduction was granted, but the headman was executed for his temerity in asking. It is small wonder that there were frequent peasant rebellions—as many as twenty in different parts of the country in one year—and "smashing raids" in the cities. Improvements in the lot of the small farmer and the yield of his land led, in a manner not unfamiliar elsewhere, to a glimpse of better conditions and rising demands for greater freedom and further improvements.

There were thus a number of converging factors which tended to under-mine from within the carefully constructed solidarity of the Tokugawa regime—the presence of numbers of *ronin*, unemployed and congregating in the large cities; the rise of the merchant class, for which the Japanese feudal system provided no recognized place; the introduction of Western knowl-edge and techniques, which were of their nature disruptive to the traditional Japanese way of life; and the peasant unrest breaking out into open re-bellion. The *bakufu*, already faced with these internal problems, had now to face another, this time a threat from outside, with the arrival of Com-modore Matthew C. Perry of the United States Navy in 1853.

Commodore Perry's mission has sometimes been treated as though it were the sole reason for the change in Japan's attitude from one of seclusion to one of participation in the modern world. That this is an oversimplified interpretation may be seen from the foregoing account of internal changes within the country. Nor was Perry the first to knock on the door of a closed Japan, though he was the first to gain an entrance.

Russian geographers learned about Japan only in the late seventeenth century, and in 1702 Peter the Great interviewed a shipwrecked Japanese sailor. In spite of the Japanese ban some secret trading took place in the eighteenth century between Japanese and Russians, whom the Japanese called the "Red Northern Islanders" (from the Kurile Islands). A Russian officer, Lieutenant Adam Laxman, was sent to Hokkaido by Catherine the Great to try to open trade negotiations in 1793, but was told he must go to Nagasaki to gain a hearing. When a later ambassador went to Nagasaki in 1804, however, he met with no more success. The British sailed a frigate, H.M.S. *Phaeton*, into Nagasaki harbor in 1808 in chase of a Dutch vessel during the Napoleonic Wars, demanded and received supplies, and sailed away. A British survey vessel in 1845 reported courteous treatment by the Japanese; but in neither case did the British attempt to make any trade arrangements. The *Morrison*, a ship chartered by American missionaries, had been fired upon when attempting to return Japanese castaways in 1837. The only approach made by the United States government prior to Perry's mission had been an abortive one under Commodore James Biddle in 1845.

Commodore Perry's success in using negotiation backed by force to compel Japan to open her doors has received more than usual attention in Western history because it was one of the rare occasions at this early date in which America rather than one of the European powers took aggressive action. The action itself took its rise from causes which might seem at first relatively minor. The United States was very dissatisfied with the treatment being meted out by the Japanese authorities to shipwrecked sailors and to ships in need of shelter and supplies. Whaling ships and vessels involved in the fur trade of the American west coast required victuals and fresh water when they faced the vast and typhoon-ridden stretches of the Pacific Ocean. With the coming of steam, coaling stations in Japan were going to be of increasing importance. But from the beginning other and larger factors were also operative. Expansion of overseas trade was made possible and necessary by surplus goods turned out by the new manufacturing methods of the Industrial Revolution. New markets were vital. America had extended her frontier to the west coast; the next logical extension was over the Pacific Ocean. The example of Britain's easy success a decade earlier in forcing China to open her gates to trade was not lost on the other great powers. Moreover, the United States was well aware that Russia had designs on the Japanese market. Commodore Perry's instructions from President Fillmore therefore covered the immediate matter of the treatment of distressed mariners and also the question of a trade treaty.

Perry himself had not wanted the command of this squadron. As a senior officer he had hoped for a pleasanter assignment in European waters; but he was admirably cut out for his delicate task in Japan. He combined tact with dignity and firmness, and had sufficient patience to counter the delaying tactics of the Japanese. He had as his interpreter S. Wells Williams, a pioneer American missionary in China who had been on the *Morrison* and had acquired some knowledge of Japanese. As it turned out, most of the negotiations were carried on in Dutch. When Perry's squadron, consisting of two steam frigates and two sloops, sailed up to Uraga near the mouth of

Edo Bay, there was consternation and curiosity among the Japanese. In a short time the common people began swarming out in small boats to view the strange warships, but Perry gave orders that no one was to be allowed aboard. Commodore Biddle in an earlier attempt to establish relations had made the mistake of allowing the people to take liberties and thus had lost the respect of the officials. Those in authority were deeply concerned. They were impressed by steam propulsion and they knew enough about artillery to realize the greatly superior fire power of the American vessels. They also knew, better than the Americans, how dependent the large capital of Edo was upon seaborne supplies.

Commodore Perry wished to deliver President Fillmore's letter to "the Emperor," by which he meant the effective ruler, who was really the Shogun. The Japanese appeared to agree, but kept sending junior officials with whom Perry wisely would not deal. At length an official of adequate rank received the letter with its demands (see Plate 30) and Perry, with a shrewd concession to Oriental face, said he would give the authorities time for consideration and return in a year for their answer. He made it clear, however, that when he returned it would be with a more powerful force.

The Shogunate was now in a dilemma. Patriotism, national pride, and the policy of isolation all pointed to a strong negative to the American demands. But the Shogun's advisers were well aware that America possessed superior weapons; the question was whether she would use them or not, and all indications were that she intended to back up her demands by force, as the British had done in China. In this situation the Shogun took the unprecedented step of consulting the emperor's court and all the *daimyo* throughout the country. He must have known that this would further weaken his position of control, which was already much less strong than in the early days of the Tokugawa Shogunate. But Abe Masahiro, his principal adviser, felt that it was absolutely necessary in the national interest to have as much agreement as possible on the correct policy toward the aggressive foreigners. The majority of those who replied to the Shogun's question were in favor of resistance, though some *daimyo* who had already had Western contacts showed an awareness of the need to temporize. The emperor's court was strongly in opposition to any concessions. However, Abe felt that his assessment of American power and determination made it necessary to compromise. Thus, when Perry returned in 1854, as he had promised, the Shogun's officials employed the usual delaying tactics but ultimately conceded the main items of the American demands. By this Treaty of Kanagawa two rather inadequate ports were opened to limited trade—Shimoda, small and isolated, and Hakodate, far away on Hokkaido; American shipwrecked sailors were to receive good treatment; and an American consul was to be permitted residence at Shimoda.

The signing of the treaty and the attendant celebrations proved to be a colorful affair. Honor guards from both sides were drawn up on the beach at Kanagawa. There was an elaborate exchange of presents and entertainment. Sumo wrestling and a minstrel show were the forms of amusement each nation thought suitable to offer the other. The *pièce de résistance* was an American scale model of a steam locomotive and train large enough to ride upon. The track was laid out on the seashore and officials in Japanese dress were to be seen flying round curves on the cars in evident pleasure, the more so as they had been enjoying the champagne and whiskey which also figured prominently among the American gifts. Another present was a Morse electric telegraph system which was set up and demonstrated. It may be imagined that the lesson of these modern marvels of steam and electricity was not lost upon the observant Japanese.

The Perry squadron departed, but the implementation of the new treaty proved to be a long and laborious business. In the man chosen to represent her in the new relations with Japan, America was again fortunate. Unlike Commodore Perry, the first American minister, Townsend Harris, had actively sought the post. He was fascinated by Japan and possessed the necessary tact and patient determination to carry his work to successful completion amid the most harassing and frustrating conditions. A recent book (Oliver Statler, *Shimoda Story*) represents Harris as arrogant, small-minded, and given to deceit. There is doubtless an element of truth in this view, but a large amount of proper pride was an asset, not a liability, in dealing with the Japanese at this juncture. As part of the Perry treaty a plot of land and a house for a resident minister had been stipulated. But when Harris arrived, the Japanese claimed nothing had been said about servants. The possession of a sufficient retinue was necessary not only for the household tasks but for the maintenance of such style as would entitle the minister to respect for his position. So Harris doggedly set about winning permission to employ servants. He then had to secure an audience with the Shogun to present his credentials. In the end the persistence of Harris and the good sense of the more moderate Japanese officials prevailed; at the close of 1857 Townsend Harris proceeded in style from his residence at Shimoda to the Shogun's court at Edo and was duly received.

Negotiations for a full treaty of commerce had already been begun. During these Harris made full use of the argument that it would pay the Japanese to conclude an agreement with a nation as reasonable as America rather than submit to the imperialist ambitions of Britain and other European nations, as seen in China. Nothing was said of the fact that all Western nations, including the United States, had benefited from the concessions extracted from China by the British. In July 1858 a commercial treaty was signed between Japan and the United States which included among its terms the opening of additional ports, the rights of extraterritoriality and foreign residence in Edo and Osaka, agreement on customs dues and provision for the United States to supply Japan with ships, armaments, and technicians. Subsequent treaties were concluded with four other Western powers, Russia, Britain, France, and Holland. The terms of these were similar and in some cases they tended to favor the foreign merchants—20 percent import duty, lowered to 5 percent on all goods in 1866, was a cheap price to pay for the opportunity of a new market. From the beginning the Japanese sought a graduated scale of import duties and the abolition of the galling provisions of extraterritoriality, the foreign right to have all cases involving their nationals tried in consular courts outside the jurisdiction of Japanese laws. These objectives were at length gained with the abolition of extraterritoriality by treaties in 1894, becoming effective in 1899, and with complete tariff autonomy in 1911. Tariff autonomy became effective in China in 1933, but extraterritoriality was not abolished there until the end of World War II hostilities in 1945.

The Harris commercial treaty engendered considerable controversy in both shogun and imperial court circles. Political attitudes were now crystallizing—the hereditary lords (*fudai*) along with the Shogunate favoring foreign trade, and the collateral (*shimpan*) and outer (*tozama*) lords rallying round the emperor and fostering resistance to foreign demands. This latter policy was summarized in the slogan, *Sonno-Joi*, "honor the emperor, expel the barbarians." In 1858 Ii Naosuke, one of the most powerful of the hereditary *daimyo*, put into effect strong measures to reassert the power of the Shogunate. His work was effective enough to provoke violent opposition, and his enemies took advantage of a snowstorm to set upn him and kill him while he was on his way to attend the Shogun. The *ronin* were becoming more and more truculent. Heusken, Harris' Dutch interpreter, was killed at night in an Edo street, and in 1863 a band of *ronin* set fire to the British legation.

Meanwhile the authority of the Shogun was being attacked on theoretical as well as on practical grounds. The Mito fief had for some time been known as the home of a group of nationalist historians who asserted the native traditions and values over against the Confucian learning from China. Their work had been reinforced by the researches of Motoori Norinaga (1730–1801), who published an extensive commentary on the text and meaning of the Shinto classic, the *Kojiki*. Although early Japanese history had not been forgotten during the long years of the Tokugawa, new research made it ever more evident that the original authority of the state had been vested in the person of the emperor and not in the Shogun, and that in fact the total control exercised at this time by the Shogun was illegal. The historical and legal foundation for a restoration of the power of the emperor was thus clearly laid down. To the *samurai*, with their strong sense of precedent and tradition, the idea made a growing appeal.

The difficulties of the Shogunate were increased by the heavy indemnities demanded by the foreign powers for breaches of the peace which the declining authority of the Shogun's government was powerless to prevent. Attacks upon foreigners and pro-foreign Japanese were being made not only by isolated *samurai* but even by *daimyo* beyond government control and acting with the support of their domain leadership. It was this independent action of prominent *daimyo*, particularly the clans of Choshu and Satsuma, which finally precipitated the fall of the Tokugawa regime.

The clans of Choshu and Satsuma were hereditary enemies of the Tokugawa and their geographical position in the extreme west made them hard to control. They could each dispose of considerable military forces; Satsuma had 27,000 warriors and Choshu 11,000. Moreover their *samurai* had not been softened by the easy living of Edo and had retained their martial spirit. Traditional in outlook, they yet commanded the use of Western-type weapons, since their domains included the ports of entry of Chinese and Dutch trade. Satsuma also controlled the Ryukyu Islands which acted as a transfer port for the entry of foreign goods. Both clans suffered, along with many others, from financial stress, but both were able by wise management to overcome the problem. Choshu developed an office for aid to needy *samurai* which added to its other functions the profitable investment of clan funds. Satsuma under able financial leadership in the 1830's and 1840's had been able to improve the quality of its crops, reduce waste, and exercise a closer control of the valuable sugar crop from the Ryukyu Islands. The clan thus succeeded in reducing its debt and also paying for military modernization.

A fresh stimulus to the independent fighting spirit of Satsuma and Choshu came from a remarkable personality, Yoshida Shoin (1830–59). Son of a Choshu *samurai* of modest rank, small and not very healthy as a boy, he became during and after his short lifetime a strong patriotic influence in his own clan and far beyond. He studied assiduously and traveled widely in Japan, forming in his own mind an explosive combination of Dutch learning and the fervid nationalism of the Mito school. At one point he tried to smuggle himself out of the country on board one of Perry's ships, armed with a plentiful supply of paper and brushes to make notes on the ways of the foreigners. When discovered he was returned to his own clan and placed under house arrest. He then proceeded to open a small school. He was an excellent teacher and his enthusiastic discussions of the meaning of loyalty to the emperor in the new context of a Japan being opened to foreign influence deeply affected some young *samurai* students. Among these were Inoue Kaoru, Ito Hirobumi, and Yamagata Aritomo, who were very shortly to become three of the most prominent leaders of the new Japan. Yoshida had more fire than sense and became involved in a plot to assassinate a Tokugawa official in Kyoto. The plot was discovered and Yoshida was taken to Edo and executed in his thirtieth year. Robert Louis Stevenson heard about Yoshida from a Japanese friend and in 1880 wrote of him and of a fellow-prisoner, Kusakabe, in *Familiar Studies of Men and Books*:

> He [Kusakabe] was led toward the place of death below Yoshida's window. To turn the head would have been to implicate his fellow-prisoner; but he threw him a look from his eye, and bade him farewell in a loud voice, with these two Chinese verses:—

"It is better to be a crystal and be broken,
Than to remain perfect like a tile upon the housetop."

So Kusakabe, from the highlands of Satzuma, passed out of the theatre of this world. His death was like an antique worthy's.

Yoshida was then tried and executed, and Stevenson sums up his character thus:

It is hard to say which is most remarkable—his capacity for command, which subdued his very jailers; his hot, unflagging zeal; or his stubborn superiority to defeat. He failed in each particular enterprise that he attempted; and yet we have only to look at his country to see how complete has been his general success. His friends and pupils made the majority of leaders in that final Revolution, now some twelve years old; and many of them are, or were until the other day, high placed among the rulers of Japan.[3]

The stage was thus set for the last series of events that were to lead to the downfall of the Shogunate, the restoration of the emperor's power, and the modernization of Japan, already begun but soon to gain momentum as a matter of deliberate policy. In this last struggle there were five groups in constant and confusing interaction: the Shogunate, the imperial court, the Choshu clan, the Satsuma clan, and the foreign powers acting in concert. A key to the understanding of these crucial years 1858–68 is an awareness of the rivalry of Satsuma and Choshu, both demanding change and both in a better position than any other clan to bring it about, but neither wishing to yield primacy of leadership to the other. When these two clans agreed to combine their efforts, events proceeded to a climax. The victim was the Shogunate; the means to victory was to possess military power and to become, on the ancient pattern, the spokesman for the emperor; and the shifts of policy were determined by the iron necessities of confrontation with the foreigners.

Satsuma at first favored the union of court and Shogunate; but Choshu, not to be outdone, took the line of out-and-out support for the emperor against the Shogun. Choshu won over some of the court nobles and received important, though temporary, support from extremist *samurai* in the domain of Tosa in Shikoku. Thus fortified, Choshu succeeded in getting the emperor to compel the Shogun to fix the date of June 25, 1863, as the day on which all "barbarians" would be expelled from Japan. As the fateful day approached, it became evident to most *daimyo* that this patriotic resolution could not be carried out. The Choshu clansmen, however, fired their cannon against American, French, and Dutch ships in the Shimonoseki Strait. The Americans retaliated by shelling the Choshu forts and sinking two new ships. A few days later French forces made a landing and demolished the forts and their stores.

At this point a *coup d'état* led by Satsuma restored more moderate forces to power at court. But Choshu on its own ground continued intransi-

3 Nottingham Society, N.Y., edition of *Collected Works*, Vol. X, p. 127.

gent, and began forming "mixed units" of *samurai* and commoners, armed with modern rifles, under one Takasugi Shinsaku (1839–67). The morale and effectiveness of these units was very high and their success was decisive in convincing conservatives throughout Japan of the necessity of modernization. Choshu's constant antiforeign provocations led to a second international action. In 1864 seventeen English, French, Dutch, and American warships again destroyed the rebuilt Choshu forts and forced the reopening of the Shimonoseki Strait to international traffic. The Choshu *samurai* Inoue Kaoru (1835–1915) and Ito Hirobumi (1841–1909), earlier students of Yoshida Shoin, had illegally left the country and spent some time studying in London. They had but lately returned and were able to exercise some influence as interpreters in relations with Western powers. Their persuasion and the cold logic of events now convinced the Choshu authorities that the expulsion of foreigners was an impossible dream.

Satsuma, meanwhile, though less openly antiforeign, had become involved in trouble with the British. A cultural misunderstanding, typical of the times both in China and Japan, had developed in 1862, when an Englishman, Charles Richardson, out riding with some companions, had failed to dismount and show proper respect by making an obeisance to the lord of Satsuma as his procession passed by. Angry Satsuma *samurai* guards had set upon and killed him. The British government demanded a large indemnity from the Shogun and a further sum from the Satsuma *daimyo*, along with the punishment of the guilty parties. A British naval force of seven ships stood off Kagoshima, the Satsuma capital, to enforce payment and were fired upon. They replied with a severe bombardment of Kagoshima and the sinking of a large number of ships in the harbor. The reaction of the Japanese was not one of grievance but of unbounded admiration for the efficiency of British naval power. British warships were subsequently purchased by Satsuma and a number of volunteers trained by the Royal Navy. When the new Japanese Navy was formed, the majority of its officers were British-trained Satsuma *samurai*, while a large number of army officers came from Choshu and were trained by the French.

The Choshu clan had clearly shown its opposition to the Shogunate. Punitive action had to be taken, and in 1864, on the authority of an imperial order, the *daimyo* of Nagoya was chosen to lead a large combined force from several domains against Choshu. The moderate group in Choshu were ready to come to terms and an agreement was made through the offices of a Satsuma warrior, Saigo Takamori (1827–77), risen from humble origins but now prominent in the Shogun's service. The terms arranged were not harsh, probably because Saigo, as a Satsuma man, had no desire to see the Shogunate too powerful nor Choshu too weak. But the terms did include the disbanding of the "mixed units" and these units were in no mood to obey. Instead, after several successful engagements against the moderates of their own clan, they took possession of the Choshu capital of Shimonoseki and formed a new domain government in which the extremists were the dominant force. Their independence of authority led to a second punitive expedition against them in the summer of 1865. But this time Choshu was in an even stronger position. A member of the domain government, Kido Koin (1833–77) had proved an effective leader, tightened discipline over the independent "mixed units," and modernized the whole of the domain forces. The Satsuma and other *daimyo* withheld or withdrew their support from the Shogun, whose government was at the same time embarrassed by the economic burden of the expedition against Choshu and by rice riots in several cities. Choshu emerged victorious and the Shogun's forces withdrew.

Two *ronin* from Tosa now began to work for a coalition between Satsuma and Choshu. A secret agreement was entered into in 1866, and this marked the beginning of the end for the Tokugawa Shogunate. The thirteenth Shogun Iemochi died that year and was succeeded by Keiki, a wise and vigorous leader. Léon Roches, the French minister, supported Keiki in the reorganization of his administration and military forces and in the building of a modern dockyard at Yokosuka. Sir Harry Parkes, the British minister, in a rival move, supplied Satsuma and Choshu with arms. But it was too late for the Shogunate to stage a recovery. On January 3, 1868, Satsuma and Choshu, aided by the collateral domains of Echizen and Nagoya and the outer domains of Tosa and Hiroshima, took possession of the palace and proclaimed an "imperial restoration." Keiki himself was inclined to capitulate, but some of his supporters insisted on making a fight of it. Shogun forces marched up from Osaka toward Kyoto. They were superior in numbers but inferior in modern equipment and were defeated at the hamlets of Fushimi and Toba south of Kyoto on January 27.

The imperialist forces pressed straight on to Edo. Most of the *daimyo* submitted to them. Keiki forbade resistance, but there was some fighting in Edo near the present site of Ueno Park. Keiki was treated generously. He retired and was confined to his estate in Mito. His successor in the family title was allowed to keep one-tenth of the Tokugawa lands, but even this amounted to 700,000 koku, about the same revenue as that of Satsuma and almost twice that of Choshu. The Aizu domain leaders continued to hold out in northern Honshu until November, and the last embers of resistance were stamped out in Hokkaido in May of 1869. This marked the end of the Tokugawa rule which had begun with Ieyasu's victory in the battle of Sekigahara in the year 1600.

13

THE MEIJI RESTORATION AND
THE MODERNIZATION OF JAPAN

1868–1912

A boy of sixteen was given a document of five medium-length sentences to sign in April 1868. The sentences consisted of pious hopes and unexceptionable statements—"all classes . . . shall unite," "no discontent," "the just laws of Nature." It is true there was one mention of "public discussion," but subsequently this feature was not encouraged. Nevertheless the Charter Oath was a revolutionary document and the consequences of it enormous, for the signatory was the Emperor Meiji ("Enlightened Rule").[1]

The young and vigorous *samurai* leaders of the new state had immense problems to face, but they lost no time in addressing themselves to the task. Edo was not subdued until July of 1868, but already in April the first principles of the new regime had been enunciated in the Emperor's name in the Charter Oath, also known as the Five Articles Oath. In general moral tone, in intentional lack of specifics, and in deliberate borrowing from another culture, it was faintly reminiscent of the "constitution" of Prince Shotoku in the seventh century.

ARTICLE I. Deliberative assemblies shall be widely established and all matters decided by public discussion.

This would appear to indicate a first step toward full democracy, but such was not its intention. It was rather a bid to rally support for the new government. Since the main policy makers came from not more than seven domains, this clause allowed the leaders from other parts of the country to feel they could have a part in forming national policy. Later, when the government felt more secure, the practice of holding these assemblies was discontinued.

[1] There was opposition to recent Japanese government plans to hold celebrations of the two-hundredth anniversary of the Meiji Restoration in view of its bourgeois nature.

ARTICLE 2. All classes, high and low, shall unite in vigorously carrying out the administration of affairs of state.

This appeal for unity had more significance then than now in view of the strict class structure of Tokugawa Japan.

ARTICLE 3. The common people, no less than the civil and military officials, shall each be allowed to pursue his own calling so that there may be no discontent.

More definite than Article 2, this was a promise that the frustrating class barriers of feudalism would no longer be in force and that all careers would be open to those with talent. The whole country, in fact, would become a man-power pool for the immense effort of modernization.

ARTICLE 4. Evil customs of the past shall be broken off and everything based upon the just laws of Nature.

Among the "evil customs of the past" the authors intended to include the Tokugawa Shogunate and all its works. The "just laws of Nature" is a universal phrase with a mystical appeal. The concept was familiar in the West, but was also known to the East in fundamental Confucian and Taoist thought.

ARTICLE 5. Knowledge shall be sought throughout the world so as to strengthen the foundations of imperial rule.

Here was the most deliberate break with the past. Modernization was to be a main, calculated, and official aim. The old and the new were combined in one phrase—"imperial rule" was the heritage of the past, but for the future it would be promoted by "knowledge . . . sought throughout the world." In another famous slogan it was to be "Eastern ethics and Western science"; ancient patriotism and modern, scientific application were to be the secret of Japan's rapid rise to power.

CONSTITUTIONAL PATTERN. The first efforts of the reformers to construct a new machinery of government show the marks of improvisation, for changes were made four times between January 1868 and September 1871. Finally a Council of State (*dajo-kan*, an ancient name) and six ministries were set up. The Council of State under the chairmanship of a reformist court noble, Sanjo Sanetomi (1837–91), had three divisions: the Left Chamber was concerned with legislation, the Right Chamber supervised the ministries, and the Central Chamber held control over the work of the other two chambers as well as over the recently created Office of Shinto Worship. The last provided a means for stressing publicly the divine descent of the emperor. This system of government lasted until a cabinet was introduced in 1885. But whatever the system, the stability of the government came from the fact that it was run at the beginning by a group of men similar in age (the youngest was thirty-one, the oldest forty-one), in social rank (generally the lower *samurai*, with one or two court nobles), and in political training (all with experience in their own domains in a period of upheaval and change). They were an unusually brilliant company. At first they ruled as assistants to figurehead chiefs, then gradually took the higher offices themselves, and ended for the most part as respected Elder Statesmen, *genro*, a position of unofficial power which had no real parallel outside Japan.

CENTRALIZATION. Edo was chosen as the new capital and the emperor was installed in the Shogun's castle, which underwent suitable alterations. To mark the break with the past the city was renamed Tokyo, "Eastern Capital." The main obstacle to centralized government was a psychological rather than an administrative one, namely the proud separate existence of the numerous domains. The first steps to centralization were taken in the ex-Tokugawa domains, which were very extensive and entirely at the disposal of the government. These were divided into prefectures. The administration of the other domains was then gradually brought into line with the system used in the new prefectures. Tolls and economic barriers between domains were abolished.

The leaders of the central government had already been policy makers in their home domains and were therefore able to exercise considerable influence. Kido Koin of Choshu and Okubo Toshimichi (1830–78) of Satsuma persuaded their respective *daimyo*, as well as those of Tosa and Hizen, to give back their lands to the emperor in March 1869. In one sense this was a token change, for the *daimyo* were reappointed as governors of the territories. Many other *daimyo* followed this lead, because they did not want to incur the displeasure of the government or lose any future privileges or benefits under the new regime, which had obviously come to stay. The central government, moving with caution but increasing confidence, sent special envoys to the leading domains of Satsuma, Choshu, and Tosa to assess the degree of support for their policies. One of the envoys was the court noble Iwakura Tomomi (1825–83) who had close associations with Okubo. Both were to hold very important posts in the Meiji government in the next few years. Then in August 1871 the emperor announced on behalf of the government the abolition of all the domains. The ruling came as a shock, but there was no major resistance. The country was divided into seventy-five prefectures (three of them urban), but this number was later reduced to forty-five. These form the present-day units of local government.

COMPENSATION AND FINANCE. That there was so little resistance to changing the age-old feudal pattern is surprising, but the domains were not organized to combine against a central government riding the crest of a popular, patriotic movement. The absence of resistance must also be taken as an index of the penetration of Western knowledge and its international implications among the educated local leaders throughout the whole of

Japan. Moreover the compensation to the former *daimyo* was generous. The majority of them, as governors of prefectures, received 10 percent of the area taxes as personal income. Most were actually better off financially, since they were relieved of the *samurai* payroll responsibilities, administration costs, and especially the domain debts.

The *samurai* were not treated so well; their stipends were cut by 50 percent. They had been paid less than the full book value of their salaries by the former *daimyo*, but the new salaries still represented a considerable drop from what they had actually been receiving before the change in 1871. This caused considerable discontent and some real hardship, particularly among the lower *samurai*.

Paying salaries, taking over the obligations of the domains, and at the same time building up modern defense forces placed upon the central government a heavy financial burden, for which tax income was inadequate. Japan did not want to become dependent on foreign capital, but a small loan of £2,400,000 ($6,000,000) was contracted with Britain in 1872, in addition to another British loan of less than half that amount already entered into for the building of a railway between Tokyo and Yokohama. These loans and considerable sums raised from Japanese merchant houses enabled the government to carry on during the first few crucial years. Internal trade, now free of restrictions, showed marked improvement, and was further stimulated by the new export-import commerce. Within ten years the government had begun to reach a sound financial position.

Feudal taxes and restrictions on land use and sale were removed and the taxpayer on any given piece of property was constituted the owner. A new land-tax system, based on money not crop yield, came into operation in 1873. The tax was fixed at 3 percent on current assessed land values, but this was later reduced to 2½ percent. Four years were taken up in assessing the arable land of Japan and four years more in applying the system to mountain and forest land. There was some peasant unrest at first, since it proved harder to evade the new regulations than the old.

In 1876 all *samurai* stipends were transferred into the form of government bonds; but the interest on the bonds only amounted to about half the value of the already reduced stipends. The *daimyo*, again, were treated more generously in the bond amounts they received. In 1871 *samurai* were permitted and in 1876 compelled to cease wearing the pair of short and long swords which had been the jealously guarded social privilege of their class.

THE ARMY AND NAVY. The overthrow of the Shogunate had been accomplished with the aid of forces from the domains and only a small nucleus of imperial troops. But once the Restoration had been effected, the new leaders at once began to build up the imperial forces. The pioneer in this was Omura Masujiro, who set up arsenals and military academies. He was assassinated by conservative *samurai* in 1869, and his work was taken up by Yamagata Aritomo (1838–1922). After studying under Yoshida

Shoin and commanding the Choshu mixed units, he spent some time in study in Europe. He became commander of the Imperial Guards, nucleus of the new army, a force of over 9,000 recruited from Satsuma, Choshu, and Tosa domains and organized on the French model. In 1873 he was made army minister and was prominent in the government for many years. When the domains were abolished, the country was divided into four garrison regions and standard regulations were enforced in order to unify the diverse domain forces now incorporated into the army.

Shogunate warships and flotillas from various coastal domains formed the first units of the new navy, which took the Royal Navy as its model. The former Satsuma fleet for many years supplied the majority of senior officers for the Japanese Navy. A fishing and sea-going tradition in Japan was of help in the rapid development of an efficient modern navy, as a similar island-nation tradition had earlier helped Great Britain.

Yamagata in 1873 introduced a revolutionary law of universal conscription. This spelled the ultimate end of *samurai* military privilege, but it was a necessary part of the modern state which Japan aspired to become. The measure was incidentally useful in extending government control into the most remote hamlets of the countryside. It also provoked considerable peasant discontent but no serious incidents. All, regardless of social origin, were liable to call-up, for three years of active duty and four years in the reserves.

The Japanese leaders intended not to Westernize, but to modernize; that is to say, they decided to choose the best model in each field of technology and administration which would make Japan powerful and a match for other nations. They did not intend to sacrifice or to alter fundamentally "the spirit of Old Japan," *yamato-damashii*, the soul of the nation, or the basic structure of their society under the emperor through which this spirit was expressed. Deputations of leading statesmen and students were sent abroad to bring back information and ideas upon which the reforms could be based. The Shogunate and certain domains had already sent individuals such as Ito and Inoue abroad prior to the Restoration and this process was stepped up after 1868. The largest and most important group to go abroad was the Iwakura Mission, which left in 1871 and spent two years in the United States and Europe. The delegation was composed of forty-eight members and fifty-four students, and included, in addition to the leader, Iwakura, such prominent government figures as Okubo and Kido, as well as future leaders such as Ito. They gathered extremely useful information, but failed completely in their second objective, to persuade the Western powers to alter the unequal treaties entered into by the Tokugawa.

In this process of conscious cultural borrowing in the nineteenth century —undertaken not for the first time in Japanese history (see Chapter 3)— two points are noticeable: first, the impartial selectivity of the Japanese, and second, their willingness to change their plans if they found a better model in another country. For the formation of their navy, they looked to Britain, as has been noted. For the army, France was the model; but Yamagata made important changes in 1878 when he adopted the German general staff organization. A French legal expert, Gustave-Émile Boissonade, assisted the patient committee that worked out a new civil code of law, beginning in 1875 and issuing a final draft in 1888. Further alterations stemming from German law were made and the resulting code was put into effect in 1896. German doctors were brought to Japan to give instruction in medical schools; and until recently most Japanese doctors had to be able to do a large part of their reading in German.

Several government departments made use of experts invited from abroad. The Bureau of Mines, for instance, employed 34 foreigners, and the Ministry of Industry spent a large proportion of its budget in 1879 to hire 130 Western advisers. Efforts were made to replace the foreign experts as quickly as possible with trained Japanese, since the foreign salaries were so high.

EDUCATION. In order to bring about a basic and permanent change in the attitude of the Japanese toward modernization, reforms in the field of education were of the first importance. A Ministry of Education was set up on the Western pattern in 1871. The French system was adopted at first, with eight school districts, and compulsory elementary education for boys and girls, for three years of schooling, later increased to six. Here again a change in Japanese policy occurred and more liberal ideas of education from America supplanted the rigid French pattern. Dr. David Murray of Rutgers University, New Jersey, exerted a profound influence on the educational system during the six years he spent in Japan. The missionary societies from America were also influential, especially in pioneering higher education for women.

The Confucian University in Edo was amalgamated with the Shogunate medical school and the language study at the Institute for the Investigation of Barbarian Books to form in 1869 a new government university, later named Tokyo University. Other government universities were added, from Kyoto University in 1897 to Hokkaido University in Sapporo in 1918. All maintained a very high standard. In the 1880's a further change in educational style took place; a convergence of nationalistic, Confucian, and German influences emphasized the supremacy of the state. The highest value was put upon the good of the nation as a whole, while the free development of individual personality through education was accorded a lower place. An Imperial Rescript on Education was issued in 1890 in which harmony and loyalty were stressed above all else. The schools thus became a means of official indoctrination ready to the hand of future governments.

The man who did most to popularize Western knowledge in Japan was Fukuzawa Yukichi (1835–1901). His books, *Conditions in the West* and *Encouragement of Learning*, were best sellers, for he described the ordinary social customs of the West, concerning which the average Japanese felt a consuming curiosity. His engaging autobiography, recently reissued, is an epitome of his age. His father was a *samurai* with scholarly tastes, belonging to the Okudaira clan in Kyushu. He sent his children to a teacher for calligraphy and general education.

> The teacher lived in the compound of the lord's storage office, but, having some merchants' children among his pupils, he naturally began to train them in numerals. "Two times two is four, two times three is six etc." This today seems a very ordinary thing to teach, but when my father heard this, he took his children away in a fury. "It is abominable," he exclaimed, "that innocent children should be taught to use numbers—the tool of merchants. There is no telling what the teacher may do next." [2]

Yukichi was sent to Nagasaki in 1854 to study Dutch and gunnery. After further study in Osaka, he was called to Edo to act as Dutch interpreter in the business of his clan. He was shocked to find in Yokohama that all the foreigners spoke English, not Dutch. With some fortitude he immediately embarked on the study of English. Since foreign books were in very limited supply, students had to copy laboriously by hand the section of the common textbook which they wished to study, writing out as best they could "the strange letters written sideways."

Considering Yukichi's determination and competence, it is not surprising that he was sent by the Shogun on two missions abroad, to the United States in 1860 and to Europe in 1862. He says he was not taken aback in these experiences in the way his guides expected. He was already familiar with the principles of the electric telegraph and understood the method of refining and bleaching sugar. What astonished him was the waste of iron, which he saw lying about in garbage piles and on the seashore, and the lack of reverence for the descendants of George Washington, even the lack of knowledge of their whereabouts. On his return he found the antiforeign feeling running so high that the captain of his ship was advised not to show a foreign umbrella in the streets, for fear he would be cut down by *ronin*. Yukichi went farther than most in his hatred of the Chinese Confucian heritage and the dead hand of the past. He met a farmer one day riding along the seashore. On seeing a *samurai*, the farmer dismounted at once in order to show respect; but Yukichi explained that under the new laws this was not necessary. Much against the man's will, he forced him to mount again and drove him off, Yukichi reflecting sadly "what fearful weight the old customs had with the people." He devoted the rest of his life to writing and translating and to the affairs of the school he founded, which became Keio University, the first private university in Japan. He summed up his aim in life as follows:

[2] *The Autobiography of Yukichi Fukuzawa*, tr. Eiichi Kiyooka (New York: Columbia University Press, 1966), p. 3. In the book title the surname Fukuzawa has been placed second to accord with Western practice.

After all, the purpose of my entire work has not only been to gather young men together and give them the benefit of foreign books but to open this "closed" country of ours and bring it wholly into the light of Western civilization. For only thus may Japan become strong in the arts of both war and peace and take a place in the forefront of the progress of the world.[3]

Gradually the people of Japan as well as the leaders became aware of changes in the air. New fashions in dress and style, in habits and customs, began to enjoy a great vogue, the high point being reached in the 1880's. The *samurai* haircut, with the top of the head shaved and the rest of the hair brought up into a topknot, proved quite impractical with the introduction of the modern army uniform cap, so Western-style haircuts were adopted. The term *haikara*, "high collar," was used to mean "fashionable"; "business suit" appeared in Japanese as *sebiro*, a corruption of the words "Savile Row," the tailors' street in London, leading city for men's clothes. The emperor was even induced to eat beef, in order to overcome in the average Japanese a prejudice derived from Buddhism against this diet. Prints are to be found from this period showing modern young men about town eating beef, sporting umbrellas and big "turnip" watches. Women learned to use the new sewing machines to turn out Western-style dresses with large bustles. There was even a short period when leaders of Tokyo society felt it incumbent upon them to attend Assemblies every Sunday night in the Rokumeikan, a building put up by the government, to dance waltzes and quadrilles. They were prepared to dress up in uncomfortable evening dress; but fancy dress was something else. When an elaborate fancy-dress ball was held in 1887, attended by members of the government, Japanese opinion was so shocked by the undignified absurdity of the proceedings that the whole practice of ballroom dancing was dropped.

In literature there was a growing demand for translations of Western works. Among the earliest translations were *Robinson Crusoe* (1859), Samuel Smiles's *Self-help* (1870), and John Stuart Mill's *On Liberty* (1871). Jules Verne's writings were among the most popular. Novels were written by Japanese depicting new and daring behavior, and one of them dealt with revolutionary movements in different parts of the world. Few were of any literary merit.

It is possible, amid the amusing vagaries of fad and fashion, to miss the serious purpose behind the efforts at social modernization, for the motive was an important one. It was to become accepted by the leading nations of the world so that the unequal treaties would be revised, tariff rates improved, extraterritoriality abolished, and Japan accorded her full place in the comity of nations.

The course of reform and modernization was by no means all plain sailing. Peasant unrest has already been mentioned; it was considered an

[3] *Ibid.*, p. 246.

acceptable risk by the government. But the distress of the former *samurai* gave grave concern to the leaders, themselves for the most part from the same class. The launching of an overseas venture was discussed as a possible means of employing the *samurai* and restoring their morale. Diplomatic missions had already been sent to Korea after the Meiji Restoration to renegotiate trade and foreign relations and bring them more into accord with the new situation in Japan. When these approaches were rejected by the conservatives in Korea, Saigo Takamori actually suggested that he be sent over alone, so that his expected murder might give a valid excuse for Japan to attack. This offer was not accepted, but a chance to act seemed to come when the Iwakura Mission drew off to the United States and Europe the more moderate members of the ruling group. The remainder, including Saigo, decided in the summer of 1873 that a military force should be sent to Korea. Members of the Iwakura Mission returned just in time to have this provocative decision reversed. It was clear to them, after comparing Japan with Western countries, that the plan was premature and most unwise. Saigo resigned and returned home to Kyushu.

As a milder show of force an expedition was sent against Taiwan to exact punishment for the murder of some shipwrecked seamen from the Ryukyu Islands. China gave in and agreed to pay an indemnity. Later a naval force was sent to Korea and, by the Treaty of Kanghwa of 1876, two ports in addition to the existing one at Pusan were opened to Japanese trade and Korea was declared independent, although without any attempt to secure the agreement of China, the nominal suzerain.

To the discontented *samurai*, however, conquest by treaty was no substitute for the glories of war. Following Saigo's resignation from the government there were several revolts in Satsuma, Tosa, and Hizen over Korean policy, the commutation of *samurai* stipends into government bonds, and the ban on wearing swords. In these revolts Saigo himself took no active part, for he was unwilling to come out against the government and his former colleagues. He built up a chain of schools in the south devoted to military training and the fostering of conservative *samurai* ideals. In the end these became so successful and so powerful that he could no longer control the more eager of his followers. When the government took the precaution of removing military stores from Kagoshima, the provincial capital, supporters of Saigo seized the government depots there, put their hero at their head and began a march on Edo with 40,000 troops. They did not get very far. They were held up by local government forces at Kumamoto and the central authorities had time to muster an army. Conscript regiments with naval support fought a hard campaign of six months and forced the rebels back on Kagoshima, where Saigo and his chief supporters were killed after desperate resistance. Saigo Takamori became a legend; but there were no more feudal rebellions. The Meiji government was undisputed master of Japan.

Rebels such as Saigo had neither the foresight nor the political realism of the government leaders whose cardinal policy was summed up in the contemporary slogan *fukoku-kyohei*, "rich country-strong army." These leaders early grasped the fact that modernization was a total and indivisible process, that certain constitutional, legal, and economic ideas and methods from the West would have to be incorporated into their new system, even though they intended to retain "the Japanese spirit." Above all they realized, in contrast to the limited modernizers in China, that a modern war machine required not only arsenals and shipyards but the whole apparatus of modern industry to undergird it. Their slogan led directly to what is now known as a military-industrial complex, though they would not have necessarily approved the uses to which their more chauvinistic successors put the military-industrial tool which they so skillfully forged.

INDUSTRY. The Meiji government provided secure political conditions and a reliable financial framework in the country. It also sponsored and supported early developments in some industries, especially the heavy industries needed to fill modern army and navy requirements. The private sector was nevertheless responsible for the major development of industry in Japan.

A modern furnace for iron smelting was constructed by the Hizen domain as early as 1850 from instructions contained in a book from Holland. Soon afterward the iron from this furnace was used to cast cannon which were more efficient than the older bronze models. Tokugawa Nariaki, lord of Mito, was running a small iron and shipbuilding concern in his own fief by 1858. The new government built on these foundations by developing large arsenals in Tokyo and Osaka, and by adding to the two earlier shipyards at Nagasaki and Yokosuka a new one at Hyogo (Kobe). Even before the new government began operations there were already, by 1868, 138 modern ships in use, some bought from abroad and some made in Japan.

The early railroads showed only a slow growth in mileage of track laid down owing to the mountainous terrain and the high cost of tunnels and bridges; but such track as there was immediately began to bear heavy traffic. The short Tokyo–Yokohama railway built in 1872 was carrying two million passengers by 1880, in addition to large quantities of freight. Kobe was linked to Osaka in 1874 and to Kyoto three years later. Small sections of the Tokyo–Kobe projected line were completed by 1877. After this date private companies began to enter the railroad field, which had hitherto been government-financed, and private construction soon outstripped that of the government, as the following chart indicates:

YEAR	PRIVATE COMPANY TRACK	GOVERNMENT TRACK	TOTAL
1881	none	76 miles	76
1885	130 miles	220 miles	350
1895	1,500 miles	580 miles	2,080

After 1906 the railroad system was nationalized for strategic reasons in times of national emergency.

A coal mine was started by the Hizen domain in 1869 and operated at first with British assistance; but the government took it over in 1874, and was soon operating eight other mines. This and some significant development in textiles occurred under the direction and with the encouragement of Ito, who was minister of the newly created Ministry of Industry from 1870 to 1878. The textile industry provides the clearest pattern of cooperation between the government and the private sector. Woolen manufacture, required for uniforms for the military and for government employees, was entirely a government responsibility. Silk, on the other hand, required much traditional handwork, the only major innovation being machine reeling. Enough private capital was available to finance the expansion caused by heavy foreign demand, and the government took very little part in this industry. In 1880 silk formed 43 percent of Japan's export trade. In the cotton industry, one of the greatest growth industries of the period, both government and private finance were involved. Private capital was attracted since the factories could be large or small and the technology was comparatively simple. The Satsuma domain opened a factory in 1868, and there were three government mills by 1880, as well as numerous private concerns. Cotton machinery was purchased from abroad in 1878 with a large government loan of 10 million yen, and then sold on easy terms to private companies. The growth of the cotton industry as a whole is indicated by the number of spindles being operated, as follows:

1877   8,000
1887   77,000   (equivalent to the number of spindles in one Lancashire mill)
1893   382,000

Cheap labor was forthcoming for both cotton and silk manufacture from the daughters of poor farmers who were indentured to the factory owners, housed in dormitories, and made to work long hours with very little freedom. Conditions in the factories themselves, however, were probably no worse than at the corresponding stage in Europe during the Industrial Revolution. The girls in the cotton and silk mills of Japan undoubtedly suffered from virtual imprisonment and from tuberculosis, as is vividly portrayed in Kagawa Toyohiko's novel *A Grain of Wheat*; but their fate in the factories was better than the earlier destiny of girls from impoverished families who were sold to brothel keepers.

The industrial development sponsored and financed by the government proved a costly item. It was only made possible by a deliberate decision to favor industry at the expense of agriculture. In 1880 about 75 percent of the population was engaged in farming and 80 percent of the tax revenue came from the agricultural yield. This tax revenue enabled the government, among other things, to pay for imported industrial machinery and the

20, 21 The Four Seasons, manner of Kano Motonobu (1476–1559). Pair of six-panel
screens (*byobu*). Ht., 5 ft 1 in.; ink and light color on paper. Plate 20: spring (left)
and summer. Plate 21: winter (left) and autumn (*The Asia Society, New York: Mr.
and Mrs. John D. Rockefeller 3rd Collection. Photography by Otto E. Nelson*)

22 Moss garden of the Saihoji Temple, Kyoto. One of the oldest of the moss gardens, this was also designed by the fourteenth century Zen monk, Muso Soseki, and was the inspiration for the moss garden beside the teahouse in the Silver Pavilion grounds. (*Japan Information Center*)

23 Tea ceremony (*chanoyu*). Note the iron kettle, water jar, cup, bamboo whisk and ladle. (*Japan National Tourist Organization*)

24 Himeji Castle. In the sixteenth and seventeenth centuries, when muskets were in use but heavy artillery had not yet been introduced, moated castles such as this provided the feudal lords, or *daimyo*, with protection and a degree of interior luxury. Sloping tile roofs prevented the lodgment of fire arrows. (*Japan National Tourist Organization*)

26 Garden of the Sanzen-in Temple, Ohara. The original temple goes back to the eighth century. This and the following plate illustrate how the Japanese create an intimate connection between buildings and Nature. (*Japan National Tourist Organization*)

25 Tea jar (*chatsubo*) by Ninsei Nomura, active mid-seventeenth century; light grey stoneware with decoration in overglaze polychrome enamels. Ht., 12 in. Seven quarrelsome crows (a bird of good luck in East Asia) are disposed around the jar in such a way as to leave plenty of restful space among them. (*The Asia Society, New York: Mr. and Mrs. John D. Rockefeller 3rd Collection. Photography by Otto E. Nelson*)

27 Garden of the Shisendo Villa, Kyoto. Japanese architecture, by the use of verandahs and removable screens, succeeds in bringing the house into the garden and the garden into the house. (*Japan National Tourist Organization*)

28   The *Kabuki* play *Musume Dojoji*, centering round a temple bell. Chorus of monks in the foreground and orchestra behind them. *Kabuki*, which became popular in the Tokugawa period (1615–1867) has more characters and more action than *No* drama. (*Japan National Tourist Organization*)

29   Flower arrangement, an art of theoretical complexity in Japan, but one which is appreciated worldwide simply for its aesthetic value. (*Japan National Tourist Organization*)

30 Commodore Matthew C. Perry at Uraga, July 14, 1853. The first landing of the
American expedition. The Commodore is immediately behind the two sailor boys.
Note two of the ships have both steam power and sails, the remainder sails only.
(*Courtesy U.S. Naval Academy Museum*)

31 Glover House and Nagasaki Shipyards. The house was built for a British
engineer-consultant in the nineteenth century, and is associated with Puccini's opera,
Madame Butterfly. (*Japan National Tourist Organization*)

32 Tokyo: old and new. A guardhouse of the Imperial Palace, the moat and a modern hotel in Tokyo, the capital under its present name only since 1868. Previously the capital was at Kyoto. (*Japan Information Center*)

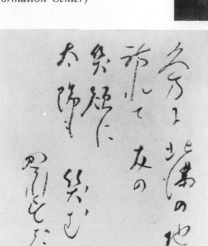

33 Calligraphy. 1940 poem by Kagawa Toyohiko, representing the idealistic hopes of many Japanese for the peaceful development of Manchukuo. (Translation: "As I visit, after a long interval, the northern land of Manchuria, in the smiling faces of my friends the sun too smiles for me.") (*From the author's collection. Photography by Keith Scott Morton*)

34 Yawata industrial area in northern Kyushu, containing chemical plants and the Yawata Iron and Steel works, largest steel firm in East Asia and fourth in the world. (*Japan Information Center*)

35 Machine control room, Yawata Iron and Steel Works, with remote and automated control of steel production on the factory floor below. (*Japan Information Center*)

36 Electronics industry in Japan: the inspection of transistors. (*Japan Information Center*)

37 Tokyo, Marunouchi Business Center and traffic in the Imperial Palace Plaza. The population of Tokyo is over 8.3 million (1980) (*Japan Information Center*)

services of foreign experts. Foreign loans could be negotiated, but these were expensive and involved an unacceptable measure of dependence on foreign governments; no one had invented foreign aid, and Japan had to pay as she went. The 1870's had been a decade of unprecedented expenditure. In addition to the payments to *samurai* and *daimyo* and the industrial financing, it had been necessary to make new outlays for the development of Hokkaido, the northern island. These had included subsidies to immigrant farmers, whose influx in considerable numbers successfully held off Russian encroachment which was threatening from the north. Then at the end of the decade came a period of serious inflation, which added to the difficulties of the government. In 1877 the price of rice was 5.7 yen per koku, but in 1880 it had risen to 12.2 yen. The members of the government considered requesting a foreign loan, which they could have secured from London, but on the advice of the able finance minister, Matsukata Masayoshi (1835–1924), they decided on a policy of retrenchment and economy instead. This policy was firmly carried out and gradually improved the government's financial position, until by 1886 the state of affairs could be considered normal.

Among the economy measures introduced by Matsukata was the sale to private buyers of factories and enterprises which had originally been financed by the government. For some of these enterprises it was not easy to find purchasers and the prices were not advantageous to the government, as sales were made at figures varying from 11 to 90 percent of the original investment. Ready cash, however, was made available to the government, and the losses were more than balanced by the advantage of new industries to the nation as a whole. Manufacture involving national defense remained in government control. There was inevitably a certain amount of political graft bound up with these sales arrangements, factories being sold at low prices to friends of those in the government ministry concerned. In some cases these were the very men best able to carry on the industry in question; in other cases they had to wait for years for the ultimate profits. In one instance at least, involving government property in Hokkaido, the price was so absurdly low that a scandal erupted and the sale was blocked.

Some of the firms which benefited most from the purchase of government-financed concerns were the great business houses which emerged as the so-called *zaibatsu* ("financial clique") firms. The first in order of size was Mitsui, which started in Tokugawa times as a *sake* brewery and branched out into the sale of dry goods and into banking. In the mid-nineteenth century a brilliant manager, Minomura Rizaemon, had the firm adopt modern banking methods and diversify its operations. His friendship with Inoue gave him valuable government connections. The firm bought the Tomioka silk-reeling mill from the government, began to engage in heavy industry, and set up the great Mitsukoshi department store business as a separate entity. The second *zaibatsu* firm of Mitsubishi owed its origin to a Tosa *samurai*, Iwasaki Yataro (1834–1885), who, with the help of the resources of the Tosa domain and government subsidies, set up his own shipping line. From this in turn developed the famous N.Y.K., Nippon Yusen Kaisha, or Japanese Mail Line. The third largest firm was founded by a well-to-do peasant of consuming ambition, Shibusawa Eiichi (1840–1931), who rose to prominence under the patronage of Keiki, the last Shogun. Shibusawa engaged in banking and trading, served in the government, and became president of the First National Bank. He founded the Osaka Spinning Mill, which became in the 1880's remarkably successful by reason of its large size, up-to-date technology, and efficient management. In addition to these activities Shibusawa played a part in the affairs of some hundred other companies. Two other main *zaibatsu* firms were Yasuda in banking and railroads, and Asano, the firm which purchased a government-built cement factory and turned its losses into profits.

POLITICAL EVENTS: TOWARD A CONSTITUTION. In the realm of politics the movement toward representative government was slow and tentative; indeed at one point President Ulysses S. Grant of the United States advised the emperor to make it slow. The government of Japan from the Meiji Restoration in 1868 to the promulgation of the Meiji Constitution in 1890 was in the hands of a few men, an enlightened and progressive group but a distinct oligarchy nonetheless. It is doubtful whether any other political arrangement would have worked. A demand for representative institutions, however, was steadily growing, stimulated by the study of Western models.

When Saigo Takamori left the government in the 1873 crisis over Korean policy, Itagaki Taisuke (1837–1919) went with him; but thereafter the two men moved in very different directions, Saigo toward an unwilling military resistance and Itagaki toward progressive political action. With support from his own clan of Tosa, Itagaki formed a political club called the Society of Patriots. From local beginnings it reached national proportions and formed a valuable training ground for the future political party movement. Any training in legitimate activity of this kind was of benefit, for the notion of "a party" was still an unfamiliar one. The authorities tended, in the traditional manner, to regard associations of persons advocating change as automatically subversive, while those zealous for change wanted to proceed immediately to extremes and had no concept of a "loyal opposition." The limits of valid political activism had still to be discovered and laid down, as may be deduced from the tenor of a newspaper headline of the time: "Tyrannical officials must be assassinated."

While Itagaki and others were carrying on the movement for "people's rights," the government was making experiments of its own. In 1879 prefectural and later town assemblies were elected. There was a small property qualification to determine electors, and only matters concerning taxes and budget were permitted on the agenda; but it was a beginning in representative government. Yet again the leadership was revealed as a true oligarchy, for they were determined to keep control in their own hands and decide the pace of advance. Newspapers had been increasing in numbers and influence during the seventies, and from the start they exhibited the tendency they still display, of being antigovernment and antibureaucratic. Reacting to this, the government passed a Press Law in 1875 which gave wide powers of censorship. The law of libel was made strict and police permission was required for public gatherings. All this apparatus was used against the budding parliamentary movement on numerous occasions. On the other side, the movement for the "people's rights" was strengthened by the translation of Jean-Jacques Rousseau's *Contrat Social* which appeared in 1877. Intellectuals inspired by it formed a radical wing depending on French rather than on British parliamentary ideas.

The conflict between the conservative government leaders and their opponents came to a head in the crisis of 1881. Okuma Shigenobu (1838–1922), who was heading the parliamentary movement from within the government itself, proposed that elections be held in 1882, that a parliament meet the next year, and that a cabinet be responsible to parliament in the British manner. This was most alarming to the oligarchs and after some discussion Okuma was dismissed from office. As a concession to the parliamentary party it was arranged that the emperor should announce that a constitution providing for a parliament would be set up in the year 1890. Regular political parties were now formed, the Jiyuto, or Liberal Party, under the leadership of Itagaki and Goto Shojiro and with some of the characteristics of French radicalism, and the Rikken Kaishinto, or Constitutional Progressive Party, led by Okuma and more akin to English ideas. A warning had already been issued in the emperor's name against "those who advocate sudden and violent changes." In 1887 a Peace Preservation Law authorized the police to remove from the area of the capital any person "judged to be scheming something detrimental to public tranquillity." This wide provision was obviously subject to abuse, but in extenuation of the government's action it must be said that assassination was a constant threat; Okubo Toshimichi, a highly respected member of the government, had been murdered in 1878. Furthermore, though the government had its own cautious timetable, its members did agree in principle to the establishment of a representative national body; the disagreement was over the date and the nature of the body and its powers. Democracy in some form was felt by all to be a reason for the success of the Western nations. Representative government was something you had to have, like *moningu*, "morning coat," the formal Western dress officially adopted during this era.

Ito now began serious work on the drafting of the promised constitution. He led a mission to Europe in 1882 to make a comparative study of government systems. He already knew in broad outline what he was looking for, and spent most of the time in Prussia, where he met Bismarck and studied under Albert Mosse, and in Austria, where he received the advice of Lorenz von Stein. He spent only six weeks of the eighteen months abroad in London, for the Germanic system, with tighter centralization and greater powers for the monarch and the bureaucracy, seemed to him better suited to the needs of Japan than the British parliamentary system, which involved political parties of some experience and self-restraint.

When Ito finally returned to Japan, he superintended several steps leading toward the controlled democracy he was so carefully planning. In 1884 a new peerage, required to form the Upper House in the proposed constitution, was created. It had five ranks—prince, marquis, count, viscount, and baron. Five hundred persons were included in the first grant of titles of nobility, of whom no fewer than 470 already belonged to the old court nobility. The remaining thirty belonged mainly to the government group, and leaders of the new political parties were intentionally left out. Then the civil service was reformed, with the institution of examinations and the passing of regulations designed to prevent nepotism. The Law School of Tokyo University became the chief avenue of entrance into the higher echelons of the civil service and the bureaucracy gained steadily in political significance. Next a cabinet replaced the dajo-kan as the supreme organ of government under the emperor. This gave the premier, Ito, more power; and since the cabinet was set up prior to the constitution, the precedent was the more easily established that the ministers should be responsible to the emperor and not to the elected representatives of the people. Finally, in 1888, a Privy Council was created to advise the emperor. Since its first task was the final drafting of the constitution, it seemed to Ito to take precedence over everything else and he resigned the premiership to take over its chairmanship. Most of the members were in agreement with Ito's views and they had an unrestricted field of action, since the Privy Council was specifically enjoined from receiving petitions from the public.

The Meiji Constitution was promulgated in February 1889, the first system of representative government to be adopted in Asia. In spite of numerous safeguards it was regarded by many as too liberal; but Ito ingeniously warded off criticism by the conservatives through his arrangement that the constitution was made as a gift from the emperor to the people of Japan. Sovereignty was fixed in the person of the emperor, declared to be "sacred and inviolable." He was to convene and dissolve the Diet or parliament, and could pass emergency laws when the Diet was not in session. These, however, had later to be submitted to the Diet. He was supreme commander of the army and navy and the government ministers were individually responsible directly to him and not through the cabinet as a whole. The constitution set up a Diet with a House of Peers, appointive, and a House of Representatives, elective. Each was of equal status, which meant that the upper house had the power of veto, in addition to the veto power vested in the emperor. The House of Peers consisted of the upper nobility, representatives of the lower nobility (counts, viscounts, and barons), distinguished public figures, often scholars, and representatives of the highest taxpayers. The House of Representatives consisted of 300 members, later raised to 466, elected by all adult males in Japan over the age of twenty-five and paying at least fifteen yen per annum in taxes. In practice this turned out to be at first only one percent of the population. The premier was to be appointed by the emperor on advice from the elder statesmen. An important provision was inserted in order to insure to the government some freedom from Diet control, namely the power reserved to the government to carry on with the budget of the previous year if the Diet failed to pass the new budget proposed.

Since the time of their formation the political parties had declined rather than gained in influence. They suffered from internal faction, felt the adverse effects of public opinion after the riots of 1884, and were harassed by the operation of the Peace Preservation Law. Nevertheless, when the first Diet was elected in 1890, the members proved much less amenable to government persuasion than Ito had expected. The Diet used its budgetary powers to show its resistance to the government; but the government found that the weapon it had counted on, namely the right to operate in case of need with the budget of the previous year, proved almost useless, for the simple reason that, in an expanding economy, the previous year's budget figure was never enough. A succession of premiers fell back upon their second weapon, the proroguing or dissolution of the Diet. The government leaders, in their frustration, did not hesitate to use more extreme methods. The second election, which took place in 1892, was accompanied by bribery and the use of police force, in which 25 persons were killed and almost 400 wounded. Two factors, however, made for a series of uneasy compromises: the government leaders were unwilling to see the new constitution fail, and the parliamentary party leaders did not want to incur the constant expense of new elections. (There were four premiers and two elections in the year 1898, but this was exceptional.) The machinery of representative government, although creaking, did function, and gradually the political parties began to operate more normally by opposing each other rather than by combining to hamstring the executive branch. The pattern of control already established in the hands of the members of the Choshu and Satsuma clans continued, for the premiership alternated between Choshu and Satsuma men from 1885 to 1898, the former being represented by Ito and Yamagata and the latter by Kuroda Kiyotaka and Matsukata Masayoshi.

EXPANSION OVERSEAS. Japan's turbulent and phenomenal advance in both the economic and political realms inevitably created new pressures and new demands. This growth, combined with national pride and ambition, produced a drive to control or acquire new territory overseas, which is the salient factor in Japanese history from the 1890's until the end of World War II. Korea, traditional target of Japanese conquest, was the starting point. In 1894 the king of Korea, involved in factional strife at the court, appealed to his suzerain, China, and a small contingent was sent in answer to his plea. The Japanese then sent a larger army and demanded reforms in

Korea on behalf of the progressive party which they were supporting. China refused agreement and war was declared in August. The Japanese were successful on land and their troops penetrated into Manchuria. The decisive action took place at sea, off the mouth of the Yalu River. Japan was again victorious, and went on to destroy the rest of the Chinese fleet at Weihaiwei in Shantung province and to capture Port Arthur on the Liaotung Peninsula. China had been easily defeated. The spoils of war obtained by Japan at the Treaty of Shimonoseki in April 1895 were considerable—the islands of Formosa and the Pescadores, the recognition of Korea's independence, an indemnity of 30 million pounds, and a commercial treaty. During the negotiations the Japanese had also secured the cession of the Liaotung Peninsula in South Manchuria, but before the treaty was ratified Russia, France, and Germany combined to compel Japan to relinquish that claim. The Japanese bowed to the inevitable, but the insult rankled, the more so as Russia proceeded to develop her own interests in Manchuria. Japan annexed Korea outright in 1910, and meanwhile found the indemnity very useful in expanding her foreign trade.

The last years of the nineteenth century were comparatively quiet. Ito at length secured the consent of his *genro* colleagues to form a new party favorable to the government, naming it Rikken Seiyukai, Friends of Constitutional Government, thus recognizing what had long been the case, that the original dream of having a cabinet above and independent of the political parties was an impossible idea. In the same year, 1900, Yamagata, while premier, had a ruling adopted that those appointed as army and navy ministers in the cabinet must be officers on active duty. This was to have ominous consequences, for its effect was to increase the leverage of the military upon the political process. At the same time the sense of grievance at the terms of the Treaty of Shimonoseki had made it easier for Yamagata and his military colleagues to raise the figure for the defense budget.

The significance of Japan's easy victory over China in 1895 was not lost upon Western observers; but the point at which the nations of the world recognized that Japan had joined "the club" of powers possessing modern weapons was the occasion of the Relief of the Legations which marked the end of the Boxer Rebellion in Peking in 1900. The full story of that tragic but understandable anachronism belongs to the history of China. The shrewd and formidable Empress Dowager had skillfully turned the hatred of the Boxer rebels away from the Manchu regime and toward the foreigners. When to the persecution and killing of Christians was added the murder of the German ambassador and the subsequent siege of the legation quarter in Peking, world opinion was fully aroused and summary action taken. A Japanese contingent formed half the international force which set out from Tientsin and succeeded in relieving the beleaguered legations on August 14, 1900. A speech of Kaiser Wilhelm II on July 27 to the troops of the German contingent sheds an interesting sidelight on his mentality and his outlook upon Asia:

Let all who fall into your hands be at your mercy. Just as the Huns a thousand years ago, under the leadership of Attila, gained a reputation by virtue of which they still live in historical tradition, so may the name of Germany become known in such a manner in China, that no Chinese will ever again dare to look askance at a German.[4]

By taking her place at this juncture alongside the Western powers Japan felt she had successfully claimed recognition as a modern, industrialized nation. It is ironical that the possession of armed might was the chief passport to recognition. To be fully in fashion, trade and territorial ambitions were expected to go along with military potential. Japan was well established in Korea. Russia's expansion eastward and her attempted domination of Manchuria were considered a threat not only by Japan but also by the major powers. By a secret treaty of 1896 and a handsome bribe to Li Hung-chang, Russia had secured from China the right to build the Chinese Eastern Railway across Manchurian land, thus saving the expense of the longer and more difficult route north of the Amur River, and connecting the Trans-Siberian Railway with the port of Vladivostok on the Pacific. At about the same time she obtained a lease of the Liaotung Peninsula, with the port of Dairen and the Port Arthur naval base, as well as the right to connect these ports with the railway in the north by means of the South Manchurian line. This was a vital concession, for the port of Vladivostok is ice-free for only about four months of the year, while Dairen is open to navigation all the year round.

Manchuria has figured prominently in the international rivalries between Japan, Russia, and China from the end of the nineteenth century until the present. It is significant that both Manchuria and its chief city, Mukden, are designated in the West not by Chinese but by Russian words, based on the original Manchu language. (The Chinese refer to Manchuria as the "three eastern provinces," Dong San Sheng, or more often simply as "the Northeast," Dong-bei.) Geographically the region consists of a great and fertile plain, in which large-scale land development was begun only in modern times at the hands of Chinese farmer immigrants, mainly from Shantung Province. This plain produces the staple grain of the north, millet, and soybeans, legumes of high nutrient and vitamin value used also in the manufacture of paint and many other industrial products. The plain is surrounded on the east by virgin forests near the Korean border, by the Mongolian steppes to the west, and by the Great Wall and the Gulf of Chih-li to the south. It has valuable deposits of gold, iron, soft coal, and other minerals, the largest open-surface coal mine in the world being situated at Fushun near Mukden. Both the situation and the undeveloped resources of Manchuria, therefore, made it a most desirable area for exploitation by the Japanese.

There were two views in Japan as to how she might best proceed in the

4 W. L. Langer, *The Diplomacy of Imperialism*, Vol. II (New York: Alfred A. Knopf, 1935), p. 699.

complicated diplomatic maneuvering going on at this time for "spheres of influence" on the Asian continent. Ito favored an alliance with Russia on the basis of a simple division, Korea for Japanese development, Manchuria for Russia's share. Yamagata and Katsura Taro, on the other hand, felt that a military showdown was the only way to halt Russia's expansion. They concentrated on still further strengthening the army and navy, which were already by 1894 receiving one-third of the national budget. Yamagata's hard-line policy won out, and the Anglo-Japanese Alliance was signed in 1902. By this agreement the Japanese gained prestige and security, while the British were glad of an ally as further insurance in their rivalry with Germany and Russia. The new alliance did not require Britain to intervene in a purely Russo-Japanese conflict, but guaranteed British aid if any other power joined Russia.

Japan and Russia then entered into direct negotiations in 1903, in which Russia recognized Japan's right to freedom of action in Korea, but Japan, with Britain at her back, sought to restrict Russia's sphere of action in Manchuria to the railway zone only, while the rest of Manchuria was to remain under Chinese control. While the bargaining dragged on, Tsar Nicholas II began pouring a steady stream of troops to the East via the Trans-Siberian Railway. Japan was unwilling to lose the military advantage and broke off the negotiations in February 1904. She immediately struck at the Russian fleet in Port Arthur by a night attack, and succeeded in blockading the enemy ships in the harbor. Japanese land forces crossed the Korean-Manchurian border at the Yalu River, while other Japanese troops occupied the port of Dairen and besieged Port Arthur from the landward side. The Japanese forced the Russians to withdraw northward along the railway line by repeated flank attacks. Port Arthur fell in January 1905. Casualties on both sides had been heavy, and casualties among Chinese civilians would have been still heavier than they were had it not been for the efforts of a Scottish missionary doctor, riding ceaselessly on a Mongolian pony between the lines to arrange for civilian evacuations. The land war culminated in the Battle of Mukden, which lasted for over two weeks in March 1905 and produced a stalemate.

Meanwhile the Russians had dispatched their Baltic fleet to reinforce the squadron at Vladivostok. Britain refused to allow the fleet to use the Suez Canal or any British ports en route. The Russian admiral had to round the Cape of Good Hope and refuel at French ports in Madagascar and Indo-China. Admiral Togo Heihachiro guessed, correctly as it turned out, that the Russians would take the shorter route inside the Japanese islands, and he lay in wait with a powerful battle fleet in the Tsushima Straits between Korea and Japan. He achieved surprise and executed the tactic known as "crossing the T," namely steaming in column across the enemy line of advance, which enabled him to fire successive broadsides, while the rear ships of the enemy, blocked by their own vessels in front, could not bring their guns to bear. Torpedo boats then went in to administer the *coup de grace.* The result was an overwhelming disaster for the Russian fleet, in which thirty-two out of thirty-five ships were put out of action. This naval battle, in May 1905, ended the war.

Western public opinion had been pleased to see the plucky Japanese stand up to the great Russian bear. At the conclusion the British Navy was proud of its brilliant students, but the powers generally were shocked to see a European nation so thoroughly and rapidly defeated by an Asiatic race. Some swift reappraisal had to be undertaken in the chancelleries of Europe and the United States. President Theodore Roosevelt arranged a peace conference in Portsmouth, New Hampshire, which agreed to recognize Japan's "paramount interests" in Korea, handed over to her the southern half of Sakhalin, the Russian lease on the Liaotung Peninsula, and the South Manchurian Railway as far north as Ch'ang Ch'un. But the Treaty of Portsmouth gave Japan no indemnity, a fact which aroused intense feeling in the country. The Russian people had never been in sympathy with the war; defeat precipitated the Revolution of 1905.

When it was announced that Japan was not to receive an indemnity from Russia, there was rioting in the streets of Tokyo, which produced 1,000 casualties, and the premier, Katsura, was compelled to resign. An associate of Ito in the Seiyukai party was appointed to the post. The new incumbent, Saionji Kimmochi (1849–1940), a member of the former court nobility, had had a varied career. After ten years' study in France, he returned to publish his liberal ideas through the medium of journalism. This was considered undignified for a man of noble family, and he was persuaded to join the government. He served as education minister and later as president of the Privy Council. Similar opposition was voiced to his activity in political party affairs, but he maintained a close connection with the Seiyukai, and it was in this capacity that he succeeded to the premiership, although the oligarchs brought forward other reasons. Katsura had been premier from 1901 and Saionji held the office from 1906 for two years. Thereafter the two, by an amicable arrangement, occupied the post alternately until 1913.

Ito Hirobumi, by now Prince Ito, had just laid aside his last office of resident-general in Korea, when he was cut down at the age of sixty-eight by a Korean assassin's bullet in Manchuria in 1909. The lifetime of this man of peasant birth, who had reached a place second only to the emperor himself, had seen his country pass from being an almost unknown land to the position of a world power. The Emperor Meiji, also a man of vigor and talent, died in 1912, thus bringing this remarkable era to a close.

14

EXPANSION, LIBERALISM, AND MILITARISM

1914–1931

The planned revolution carried through by the Meiji leaders and the obedient, even enthusiastic, response of the people had by 1912 proved an outstanding success. The political outlook was uncertain as the original Elder Statesmen were removed by death; but Japan had gained impressive military strength and her economy had reached what is now known as the take-off point. Hard work and thrift enabled her industry to reinvest as much as 15 percent in plant and machinery in good years, after 1900, and still have enough left over to raise the standard of living of the country as a whole. Japan thus proved able to support her growing power upon an adequate industrial and commercial foundation.

The quarter of a century prior to World War I was the period of a worldwide scramble for colonies, concessions, and spheres of influence in Asia and Africa. As the accompanying table shows, Japan joined the other great powers in making very considerable expenditures on "defense" from 1890 to 1914. The Japanese total was increased fourfold and the amount per capita rose from 60 cents to $1.75. While the latter amount was less than the American figure of $3.20 and far below those of the major competitors for world power, Great Britain and Germany, it represented an impressive effort considering the fact that Japan had only begun to attempt modernization as a definite policy after 1868.

When World War I broke out in August 1914, the Okuma government immediately entered on the side of the Allies, declared war on Germany, and sent a force to attack the German holdings in Shantung without any regard for China's neutrality at that time. The British cooperated in the capture of the port of Tsingtao, and within three months Japan had obtained possession of the German assets in Shantung and had placed police along the railway lines to secure them. In this campaign, incidentally,

Military Expenditures of the Great Powers[1]

	STAND-ING ARMY (000)	ARMY APPRO-PRIATION ($000,000)	NAVAL TON-NAGE (000)	NAVAL APPRO-PRIATION ($000,000)	TOTAL DEFENSE EXPENDI-TURE ($000,000)	GROWTH FACTOR	COST PER CAPITA HOME POPULA-TION ($)
JAPAN							
1890	70	18	41	6	24		.60
1914	250	48	700	48	96	x4	1.75
GERMANY							
1890	487	121	190	23	144		2.95
1914	812	442	1305	112	554	x3.1	8.52
BRITISH EMPIRE							
1890	355	88	679	69	157		4.03
1914	381	147	2714	237	384	x2.4	8.53
FRANCE							
1890	502	142	319	44	186		4.87
1914	846	197	900	90	287	x1.5	7.33
RUSSIA							
1890	647	123	180	22	145		1.32
1914	1300	324	679	118	442	x3	2.58
UNITED STATES							
1890	27	45	40	22	67		1.06
1914	98	174	895	140	314	x4.7	3.20

[1] Adapted from Black and Helmreich: *Twentieth Century Europe*, Alfred A. Knopf, New York, 1966, pp. 25–26.

military aircraft were first used in warfare. Japan at this time also occupied the Pacific Islands formerly held by Germany, namely the Mariana, Caroline, and Marshall islands.

The moment seemed propitious for Japan to follow up these gains by consolidating her power on the continent. The government in 1915 secretly presented Yüan Shih-k'ai with Twenty-One Demands in five groups. Groups 1 through 4 concerned rights or limitations in Shantung, Manchuria, the central Yangtze valley, and on the China coast. Group 5 involved the appointment of Japanese as advisers in Chinese government affairs, joint Sino-Japanese control of police, and certain conditions affecting arsenals and the purchase of arms. This last group was such a clear infringement of China's sovereignty that the Western powers, preoccupied though they were with the war, could not possibly ignore the matter. When Yüan Shih-k'ai intentionally informed the world press of the contents of the Twenty-One Demands, Japan was forced to withdraw the more controversial of her "requests," but she obtained valuable concessions in Shantung, South Manchuria, and the eastern part of Inner Mongolia. Japan's aim in all this was mainly economic, but there were serious political repercussions in China, where Japan was suddenly marked out as the main imperialist enemy. Japan had secured agreements one by one from the main powers to have a special position accorded her in China in exchange for help in World War I. The climax came in 1917 in the exchange of the Lansing-Ishii Notes with the United States. By this agreement the parties were to respect the territorial integrity of China, but recognized that the "territorial propinquity" of Japan gave her "special interests" on the Asian continent which she was entitled to protect.

In the Peace Treaty of Versailles Japan succeeded in obtaining the League of Nations mandate over the former German Pacific islands and the recognition of special rights in Shantung. She failed to have a clause guaranteeing racial equality included in the League of Nations Covenant, owing to opposition to nonwhite immigration into Australia and California. This caused no little resentment in Japan. Japan, however, was recognized at the end of the war as one of the "Big Five" powers, with a seat on the Council of the League of Nations, and emerged, after very little expenditure of men or money, more powerful than before.

The chief gains of the Japanese were not political but economic. They were aware that they had done very well from World War I. They had made immense strides in the building and operating of a great merchant fleet, having, in fact, become one of the world's great carriers through the heavy shipping losses experienced by Britain, Germany, and the United States in submarine warfare. The Japanese had been able in their new construction to take advantage of the latest technical advances. They never, for instance, had to invest much capital in ships with reciprocating engines but moved directly to steam turbines and then to diesel engines. During World War I Japanese merchant marine income had multiplied ten times. Japan had captured a large share of the world textile trade, and had ended the war as a creditor nation with gold reserves which had increased sixfold in six years.

Such were the events and the changed directions brought about by the participation of the new Japan in the international arena. A change had also come over the domestic political scene. The small, gifted, and comparatively stable group of the Meiji oligarchs had guided affairs all the way from the Restoration until the outbreak of World War I; but by the end of the war authority was more widely distributed over a much larger number of persons grouped in sets of the elite, such as the bureaucrats, the businessmen, the military leaders, the Privy Council and peers, and the intellectuals. No one of these sets had the degree of authority which the oligarchs had been able to command, and therefore all had to rely on the various combinations of power that could be set up and traded through the machinery of political parties. The Diet was the mart in which this bargaining took place; or rather, the Diet was the place in which speeches were made for public consumption, while the bargaining went on in the back rooms. Although not always harmonious, the process led to the participation of many more

Japanese in the operation of government. The decade of the 1920's, and especially the earlier half of it, was the era of liberal politics in Japan, and this tendency to rely to a greater extent on political parties was reinforced by the fact that the democratic countries had been seen to be the victors in the recent war.

The new tendency found expression in the premiership of Hara Kei (born 1856), president of the Seiyukai party and the first commoner to become premier. He held the post for three years until murdered by a rightist.

In the circumstances of party politics business interests tended to dominate, sometimes by means which were more than dubious, for frequent cases of corruption were uncovered in both main parties, the Seiyukai and the Kenseikai, the latter named Minseito after 1927. The businessmen were opposed to expansionist military schemes, because they cost money in taxes and because they led to boycotting of Japanese goods by Chinese nationalists. Thus part of the Seiyukai program in 1922 was to withdraw the Japanese forces that had gone to Siberia with an Allied anti-Bolshevik expedition in 1918 and had remained on with a vague hope of territorial gains after the other Allies had recalled their troops.

The cabinets of the 1920's represented on the whole the complexion of the political parties, and both of these were pacific rather than warlike and cautious rather than adventurous. There was little ideological difference between them. Although the parties received financial support from the big business sector, their membership was drawn from the smaller businessmen and the rural landowners, who had no other means of political expression. The poorer urban workers, below the property level which would entitle them to vote, had neither the experience nor the expectation of taking part in governing themselves. But their numbers were growing. Agricultural production, which had shown a rise of 50 percent in yield per acre from 1880 to 1914, was now leveling off. In 1920 only about half the working population was engaged in farming and there had been a steady move to the towns. By 1913 28 percent of the people lived in towns of over 10,000, as opposed to 16 percent in 1893. The figures for the production of manufactured goods tripled between 1914 and 1929.

The workers' cause was championed by new political parties. Oi Kentaro, an early radical pioneer and supporter of Sun Yat-sen, had founded the Oriental Liberal party in 1892, but it was short-lived. The Social Democratic party, founded in 1901 under mainly Christian auspices, had a program which today seems eminently reasonable, namely free education, an eight-hour day, and the abolition of child labor; but it was suppressed by the police on the day following its founding. The Communist party, established in 1921 (the same year as the Chinese Communist party), suffered from faction as well as the attentions of the police and went into voluntary liquidation in 1924. (It was revived the next year, but as an illegal, underground organization.)

It was the labor unions rather than any political party which gave the workers their means of self-expression. The booming war years supplied an impetus to the formation of these unions in industry and membership reached 300,000 by 1929. Strikes, beginning in 1919, recurred throughout the 1920's. Moreover the poorer classes began to find aid in several quarters, in a combination which was typical of the early twenties and was never to occur again in the same form. The varied elements in this combination included the intellectuals and liberal party men, the spokesmen of the labor unions, the Christians with an active social concern, and the political leftists. One of their goals, universal adult (over twenty-five) male suffrage, was attained in 1925, which at one stroke increased the voter rolls from 3 to 14 million.

One of the most outstanding of the liberal party politicians was Ozaki Yukio (1859–1954). It was he who, as mayor of Tokyo, presented Washington, D.C., with the famous cherry trees. His career as a national politician began in association with Okuma. In 1898 he was forced to resign from the cabinet on account of a speech in which he mentioned republicanism in Japan. He touched again on the delicate subject of the emperor's position when he led the Seiyukai party opposition to Premier Katsura in the Diet in 1912–13. He was working on behalf of a strongly supported movement for a democratic Japan, timed to coincide with the accession of the Emperor Showa. Katsura, to gain time for party maneuvering, had used the weapon of an imperial rescript to prorogue the Diet for fifteen days, and Ozaki challenged him in a famous speech which contained the words: ". . . they hide themselves behind the Throne, and shoot at their political enemies from their secure ambush." Ozaki was protected by his own sincerity, for no one ever doubted his personal loyalty to the emperor, and he lived to a ripe old age. But in these actions he laid his finger upon the central question of Japanese history, from the times of the Fujiwara through the Shogunate to the Meiji oligarchs and the party politicians, namely, "Who really speaks for the emperor?" The main point of Ozaki's life was made when some power to affect national decisions was given to all the men of Japan in 1925.

Among the radical Christian leaders were Suzuki Bunji, Kagawa Toyohiko, and Abe Isoo. Suzuki, an attorney, founded a labor organization on a national scale, and Abe was on the faculty of Waseda University. The most colorful and many-sided personality of the three was Kagawa (see Plate 33). Illegitimate son of a cabinet minister and a geisha girl, he became a Christian pastor and worked in the slums of Kobe, living for a time in a room six feet square. Socialist thought was introduced into Japan mainly by Christian leaders, and Kagawa aided Suzuki in his labor union work. Kagawa began writing and his novels became best sellers. He was offered a high government post, but felt he could serve his countrymen better in the freedom of the pastorate. He was active in rural cooperatives and founded a chain of sanatoria for the large number of workers who contracted tuberculosis in the insanitary conditions of the factories. (The law fixing eleven hours as the maximum working day for girls in the cotton mills was not put into force until 1916.) In spite of poor health he undertook arduous preaching and lecture tours, and found time to establish and edit the *Kingdom of God Newspaper*. His writings included philosophical works as well as popular novels with a social theme. He was imprisoned in 1921 for his part in a strike of Kobe workers, and was again placed under house arrest by the military near the end of his life, this time for attempts to promote reconciliation with the Chinese during World War II. But when the High Command became alarmed at the excesses committed by Japanese rank and file in the rape of Nanking in 1937, it was Kagawa they called upon to visit the troops and speak to the men about self-discipline. Although Kagawa was clearly exceptional, his life indicates the reasons why the ideas of Christianity have been influential in modern Japan to an extent far greater than would be expected from the membership of the Christian churches, today only half of one percent of the population.

The more pacific and liberal feeling among Japanese statesmen during this era was an aid to the settlement of East Asian affairs which emerged from the Washington Conference of 1921–22. In succession to the Anglo-Japanese Alliance, which had been renewed in 1911 but was now terminated, Great Britain, France, Japan, and the United States entered into a Four Power Pact to respect each others' rights in the Pacific area and to consult in the event of a crisis. Further, a critical clause was acceptance of a limitation on capital ships in the ratio of 5 : 5 : 3 for Great Britain, the United States, and Japan, and 1.67 each for France and Italy. Accompanying this were limitations on the tonnage of warships and the caliber of guns, and a guarantee that no new naval bases would be constructed nearer to Japan than Singapore or Hawaii. Japan had wanted the ratio of ships to be 10 : 10 : 7, but even with the slightly lower ratio, the inclusion of the naval bases clause and the fact that Japan needed to deploy her naval strength only in the Pacific Ocean gave her predominance in a large area and control of the China coast. Japan then agreed to withdraw both from Shantung in China, returning the port of Tsingtao, and from Siberia, as already mentioned. A Nine Power Treaty was also signed in 1922 in favor of the Open Door policy and the territorial integrity and administrative independence of China. In all these arrangements, however, no provision was made for adequate enforcement of the agreements.

A major disaster overtook Japan in 1923 when an earthquake of extreme severity and subsequent fires destroyed half of Tokyo and almost all of Yokohama. The catastrophe continued for three days. Gaping cracks opened in the ground and swallowed up people. Fires raged out of control through acres of wooden houses. A hundred thousand lives were lost and the damage was incalculable. The ground was cleared for a new city and, when Tokyo was rebuilt, its center was transformed by the erection of modern steel and concrete office buildings, theaters, and stores, a pattern soon followed by other cities.

The era of the twenties also saw changes in the social fashions and modes of living. Women attained a new independence as secretaries and office workers. Family living began to change as fathers became less autocratic and husbands more understanding. Some were even prepared to treat their wives as their equals. There was golf and skiing for the rich and baseball for everyone. The books of all countries were available in translation in greater profusion than ever and the Japanese became the greatest newspaper-reading public in the world. Symphony orchestras and Western classical music enjoyed a great vogue, while films, jazz, and cafés (really taverns) catered to the tastes of the *moga* (modern girl) and *mobo* (modern boy).

These gilded youth were too much for the conservative farmers and the earnestly patriotic young army officers. To many Japanese the behavior of the young people was a sign of the decadence which crept in when the old authoritarian ways were given up in favor of liberalism and internationalism. They felt that the party politicians with their newfangled ideas were not fit to advise the emperor. Who could do this better than the army? It was the repository of the ancient *samurai* virtues, and it alone maintained in purity the pristine loyalty to the person of the emperor and to *yamato-damashii*, "the spirit of Old Japan."

Such a vast and sudden change as that dividing the militaristic 1930's from the liberal 1920's has to be accounted for. It is appropriate to begin with such vague and emotional reasons as those just mentioned, for the rise of militarism in Japan was accompanied, as it has been elsewhere, with unreasoning elements of feeling and prejudice, leading ultimately to mass hysteria. The background of family and circumstance among the younger officers and the common soldiers was a further factor in the strong drive behind the increasing power of the military. The young officers tended to be the sons of officers, of small landowners, or of peasant farmers. They began a rigorous military training with little intellectual content at the age of fourteen and had no understanding of the principles of democracy or representative government, which was something entirely new to Japan. The rank and file from peasant homes, unlike the city youth, were perfectly willing to be conscripted. The army gave them not only a better life physically than they had ever known, but also an emotional security under authority more comforting than Dostoevski's Grand Inquisitor could offer. As peasants they were nobodies; as soldiers of the divine emperor, directly descended from the Sun Goddess, they felt a mysterious personal dignity. To lay down their lives for their country was not hardship but glory. Not since ancient Rome had so many at one time felt such powerful truth in the sentence *Dulce et decorum est pro patria mori* ("It is sweet and fitting to die for your country"). Everything in their elementary schooling and their military training served to reinforce this motivation. The higher officers were of the same mind but for different reasons. They read the writing on the wall of liberal policy, if it were allowed to continue. In 1925 the army strength had been reduced by a total of four out of twenty-one divisions.

The army seemed to be gaining influence with the appointment of

General Baron Tanaka Giichi as premier in 1927. However, he chose an unwise China policy of trying to stop the northern advance of Chiang Kai-shek and the Nationalist government and was compelled to abandon the attempt. Then some extremist Japanese officers in Manchuria caused him acute embarrassment. They murdered the warlord Chang Tso-lin by blowing up his train, with the idea that his son, the Young Marshal, Chang Hsüeh-liang, would be more amenable to Japanese aims in Manchuria. Tanaka demanded that they be disciplined, but the High Command ignored his demand, and this loss of face compelled him to resign.

Secret societies of an ultranationalist type were becoming increasingly active. The best known was the Black Dragon Society, called after the Chinese name for the Amur River. The name indicated an emphasis on Manchuria, and one of the society's avowed objects was to incite trouble among the Chinese so that the Japanese Army would have an excuse to come in and restore law and order. Such societies were successful in fostering among the more hotheaded officers the idea of Japan's manifest destiny to rule in Asia and the notion that the army, as the direct servant of the emperor, entrusted with carrying out his will, had a right to act independently of the civilian government.

Baron Tanaka was succeeded as premier in 1929 by Hamaguchi Osachi of the Minseito party. The London Naval Treaty, a sequel to the Washington Conference and concerned with limiting cruiser strength, was signed in 1930. Hamaguchi's willingness to make concessions in regard to the Japanese Navy was considered reprehensible by the hawks. Worse still, the world depression hit Japan during his period of office. He had already been pursuing a deflationary money policy and had returned Japan to the gold standard. This magnified the devastating effect of deflation caused by the depression. Hamaguchi was shot in a Tokyo railway station and died soon afterward. His successor, Inukai Tsuyoshi, was assassinated in 1932 in a coup organized by a young officer group. The days of the liberals were at an end and "government by assassination" had taken their place.

Japan in the years 1929 to 1932 was beset by problems and the military extremists felt that desperate remedies were called for. The depression was a worldwide phenomenon, but it had certain repercussions in Japan which were peculiar to that country. Exports declined by 50 percent in the two years following 1929. The greatest suffering fell on the farmers and peasants, with silk cocoon prices dropping 65 percent in one year, 1929–30. The real incomes of industrial workers fell from an index of 100 in 1926 to 69 in 1931; but the corresponding figures for rural incomes went from 100 to 33. Peasants had to eat the bark of trees and sell their daughters to city brothels. The rage of the people was directed against the *zaibatsu*, the large business interests, identified with the landlords in the popular mind. The suffering of the farm families was felt keenly by the army officers, many of whom came from a rural background. The army men were totally opposed to that cooperation with the international economic order which seemed inevitable to the party politicians and the businessmen, but which to the young officer group appeared as the malign source of the depression and all its evils that had swept over their country.

They had the idea that the army, known for its loyalty and honor, could devote itself selflessly to carving out on the Asian continent an empire that would be independent of the rest of the world and that would assure a stable livelihood to the farmers and industrial workers of Japan. Thus the turbulent events of recent years seemed to these patriotic idealists to have given unmistakable signs that they were meant to be the saviors of their country. All the necessary elements were present. The mystique was supplied by their sense of being empowered to carry out the emperor's will; the external enemies were the decadent democracies (the Japanese, always sensitive to world trends, had noted that Mussolini had made good his criticism of democracy by the March on Rome in 1922 and his seizure of total power in 1924); the internal enemies frustrating Japan's search for her destiny were the business interests and the venal politicians; and the means to hand were the methods of violence already so successful against Chang Tso-lin and their own high government officials. There were few theoretical restraints upon direct, strong-arm methods for men who had never been trained to consider the military power as subordinate to the civilian government.

Premier Inukai made prompt moves to overcome the effects of the depression. He took Japan off the gold standard again. Exports rose sharply and Japan began to recover more quickly than any other industrial country; but an irreversible trend toward militarism had already set in. The Fates had begun to spin their threads.

15

MANChUKUO, The ChINA WAR, AND WORLD WAR II

1931–1945

The crack corps of the Japanese Army, the Kwantung Army in Manchuria, was growing impatient. The Nationalist Government of China was becoming stronger and the day of the warlords who could be bought or intimidated was rapidly passing. Two Kwantung Army officers of colonel rank, Itagaki and Ishiwara, decided it was time to strike. They had the support of the commanding general in Manchuria, but his chief of staff wanted to know the attitude of the Tokyo General Staff. A Major General Tatekawa was sent with a letter forbidding any provocative action; but then some curious things happened. He cabled to say he was coming and the colonels at the other end advanced their timetable. Tatekawa did not fly but took the train through Korea, and, on arriving in Mukden on the evening of September 18, 1931, went straight to a geisha house and made no effort to deliver the letter. That night a bomb exploded on the railway line just north of Mukden.

Colonel Itagaki ordered his troops to attack the Chinese forces in the city. The arsenal, airfield, and radio station were captured before dawn. By September 21 the army had taken Kirin in the northeast and was fanning out all over Manchuria, far beyond the railway zone where alone they had jurisdiction. The embarrassed government in Tokyo was explaining, first, that they had acted in self-defense and second, that they were returning to the railway zone. But there was never any question of their retreating; they had the war minister's support. It was later established that the whole incident, including the bomb, had been deliberately staged.

The ostensible reason for these moves was the suppression of "banditry." A certain amount of actual banditry, it is true, was endemic in the Manchurian countryside, as Owen Lattimore's studies have shown—poor farmers turning to violent means of livelihood in seasons of crop failure. The millet stalks growing five to eight feet tall provide excellent cover and make surprise attacks by bands of desperate men relatively easy. But this type of unrest posed little threat to the industrial and transport operations of the South Manchuria Railway. The Japanese were patently seeking to extend their control over the whole country, and by early 1932 this objective was attained. They then felt themselves in a position to set up the puppet state of Manchukuo, securing the services of the last Ch'ing emperor of China, Henry P'u Yi, as ruler, and seeking to maintain the fiction that this was the will of the "Manchu" people. (The Manchus had, in fact, merged with the Chinese and had almost ceased to exist as a separate race.) In September 1932 Manchukuo was recognized by the government of Japan. The pattern of government throughout the new state was simple and uniform. The number one positions, from prime minister to local mayor, were held by Chinese, but they acted merely as rubber stamps. The real power was held by their assistants in the number two position, who were invariably Japanese. The true character of the regime was indicated by the fact that His Imperial Majesty's ambassador to the new court at Hsinking ("New Capital," formerly Ch'angch'un) was coincidentally the general commanding the Kwantung Army.

The Nationalist Government of China appealed this illegal seizure and the League of Nations sent out the Lytton Commission under Lord Lytton of the United Kingdom to investigate. On the evidence of the facts and on information secured from patriotic Chinese intellectuals and others in Manchuria, it was made clear that the state of Manchukuo had not been set up by the will of its inhabitants. Upon the presentation of the commission's report in September 1932, Japan was condemned by the League of Nations for her actions in Manchuria. She replied by walking out of the meetings and leaving the League; but no sanctions were applied by the other member nations. The scene of the affair seemed remote from the centers of Western power, but the weakness of the League of Nations and her great-power member states was to have disastrous consequences. There is little doubt that Mussolini in his adventures in Ethiopia (1935) and Hitler in his occupation of the Ruhr and subsequent mounting acts of aggression looked upon Manchuria as a test case which failed to produce anything beyond harmless verbal condemnation. But it was not only the League which was powerless; the Japanese Foreign Ministry and civilian members of the government were able to do little to stem the advance of the fire-eaters among the military. They did not even know of the plans leading up to the Manchurian Incident until it was a *fait accompli*.

Manchukuo did not become a colony of Japan in the sense of attracting farmers to settle on the land. Neither the climate nor the crops were of a type with which the Japanese were familiar. But the new territory was an ideal proving ground for the new imperialism of the army. Here there was space for maneuvers and training far away from the eyes of the Japanese people and the remaining liberals in the government. There were ample natural resources which could be used as incentives and rewards for exploitation by new industrial firms. (The old established *zaibatsu* concerns were neither inclined nor encouraged to take part.) Above all a strong base on the mainland could be built up from which the Kwantung Army could move against North China when the moment was ripe.

The military leaders, however, were not by any means prepared to confine their activities to military matters. Phobias concerning "dangerous thoughts" multiplied and intellectual leaders among the Chinese came under increasing attack. Prominent persons in the Christian churches who had contacts with foreigners, professional men such as doctors and others whose connections with the Chinese nationalists were close, all found themselves under increasing suspicion. Certain intellectuals who had given evidence before the Lytton Commission were arrested in the small hours of the morning, imprisoned by the *kempeitai*, the dreaded military police, and subjected to refined torture, including a new electric shock treatment, as well as the old water torture, which involves almost drowning the victim and then bringing him around for further questioning. Many Chinese suffered severely and all Chinese felt humiliated by the contempt in which they were held by the Japanese military and police. Revelation of these facts later caused consternation among liberal and pacific Japanese at home, who could scarcely bring themselves to believe that their countrymen had acted in this brutal fashion.

It was comparatively easy for the military to carry through at home a process of "spiritual mobilization," for in Japan the people were disciplined and dedicated to the service of emperor and country. But similar attempts in Manchukuo met with little success. The Chinese made an outward surrender to *force majeure*, but inwardly they were not convinced that it was Japan's destiny to unite all countries in a "Greater East Asia Co-Prosperity Sphere." The Japanese military authorities, attempting to promote this line of thought, compelled all school authorities, both in public and in private or mission schools, to conduct the children to worship, first at the Confucian temples in an artificial bid for a new "Manchu" nationalism, and, in a later phase, to the Shinto shrines as a sign of loyalty to the emperor of Japan, to whom, understandably, the Chinese felt no loyalty whatsoever.

More sinister was the widespread use of narcotics, not merely the traditional smoking of opium but the increasing addiction to the more deadly heroin and morphine. Keepers of opium dens were afraid of the consequences of having dead men found on their premises, and so used to get rid of the moribund addicts by giving other addicts a free shot of heroin as a reward for carrying out the dying and leaving them on the garbage heaps of the city of Mukden. After the 20 degrees below zero cold of the winter night such men were, of course, corpses by the next morning. Little attempt was made by the Japanese authorities to halt this traffic, and this contrasted with the considerable efforts of the Chinese Nationalists toward stringent control of the drug market, which had flourished in the warlord era. Some Chinese in Manchuria charged the Japanese military with the deliberate distribution and sale of narcotics in Manchukuo in the 1930's in order to corrupt and weaken the morale of the people. It would be hard to substantiate this charge; but it is certain that drugs were relatively inexpensive and very easy to obtain, even in remote villages in the countryside. Over-the-counter sales were made to anyone without question.

Meanwhile, Manchuria was being developed industrially and many technical improvements were being introduced. At Fushun the large open-surface coal mine was expanded and a power station established at the pithead for the cheap distribution of electric power over a wide area of South Manchuria. At Anshan on the Mukden-Dairen section of the South Manchuria Railway the iron and steel works set up by the Russians made considerable increases in production. The South Manchuria Railway was the hub and center of technical improvements in many fields; indeed it constituted a small empire in itself. The president of this remarkable institution was Matsuoka Yosuke, who later became Japanese foreign minister. The railway in the mid-1930's ran a stainless steel diesel-powered train daily as a superexpress from the capital at Hsinking to the port of Dairen. It was scheduled with arrival and departure times printed in half-minutes on official timetables, but this utopian practice had later to be abandoned. The hospital maintained by the South Manchuria Railway in Mukden was conducted on modern lines and produced competent doctors from its affiliated medical school.

A steady transformation had been taking place in the public health situation in Manchuria ever since the disastrous bubonic plague of the early years of the twentieth century. The pioneer agent in this transformation was the Christie Memorial Hospital and Medical College operated jointly by missionaries from Scotland, Ireland, and Denmark. Men and women graduates from this college in the fields of medicine, nursing, and pharmacy staffed hospitals and set up practices all over Manchuria and gradually raised standards of hygiene, diagnosis, and treatment both in towns and in remote rural districts. After the foundation of the state of Manchukuo the college was severely restricted and downgraded because of its international contacts. Japanese medical efforts, however, hastened the adoption of modern methods of public health control throughout the country.

Japan in her policy, though not always in the sentiments of her people, continued to move toward the right. Marxism, which since World War I had made an increasing appeal to intellectuals, was ruthlessly suppressed. Some 3,000 Socialists, Communists, and labor organizers were arrested in 1932 and 1933. Many of them were imprisoned and a few tortured to death. Direct action and violence were increasingly used, accepted, and even condoned as expressions of political opinion. A financier, Inoue, and Baron Dan, chief executive of the Mitsui firm, were assassinated early in 1932, as was Premier Inukai himself some months later. The subsequent trials of the army and civilian extremists responsible for these outrages were used as platforms for the statement of their views, and the sentences passed were often absurdly light. It was felt that their patriotism, "sincerity," and "pure motives" justified their acts of terrorism. The army itself suffered from faction, one of the main divisions being between those who had attended the War College and those who had been thwarted in this prestige-carrying ambition. General Nagata Tetsuzan was responsible in 1934 for the dismissal of an extremist general. An officer of lieutenant-colonel rank simply walked into Nagata's office and killed him with his sword. At the trial he said he was only sorry he had not been able to accomplish the slaughter with one stroke. The witch-hunt extended into academic circles, the most celebrated case being that of Professor Minobe Tatsukichi of Tokyo University. This distinguished professor was ousted from his job and all his works banned, though they had been standard texts for years, because, in his books, he had referred to the emperor as an "organ of the government" instead of in more laudatory and exclusive terms.

The army did not have matters all its own way. Elections, particularly that of 1937, returned in large numbers liberal members and those opposed to the actions of the army. The navy was less extreme and army activists were forced to accept two moderate premiers who were admirals, Saito Makoto and Okada Keisuke, for the years between 1932 and 1936. The method the army used to control the government went back to the Meiji Constitution and its Prussian model, with the emperor's position as head of the armed services clearly marked out. The result was that the General Staff was placed directly under the emperor, and the army minister became directly responsible to the emperor as well as having a place in the cabinet which was chaired by the premier. The service ministers' direct responsibility to the emperor and their right of access to him gave them a measure of control over the cabinet and the civilian ministers which was impossible, for instance, in Great Britain, where the cabinet functioned as a body under the prime minister and was responsible as a whole to Parliament. In 1936 the rule that the service ministers had to be serving officers on the active list was revived. This in turn placed these ministers under the control of army and navy opinion, and made it impossible in effect for anyone to hold those offices who did not enjoy the confidence of the main body of the officers. Since the extremist faction was always invoking the name of the emperor, they made it difficult for anyone to oppose their choices for the highest posts. If a civilian premier was unacceptable to the dominant forces in the army, the nomination of an officer to the post of army minister was delayed and thus the formation of the cabinet could be hung up indefinitely. At the same time and as a result of these processes, the Diet was becoming less and less effective. Thus, no matter what the outcome of the elections, the drift to the right continued.

The climax of direct action came with the Tokyo Revolt of February

1936. Not content with the great measure of control the army had already attained and desiring the elimination of all opposition to military policy, some junior officers of the First Division with 1,400 troops staged a coup in the capital itself. They assassinated certain cabinet ministers and members of the Imperial Household Ministry, and occupied some government buildings in the center of the city, including the Diet and the Army Ministry. The navy and other important groups were completely opposed to the coup. The only surviving Elder Statesman, Saionji, supported the emperor in a firm stand and the men who had led the coup were adjudged rebels. Troops were called in from other commands and the revolt was crushed. This time there was no propaganda performance but a prompt trial and execution of thirteen of the leaders.

Japan signed the Anti-Comintern Pact with Germany in December 1936, and this was a signal that the army considered Russia a definite threat to Japanese security. Nevertheless in 1937 the army, with Manchuria now secured, embarked on a venture into China proper. This was the next step in the outline of conquest contained in the Tanaka Memorial—Manchuria, China, Southeast Asia, Australia, India. This document reflected the thinking of army imperialists, even though it is now thought not to have been a genuine state document of the government of Baron Tanaka, premier in 1927. The aim in 1937 was to lop off China's five northern provinces, in the sense of rendering them neutral and outside the control of the Chinese Nationalist Government, and thus more open to Japanese commercial penetration. Preparations with this end in view had been going on for some time. Japanese railway police were exercising controls over the movements of persons and freight beyond the Manchurian border into North China as far as Tientsin and Peking in the supposed interests of security. Trade was extended and capital invested in North China by Japanese industrial firms with the encouragement of the army. The Nationalist Government of China, involved in the enormous problems of modernization and warload control and committed to a long-continued course of resistance against the Chinese Communists, felt powerless to prevent these stage-by-stage encroachments by Japan. Finally in July of 1937 the Japanese forces mounted maneuvers in the Peking area and a clash with the Chinese garrison troops took place at the Marco Polo Bridge.

This clash has been compared to the Manchurian Incident, but it was probably not planned, at least not at high level, for the authorities hoped to secure North China without armed conflict. Their calculations proved wrong, and in the end fatal. Once committed, the Japanese brought in heavy reinforcements; but the Chinese commander in Peking resisted strongly, even though his military resources were quite inadequate. The Japanese had moved also in Shanghai, but there too encountered spirited resistance. The limited war, if war it had to be, in which the Japanese High Command had hoped for a quick victory, also proved illusory and both sides settled down to a long struggle. Thus the real beginning of World

War II was not in 1941 when the attack on Pearl Harbor brought America decisively into the war, nor in 1939 when Britain and France resisted Hitler, but in 1937 when China decided she would not submit tamely to Japanese aggression.

It was ironic that Chiang Kai-shek's foreign military advisers were Prussian officers from the country allied with the enemy, Japan. These men served China well, advocating the strategy that Chiang followed, that of trading the vast space of China for time, in which it was hoped allies would come to China's aid. Pitched battles with Japan's superior forces were avoided and a strategic withdrawal gradually executed behind the mountain barriers of Szechuan. During this retreat extraordinary efforts were made to salvage both material and manpower. Textile factories and arsenals in Shanghai and other coast cities were dismantled and the machinery transported inland in carts, on riverboats, and on the backs of coolies in an unending chain. Students and professors picked up books and laboratory equipment and set up their universities again in temporary quarters a thousand miles away.

The Japanese were never able to take possession of the country as a whole. They could bomb but could not penetrate with ground forces the mountain provinces of the southwest in sufficient strength to force a decision; but they overran the main part of the country, holding all the principal cities and lines of communication. For Japan as well as China it was a costly war. Chinese guerrilla forces, organized mainly by the Communists operating out of Yenan in the northwest, constantly attacked and overcame small, isolated garrisons of Japanese, disrupted transport, and succeeded in supplying themselves with trucks, arms, ammunition, and even uniforms from the small enemy units they had defeated. In particular, the Communists succeeded in organizing resistance and intelligence systems among the peasants of China, thus gaining experience in community organization and control at the grass-roots level which was to prove invaluable to the Communist cause at the end of the war.

With American and British aid reaching free China in small but significant quantities, first by the Burma Road, and, when it was closed, by airlift from India "over the hump" of impassable mountains, China was able to hold out and a stalemate was produced.

Once the China campaign was launched in 1937, the Japanese Army obtained full national support and was able to obtain almost any arrangements it wished. The National Mobilization Law of November 1938 gave the government wide authority in price and wage control, a plan for national registration and compulsory savings, direction of materials and labor, and the government operation of some industries. A Manchurian Industrial Development Corporation with government capital was set up in 1938, and additional supplies of coal, iron, and chemicals were obtained through the North China Development Corporation established two years later. The political parties were swallowed up in 1940 in a type of wartime coalition known as the Imperial Rule Assistance Association. In the same year even the cabinet became almost a nonentity, for key decisions were now to be made by a Liaison Conference attended by the premier, war and navy ministers, foreign minister, and service chiefs of staff. Other ministers could attend only by invitation.

In its efforts to find some way out of the stalemate position in the China war, the Japanese government at length prevailed on a Chinese politician of sufficient stature to head a puppet government in Nanking. Wang Ching-wei agreed to fill this role in 1940, but this move did not have the effect Japan desired. There was no diminution of China's will to resist, and the specter of Russia still loomed at Japan's back. There was a group of leaders in Tokyo who felt that accommodation with Britain and America offered the best counterweight to the Russian threat. Matsuoka Yosuke, however, now foreign minister in the cabinet of Premier Konoe Fumimaro, was completely convinced that Germany would be the ultimate victor in Europe. He had evidence in plenty to support his case in the year 1940. May 10 to June 4 had seen the phenomenal success of the German blitzkrieg in the Netherlands, Belgium, and France, culminating in the Allied evacuation from Dunkirk. The air Battle of Britain was then joined, and lasted from August to November 1940. The peak came in September, when Goering and the Luftwaffe failed by a very narrow margin to break the power of the Royal Air Force, and thus could not clear the way for an invasion of the British Isles, which would probably have finished the war. The impetuous Matsuoka did not wait quite long enough; he had Japan sign the Tripartite Pact with Italy and Germany in the same month of September 1940. In November, when the Battle of Britain was decided in Britain's favor, his colleagues would probably not have allowed him to sign.

In April 1941 a neutrality agreement between Japan and Russia was signed—a triumph for Matsuoka—and Japan felt she could breathe again. It was not to be for long. In June of the same year Hitler suddenly turned to attack Russia without giving warning to Japan. The Japanese were now faced with the choice of honoring the Tripartite Pact with Germany or the more recent neutrality agreement with Russia. Memories of a 1939 summer war with Russia in the Nomonhan area of Outer Mongolia were still fresh in their minds. The superiority of the Russian tanks had become clearly evident before the affair was settled by an armistice. They decided to stick with the Russian agreement. In a rearrangement of the cabinet, the pro-German Matsuoka was dropped as foreign minister.

The economic situation was now causing the Japanese leaders some anxiety. They had been stockpiling throughout the China War, but supplies of oil in particular were urgently needed. The United States in 1940 banned exports to Japan of certain strategic materials, first scrap iron, then steel, and lastly oil. Indeed it was surprising that the United States allowed exports of these items to go on as long as she did. A sour joke among the New York GI's in bombing raids later on was, "Well, here comes the Third Avenue

El [elevated railroad that was demolished] back at us." In order to secure supplies of oil the Japanese sent two missions to the Dutch in Indonesia; but the Dutch temporized and only agreed to the delivery of small amounts. In spite of the urgency of the situation the Japanese Navy counseled caution. They were not prepared to risk hostilities with the Netherlands, Great Britain, and the United States to take the oil by force. Admiral Nomura Kichisaburo was therefore sent to the United States to negotiate. But the army was impatient and confident. A decision was taken to invade Southeast Asia in July 1941, and Vichy France was forced to agree. As soon as troops were sent in, the United States froze all Japanese assets and trade between the two countries came to a standstill.

Tension now increased in Japan between the war party and those favoring negotiation, while Premier Konoe tried to hold the balance between the two. It was decided to begin preparations in September for eventual war against the United States, but meanwhile the Nomura talks in Washington were to go on. America was well aware that an explosion might occur at any time. Both American and British nationals in Japan had received warnings from their respective governments to evacuate, the first at the end of 1940, another in the spring of 1941, and a final peremptory warning in September of that year. Konoe was forced to resign and General Tojo ("Razor") Hideki became premier on October 17. Tojo, a military man first and last, at once began general mobilization and the planning of war strategy. American terms now proposed in the Nomura talks were too stringent for Japan—nothing less than withdrawal of all Japanese troops from Indo-China, China, and Manchuria. On December 1 an Imperial Council again voted to go to war with the United States if it should prove necessary. President Roosevelt made a last appeal to the emperor, but it never reached him. The attack on Pearl Harbor by Japanese Navy planes took place early on Sunday morning, December 7. In view of all the diplomatic activity which had preceded it, the achievement of complete and deadly surprise by the Japanese is the more amazing. But Nomura himself was informed of what his government had done only when he returned to the Japanese Embassy in Washington after a session with Secretary of State Cordell Hull, who was outraged by what he thought was colossal duplicity.

The Japanese Navy had conducted intensive practice for the Pearl Harbor raid in Kagoshima Bay, and the operation from their point of view was a brilliant success, the more so as the United States Navy paid no heed to the radar warnings of approaching planes. Seven battleships, numerous other vessels, and about half the United States aircraft on Hawaii were destroyed or so seriously damaged as to be useless. Simultaneous attacks were delivered on the Philippines, Hongkong, and Malaya. In the Philippines American aircraft were caught on the ground, all neatly lined up, and off Singapore the British battleship *Prince of Wales* and battle cruiser *Repulse* were steaming out of range of air cover and were ignominiously sunk.

Free for the time being of the threat of American naval power, the Japanese moved with speed over the whole Pacific area. Hongkong fell on Christmas Day and Manila on January 2, 1942, Bataan holding out till April and Corregidor till May. The defense of Singapore was all oriented toward the sea, as the jungle to the rear was supposed to be safe and impenetrable. But the Japanese had been training troops in the jungles of Thailand, and Singapore was captured from the landward side on February 15. The Dutch East Indies fell in early March and Burma by the end of April. Within six months of the initial attack Japan was making serious preparations to advance against Australia. Her lines of communication were now, however, very far extended and the American buildup for a counteroffensive was under way.

The naval Battle of the Coral Sea was approximately a draw, but its effect was to call a halt to any attack on Australia. The Battle of Midway a month later in June 1942 gave an advantage to the United States Navy, for they had had warning of the attack and were able to destroy four Japanese aircraft carriers, which seriously affected the key factor of air power. It is said that the Japanese Navy was so humiliated by the defeat at Midway, which actually proved a turning point, that they did not inform Premier Tojo of the outcome until a month after the event. On land New Guinea was gradually recaptured by Allied forces and Guadalcanal, after bitter and prolonged fighting, was regained in February 1943.

The economy in Japan had been performing prodigies of production. The engineering firms were able to meet their own needs in the domestic manufacture of machine tools before the war started in 1941. By decentralizing production in small workshops, in a typical Japanese pattern, and by working a fifteen-hour day, the new aircraft industry was able in the course of the war to manufacture 62,400 aircraft. But raw materials were growing scarce. The Greater East Asia Co-Prosperity Sphere—Asia for the Asians under Japanese leadership—was strong in propaganda appeal but often short in performance, as the Southeast Asian inhabitants and others found that the profits accrued to Japan, and that the Japanese in running affairs were tactless and overbearing. Supplies of oil, rubber, tin, and other vital war materials did not flow back to Japan in the quantities required. Moreover, American submarine strength was growing, in spite of the urgent demands of the European theater of war, and Japanese merchant marine losses were mounting. (By the end of the war Japan had suffered the loss of over 75 percent of her shipping; some estimates go as high as 90 percent.) In fact the early estimates of the Japanese naval strategists were proving approximately correct. They had informed the government at the beginning that the war could be won by a quick campaign, but they could not guarantee to maintain the effort after eighteen months.

One permanent result of the rapid and decisive Japanese victories in the early stages of the war was that the myth of white supremacy was forever exploded. The Japanese treated the defeated Dutch, British, and

American prisoners with intentional contempt and callous cruelty in front of the native inhabitants of the whole Pacific area, in Indonesia, in Thailand, in Malaya, on the so-called Railway of Death ("Bridge over the River Kwai"), in Hongkong, in the Philippines, and elsewhere. After this and after three years of intensive anticolonial propaganda, it was well-nigh impossible for the colonial powers to reassert their authority in these regions, or anywhere in the world, at the conclusion of the hostilities.

By 1943 the pressure on Japan was becoming gradually more intense. Overall strategy was not as effectively coordinated between Japan and Germany as it was between Britain, the Dominions and other Allies and the United States. The Chinese maintained pressure on the mainland. The unorthodox British General Orde Wingate and his successors penetrated Japanese lines in Burma with small but effective forces of Chindits, as the specially trained jungle troops were called. Above all, American forces pressed a relentless campaign of island hopping, capturing certain predetermined islands and ignoring others, which then become isolated and unimportant. After months of fighting, Saipan in the Marianas was reached in July 1944, and from there the islands of Japan were within bombing range. Industrial plants, especially in Tokyo and Nagoya, were severely bombed, for Japanese air defense was quite inadequate to protect them. The Tokaido main railway line was constantly disrupted and constantly repaired; but the lack of alternate rail routes was a serious handicap to war production. When Okinawa was captured in June of 1945 after appalling losses on both sides, the bombing became much more intense, and almost all the main cities of Japan were heavily damaged by fire bombs. As the enemy closed in on Japan, resistance was fanatically brave. Few Japanese prisoners were taken throughout the entire war. Pilots flew planes to destruction, aiming their bomb or torpedo loads directly at the target and perishing in the explosion. They were named *kamikaze* ("wind of the gods") pilots, after the typhoon that had destroyed the Mongol invaders in the thirteenth century.

The Casablanca Conference of the Allies had laid down unconditional surrender as the aim in the defeat of both Germany and Japan. At the Yalta Conference of February 1945 Stalin agreed to enter the war against Japan three months after Germany had been defeated. In return Russia was to be granted the southern half of Sakhalin and the lease of the Port Arthur naval base in Manchuria, approximately what she had had to give up at the Treaty of Portsmouth in 1905. The Allies at this point were reckoning on having to fight yard by yard through the Japanese islands and thought they would require Russia's help.

Japan attempted to secure better terms than unconditional surrender through the good offices of Russia. Tojo had resigned as premier in July 1944 and his successor, General Koiso Kuniaki, in the next April, to be succeeded in turn by Suzuki Kantaro, who was less intransigent and more ready to make peace on any terms. But the Allies had no reason to modify their demands and expressed themselves unequivocally at the Potsdam Conference of July 1945 as determined to do away with the "irresponsible militarism" by which the people of Japan had been misled. With knowledge of the new and deadly weapon in their hands, the Allies conveyed their answer to the Japanese overtures through Russia: unconditional surrender or "prompt and utter destruction." They gave the Japanese ten days, and then dropped the first atom bomb on Hiroshima, the southern Army Head- quarters on August 6. Russia entered the war on August 8, and the second bomb was dropped on Nagasaki, a major port, on August 9. Although the targets had some military importance, the two bombs were dropped with the idea of breaking the civilian will to fight and thus, it was hoped, saving the casualties of a long battle in Japan itself.

The Kwantung Army in Manchuria had been depleted to reinforce other areas and could not resist the Russian advance. Units of the Russian Navy attacked Sakhalin and the Kuriles.

On August 10 Emperor Hirohito was asked by the cabinet, which was deadlocked on the question of surrender, to give his counsel. He opted for surrender, and this was offered to the Allies "provided the Emperor's status is preserved." The Allies would entertain no conditions whatsoever, so, on a second intervention of the Emperor, a complete capitulation was made. On August 15 the Emperor made a broadcast speech announcing the surrender to the whole of his people, saying they must "endure the unendurable" and bidding them work together for reconstruction. The people and the area commanders accepted the situation, for further resistance was evidently hopeless. There was a small mutiny among some military leaders who broke into the palace and attempted, unsuccessfully, to steal the recording of the Emperor's speech to prevent its being broadcast. The war minister committed suicide. Prince Higashikuni was appointed premier in order, by the imperial prestige, to secure order and obedience, and on September 2 the instrument of surrender was signed in due form on the deck of the flagship, the U.S.S. *Missouri*, in Tokyo Bay.

16

POSTWAR
JAPAN

The wisdom of the decision to use the atomic bomb has been long debated. Dropping the bomb probably did shorten the war; nevertheless Asians cannot forget that this new and frightful weapon of destruction was loosed upon them by the Christian West. Conventional weapons since the beginning of time, from the stone ax through the spear and sword to the rifle, had killed men of one generation only. Mysterious horrors were now added by the fact that the atomic bomb had the power not only to destroy large numbers instantly but also to affect future generations through the damage caused to the human reproductive system by fallout. After the war the mayor of Nagasaki made clear the fact, attested elsewhere also, that the Japanese population were shocked and dazed by the bomb, but less resentful against America than might have been expected. They were deeply disillusioned by the morass into which their own military men had led them, and they experienced a complete revulsion against war and the use of force.

The defeat of Japan in World War II involved the first invasion and occupation in their entire history of the soil this proud people had been taught to consider sacred. The effect of defeat was therefore traumatic, the more so as the courage and loyalty of the officers and men of the Imperial Army had been phenomenal. Very few prisoners indeed from the officer class had been captured, death in the *samurai* tradition being preferred to capture. Since this preference of death to surrender had been strongly reinforced by orders of the High Command throughout the war, it was felt necessary to make perfectly clear the official nature of the call to surrender by sending imperial princes and members of the Emperor's family to the various theaters of war with the capitulation orders.

The Japanese people were extremely apprehensive as to what occupation by foreign troops would mean. The wildest rumors circulated about expected rape and looting, and many women left town and retreated to the country. The population was therefore pleasantly surprised when the GI's, and the smaller number of British, Australian, and New Zealand troops involved, proved to be not only correct but friendly in their behavior. As fraternization gradually increased, the authorities on both sides became somewhat alarmed by the dangers attendant on the rapid growth of bars and brothels catering to the occupation troops. But on the whole it may be said that this occupation was one of the best prepared and best conducted in the history of warfare. At the conclusion of the seven years, from 1945 to 1952, during which it lasted, few of the reforms introduced at the beginning were rescinded, and the general lines of the course charted for Japan were accepted by parties of both the right and the left. The mood and reaction of the Japanese people toward the occupation went through the phases of fear, relief, gratitude, boredom, and finally a predictable but tolerably mild resentment.

The machinery of the postwar control of Japan was supplied by a thirteen-nation Far Eastern Commission in Washington and a four-power Allied Council in Tokyo, with representatives from the United States, the Soviet Union, the British Commonwealth, and China. The Allied Council meetings frequently degenerated into futile argument, and in practice the direction of affairs was in the hands of SCAP, Supreme Commander Allied Powers, on the basis of a short document called "Initial Post-Surrender Policies for Japan." A decision was taken to work through a Japanese government and not to replace it, partly owing to the simple logistic fact that not enough Japanese-speaking personnel could be found to staff a nationwide operation. Contact with the Japanese government was maintained through a Central Liaison Office until 1948, and thereafter directly with the various Japanese government departments.

The position of Supreme Commander Allied Powers was given to General Douglas MacArthur, who had fought in the Pacific theater all through the war. He was well suited by nature and by professional training to fill his role of supreme arbiter and effective ruler. Somewhat in the style of a shogun he was punctilious in the performance of his duties, but in his bearing rather dignified and aloof. He turned up at his office in the modern Dainichi Insurance Building near the Emperor's palace promptly each morning in a black limousine and returned to his quarters after a hard day's work, without any attempt at fraternizing or even going about the country on inspection tours. This was precisely the conduct expected and appreciated by the Japanese. MacArthur's sense of history and of destiny seemed at times pompous and egotistical to the egalitarian sentiments of Americans; but these very qualities, combined with his essential fairness, impressed the Japanese and gave them a needed feeling of confidence.

The period immediately after the end of the war was a time of great hardship and difficulty for the nation. There was widespread devastation and shortage of food. City dwellers packed the trains and fanned out daily into the countryside to try to barter a few possessions for food. The number of unemployed rose to 13 million. Repatriated Japanese swelled the population requiring to be fed, and large numbers of demobilized soldiers, so far from being heroes, found themselves unwanted and despised in the aftermath of defeat. Many of them, wounded and clad in tattered uniforms, begged alms on the streets and watched the conquerors go by with Japanese girls on their arms. Even those who obtained food were liable to be arrested for dealing on the black market. Gradually American aid and Japanese hard work improved the situation, though it was to be some time before industry could begin to show significant production.

The directives from Washington required demilitarization and democratization. The first was carried out with smoothness and dispatch. Troops were demobilized and military installations dismantled. War trials and purges were conducted between 1946 and 1948 at various levels. Twenty-five were accused of major war crimes, and of these seven, including General Tojo, were hanged and the remainder imprisoned for life. Prince Konoe, former premier, committed suicide rather than submit to the disgrace of entering Sugamo Prison. Five thousand war criminals were tried in countries of Asia outside Japan and 900 were executed; 200,000 were purged from their jobs as bureaucrats on the basis of the type of work they had done rather than for any reasons of personal responsibility.

In the process of seeking to make Japan into a democracy in the fullest sense, the first question to be decided was the position of the Emperor. Here MacArthur carried out a wise decision reached earlier at a high level and did not indict him as a war criminal in spite of the clamor for this action by hotheads in America and among the Allies. He was retained in his position as a symbol of the nation's unity and as the keystone of the social arch which would preserve the country from chaos and disintegration. Emperor Hirohito was personally quite willing in the year 1946 to make a public renunciation of claims to divinity. Thereafter he made tours of the country and began to show himself to the people in a new light as a constitutional monarch and a sympathetic and modest individual of scholarly tastes, whose hobby is marine biology.

The new constitution, passed in 1946 and taking effect in May 1947, made clear in the Preamble and Article 1 the sovereignty of the people and the position of the emperor as a constitutional monarch.

> We, the Japanese people, acting through our duly elected representatives in the National Diet, . . . do proclaim the sovereignty of the people's will and do ordain and establish this Constitution, founded upon the universal principle that government is a sacred trust, the authority for which is derived from the people, the powers of which are exercised by the representatives of the people, and the benefits of which are enjoyed by the people; and we reject and revoke all constitutions, laws, ordinances and rescripts in conflict herewith.

[203]

. . .

ARTICLE 1. The Emperor shall be the symbol of the State and of the unity of the people, deriving his position from the will of the people with whom resides Sovereign power.[1]

In a prominent position in Chapter II of the Constitution came Article 9 on the renunciation of war:

ARTICLE 9. Aspiring sincerely to an international peace based on justice and order, the Japanese people, forever, renounce war as a sovereign right of the nation, or the threat or use of force, as a means of settling disputes with other nations.

For the above purpose, land, sea, and air forces, as well as other war potential, will never be maintained. The right of belligerency of the State will not be recognized.

In other articles the peerage was abolished, the Diet made the only source of legislation and provision made for the cabinet to be selected from the majority party or coalition in the Diet, on the British model. Important provisions concerning the cabinet were contained in Article 66:

The Prime Minister and other Ministers of State shall be civilians.
The Cabinet, in the exercise of executive power, shall be collectively responsible to the Diet.

Both Houses of the Diet were to be fully elective and the franchise was extended to all men and women of twenty years of age and over. A Supreme Court was set up on the United States model, but with a provision for popular review of its membership:

ARTICLE 79. . . . The appointment of the judges of the Supreme Court shall be reviewed by the people at the first general election of the House of Representatives following their appointment and shall be reviewed again at the first general election of the House of Representatives after a lapse of ten (10) years, and in the same manner thereafter.
ARTICLE 81. The Supreme Court is the court of last resort with power to determine the constitutionality of any law, order, regulation or official act.

The powers of local self-government were considerably increased by such provisions as:

ARTICLE 93. . . . The chief executive officers of all local public entities, the members of their legislative assemblies, and such other local officials as may be determined by law shall be elected by direct popular vote within their several communities. . . .
ARTICLE 95. A special law, applicable to only one local public entity, cannot be enacted by the Diet without the consent of the majority of the voters of the local public entity concerned, obtained in accordance with law.

[1] These and subsequent quotations from the constitution are taken from *Political Handbook of Japan, 1949*, Tokyo: The Tokyo News Service.

Guarantees were given in the constitution not only for the customary freedoms of person, domicile, and religion but also for academic freedom (Article 23) and the right of collective bargaining (Article 28).

As part of the process of democracy it was the policy of the occupation authorities to encourage the trade union movement. Labor legislation between 1945 and 1947 granted rights to organize in unions, to bargain collectively, and to strike. Union membership rose within a year from approximately one million to four and a half million. Not all of this could be considered a genuine increase, since unions within some firms had the employer as president of the union. Former Marxist and Communist labor leaders, released from the imprisonment to which they had been condemned by the former military regime, began to assume positions of leadership in the unions, to such an extent that the authorities became concerned, and introduced changes into the labor field after 1948. In the countryside a successful democratic base was formed by a program of land reform. In order to eliminate absentee landlords, all land above ten acres per family holding was purchased by the government and sold at advantageous prices and on easy terms to the tenants. Seven and a half acres might be owned by a farmer who cultivated the land, and two and a half acres only by a person who rented out the land. This law of 1946 resulted in a more contented farming population, and in the reduction of tenancy from nearly half to one-tenth of the farmers. The big landlords, no longer so dominant in the economic and social spheres, lost some of their political power to manipulate the village vote. In this respect the success of the Japanese land reform may be considered a model for underdeveloped countries, though it must be admitted that such results would not have been possible in Japan without the considerable advances in democracy made prior to World War II.

SCAP also arranged for antimonopoly legislation directed against the commercial empires of the *zaibatsu*. Eighty-three holding companies were broken up and family fortunes confiscated by a capital levy. In education, compulsory schooling was increased from six to nine years and new textbooks written embodying democratic rather than authoritarian trends. Emphasis was directed away from official dogma and toward the training of children to reach their own conclusions and form their own convictions. Courses in morality and ethics were dropped and courses in social science substituted for them. American policy in this last respect may have gone beyond the point of wisdom and contributed to the malaise and uncertainty of postwar Japan. Japan was used to a state orthodoxy, while America rejects any such thing. Yet social science provides no way of life to live by.

The imprint of American ideas is clearly to be seen in the educational reforms and in such important documents as the constitution. Yet these ideas found a strong echo in the minds of the Japanese themselves, for they were seeking something very different from the ideology behind the former *kokutai* or "national polity" of the days before the war. An impressive, though unofficial, delegation of seventy leaders of politics, industry, and labor left Japan to visit Europe and the United States in 1947. The delegation was received on the floor of Congress in Washington, and in Berlin and London presented to the mayors of these cities small crosses made of olive wood from the heart of a blasted tree near the epicenter of the Hiroshima bomb explosion, in token of the need for reconciliation. When they set out the Prime Minister reminded them that former delegations had gone abroad in Meiji times to return with Western technical know-how, but he asked them to try to find out how democracy worked in practice, and what was its spiritual basis. He was aware that a democratic constitution on paper was of little use unless men had the spirit which would make it function.

Although the period of occupation was not yet halfway over, a marked change came upon the international scene in the years 1948–50, which in turn had its effect on Japanese-American relations. In 1948 Manchuria fell to the Chinese Communists and in the next year Chiang Kai-shek was forced to flee the mainland and set up his government in Taiwan. Positions were being defined in the cold war and Japan was moving from the role of a former enemy to that of a needed ally for America. By 1950 the United Nations, with America in the van, were at war with North Korea and Communist China. General MacArthur oversaw the civilian government of Japan, but he was also commander-in-chief of the American forces in the whole Pacific area, and his responsibility all along had been primarily to the Defense Department and only in the second place to the Department of State in Washington. In light of the realities of world power-politics some far-reaching alterations were made in American policies. Successive Japanese governments accepted these alterations as necessary, but many Japanese regarded them as cynically opportunist. Thus was built up a resentment against America which was exploited by the Japanese political left, and which has persisted in varying degrees right up to the present.

In the first place, American authorities encouraged the growth of the Self-Defense Forces of Japan, in police reserves and in land, sea, and air arms, in spite of Article 9 of the constitution renouncing war. Action against the *zaibatsu* was abandoned and the dismantling of plants ceased. Retrenchment and government economy were instituted on American advice. One hundred thousand government workers were laid off. A no-strike law was passed for civil service and industrial workers, and, although a Public Arbitration Board was set up, SCAP would not back up the decision of this board in the case of a railroad workers' strike in 1948. The result was that the workers received a raise of only 3 percent and not the 25 percent which the board had recommended. Some government saving was undoubtedly necessary in an overextended economy, but the angle of view had shifted. Defense and rapid recovery had taken the place of demilitarization and democratization as the primary goals. Labor agitation was now dangerous and left-wing radicals had to be controlled. In one respect, however,

America provided a valuable object lesson in the working of democracy and the superiority of the civil over the military power, even in wartime. President Truman, to the astonishment of the Japanese, dismissed General MacArthur in 1951 because of the General's expressed wish to carry the war into Manchurian territory in spite of the President's instructions to the contrary. His replacement as Supreme Commander was General Matthew Ridgway.

The march of events indicated above made it desirable to conclude a peace treaty with Japan, but when this was attempted through the channels of the Far Eastern Commission, Stalin and Chiang Kai-shek objected. President Truman then appointed the international attorney John Foster Dulles to make individual approaches to the various nations concerned. Dulles worked hard during 1950 and 1951. By September of the latter year the representatives of 52 countries gathered in San Francisco to sign a peace whose terms had been in the main settled already. Russia tried to confuse and divide the delegations, but all signed save Russia, India, and mainland China. Japan renounced her claims to Korea, Formosa, the Pescadores, the Kuriles, South Sakhalin, and the former Pacific mandated islands. Reparations were to be negotiated with the separate countries who wished to receive them. Both the Peace Treaty and the whole occupation policy were nonpunitive and nonvindictive. Prime Minister Yoshida Shigeru was satisfied that the treaty was "fair and generous," and made it clear that Japan aligned herself with the non-Communist world. At the same time as the signing of the Peace Treaty, America and Japan concluded a Security Treaty, which provided for the stationing of United States forces in and around Japan for purposes of the internal and external security of the country. A separate agreement to resume diplomatic relations with Russia was signed in 1956, and at that point Japan was admitted to the United Nations.

A review of the economy of Japan shows phenomenal growth in the postwar years, once the initial difficulties were overcome. As in the Meiji era, economic growth was fostered by a combination of government and private enterprise. United States assistance, both governmental and private, was of decisive importance. The Japanese banks have made commercial loans easy to acquire, and the government has offered tax incentives and high depreciation allowances. The overall rate of economic growth averaged 10 percent annually from 1950 up to 1965, with a high of 12.1 percent in 1963 and a low of 7.5 percent in 1965. Comparative figures for other countries' growth are West Germany, 6.1 percent; France, 5.3 percent; England, 2.4 percent; and the United States, 2.3 percent. The gross national product, only $1.3 billion in 1946, rose to $15.1 billion in 1951, and then in an upward surge more than tripled to $51.9 billion in 1962, and shot up to $167 billion in 1968.

The story of the average Japanese wage earner is told by the figures for per capita real income. If 100 is taken as an index for the year 1934, he loses half his income in the year after the war (1946, 51.9), and does not clamber back to the original figure until 1954 (99.5); but by 1962 his earning power has more than doubled (215.2). Life expectancy is now sixty-five years for a man, seventy for a woman.

Japan's constantly rising prosperity has undoubtedly favored a conservative trend in politics. All the premiers since the war have been conservative, except Katayama Tetsu, Socialist in politics and Christian in religion, who held office in 1947–48. Yoshida was longest in office (1946–47 and 1948–54) and bridged the period between the Occupation and independence. He was prepared to cooperate with the Occupation authorities out of a genuine conviction that Japan's destiny lay with America and her allies. He retained the support of his countrymen and disarmed some of the opposition by what was known as the "reverse course." This phase, a turning point in Japanese-American relations, was a criticism and modification of some of the occupation policies, which could be seen in Yoshida's plans to control subversive activities, his support of a restructuring of the *zaibatsu*, and his restoration of the police force to a measure of central control. This move toward greater central control and less local autonomy was continued, particularly in the field of education, by Yoshida's rival and successor as premier, Hatoyama Ichiro (1954–56). During his period of office relations with Russia were resumed, trade with Communist China grew in volume, and the divided conservative wing in politics was reunited into the Liberal Democratic party. The next premier to hold office for any length of time was Kishi Nobusuke (1957–60). He was caught in a wave of feeling against American policy, which had already gone through various stages. Beginning in 1952 with the Security Pact and American pressure for Japanese rearmament, it had been notably increased by the incident of the *Lucky Dragon* fishing vessel in 1954. The unfortunate crew of this ship were affected by radiation sickness due to radioactive fallout in the atomic test at the Bikini Atoll. The subsequent explanations were badly handled by the American authorities and Communist propaganda made the very most of the ensuing resentment. Then during Kishi's premiership the Security Treaty came up for review, and he was accused of forcing a renewal of the treaty through the Diet for his own political advantage. So great and so violent were the demonstrations by students in the Zengakuren, a student federation to the left even of the Communist party, that the projected visit of President Eisenhower to Tokyo had to be canceled, and the Kishi government had to resign. Resentment was directed not so much against America as against the Japanese establishment and its ties with America.

Premier Ikeda Hayato (1960–64) then adopted what he called a "low posture" of caution in foreign affairs and concentrated on furthering still greater growth in the Japanese economy. He did not, however, make any fundamental change in policy, and in fact tightened the regulations on internal law and order. When he had to resign the premiership because of illness, Sato Eisaku took over. Sato crowned a number of successes with a visit to President Nixon in November 1969, in which he secured

American agreement to the return of Okinawa to Japanese rule, to become effective in 1972. He was rewarded by seeing his party, the Liberal Democrats, make notable gains in the elections of January 1970 at the expense of the Socialists. In this election the party standings were as follows:

Liberal Democrats	from 272 seats to 300
Socialists	from 134 seats to 90
Komeito (militant Buddhist party)	from 24 seats to 47
Communist party	from 4 seats to 14[2]

[2] *Time* magazine, January 12, 1970.

17

JAPAN AS A WORLD POWER

On a hill high above the harbor of Nagasaki there is a charming small house and garden built in the late nineteenth century for a British engineering advisor to the Japanese, Thomas B. Glover, whose Japanese love became the heroine of Puccini's tragic opera *Madame Butterfly*. From this vantage point, symbolically connecting East and West, one looks down on one side to the former island of Deshima, now landlocked, where the Dutch traders were kept immured and isolated from the year 1641. On the other side the view is quintessential twentieth century, one of vast shipyards with the latest technology (see Plate 31). There the giant supertankers were constructed on such a scale that bow and stern had to be launched separately and welded together in the water.

THE ECONOMIC MIRACLE. Shipbuilding was a part, but only one part, of that powerful industrial advance Japan has made after World War II to the present, often known as "the economic miracle." The Japanese are justifiably proud of what they have achieved; but some do not care for the term "miracle," since the result entailed hard work, concentrated and continuous thought and not a little sacrifice. Japan's economic expansion is the most significant factor in her contemporary history and profoundly influences her politics and society.

The engine of Japanese industry drives this remarkable expansion. How does it work, and how does it differ from industrial organization in the West?

In the first place, workers can, as a rule, look towards lifetime employment in one firm, and are expected to show loyalty by remaining with that firm. If the business prospers, they prosper. It is perceived by the workers to be in their own interest to do their best for the firm's fortunes. The managers, for their part, are expected to retain their employees and not dismiss them, even during a slump. There is therefore under-employment at intervals, but little unemployment. The larger firms provide free recreational facilities for their workers and, in some cases, free housing. Department stores offer classes gratis to employees in flower arrangement, the tea ceremony and other accomplishments considered desirable for young women. Even small firms which do not boast expensive recreation opportunities still recognize the value of the bond between boss and worker. The owner and his wife may take a dozen employees with them for a couple of weeks' free holiday at the seashore. This all seems to a Westerner paternalistic, for we have dark memories of "the company town." But it suits the Japanese style. Her feudal system in the past was founded on personal and family loyalty. Bonds of mutual obligation are woven throughout Japanese life, and these bonds carry over, even in attenuated form, into the economic network. There are company songs, company uniforms, company rewards and company social gatherings. Colleagues from the same firm often go together after work to a bar or restaurant for the evening. The firm is their life to a much greater extent than in the West. This has been the general picture, but changes are taking place, and the tie to the firm as one's family is eroding in some instances.

Lifetime employment carries, almost as a necessary condition, mandatory retirement, else the swelling ranks of workers would grow beyond control. Almost all companies employing more than 100 persons have mandatory retirement, varying between ages fifty-five and sixty. Very few indeed have a cutoff point beyond sixty years of age. Retirement income depends on a considerable proportion of personal savings, on various pension plans, and on social security, which was increased in the last decade but is still at a comparatively low level. Many retirees step almost immediately into another job. A national health service has been in place for some time, which relieves older persons of anxiety over health care.

A second distinguishing feature of Japanese industry is the greater use of subcontracting to small firms, each of which manufactures one part only of the finished product (see page 208). This business structure has grown out of premodern home and village industry, which was greatly expanded under the pressure of military procurement in World War II. It is a practice well known in the West also, particularly in the automobile industry, but has been developed to a higher degree in Japan. The small firm is relieved of certain overhead expenses, as mentioned above, but is also involved in risk, for it becomes entirely dependent on the success—and the goodwill—of the large firm. Since the oil crisis and slump the number of small business bankruptcies has increased. Small enterprises employing fewer than 100 people, some independent and some connected with larger firms, comprise 58 percent of the total business firms of Japan.

A third feature deserving comment is the peculiar nature of Japanese labor unions. These are company unions organized for each enterprise or workplace, and not nationally organized by trades, as in the West. They conduct collective bargaining with the management. Strikes and work stoppages are comparatively infrequent. Recently, however, there has been a period of short but very widespread strikes each spring for higher wages, particularly in the transport sector. Much of union activity consists in simply drawing attention to workers' grievances. Management, on the other hand, pays a good deal of attention to grievance procedures in order to maintain production and preserve group loyalty. Workers' suggestions have often been the means of improving productivity and quality control.

Union membership is not high, comprising only 30 percent of all employed personnel. The figure for the manufacturing industries is 35 percent and for wholesale and retail businesses, the lowest, at 9 percent. The sector with the highest proportion of unionized employees, 62 percent, is that of transport and communications, and it is here that most of the big strikes occur. For example, there were brief but crippling strikes annually in a "labor offensive" that became almost a spring ritual from 1973 through 1976. In one year, 38 million commuters were affected. In another, railroad, postal, telephone, airline, bus and subway workers, as well as teachers, doctors and garbage collectors all went on strike. The pay increases obtained that year, 1974, averaged 30 percent; but after the effects of the recession of 1974 to 1977 were felt, these dropped to about 9 percent. Pay increases in the spring of 1983 were only about 4 percent, since unemployment had risen to 2.5 percent. This is an extremely low figure on an international scale. Indeed some economists consider 2 percent a rate necessary to secure movement in the employment market. But the actual number of unemployed, translated from percentages into human terms, in Japan averaged 1.43 million, and this meant that in fact the workers' expectation of pay raises was low.

The accompanying table of labor costs per hour shows that Japanese firms can afford job security to their labor force and still achieve lower labor costs than those of the United States.

LABOR COSTS PER HOUR IN 1979 IN MAJOR NON-COMMUNIST INDUSTRIAL NATIONS[1]

BELGIUM, SWEDEN, NETHERLANDS, WEST GERMANY, SWITZERLAND, DENMARK	$11.30–12.10
UNITED STATES	9.50
ITALY, CANADA, FRANCE	8.50
JAPAN	6.60
BRITAIN, SPAIN	5.70

[1] Institute of the German Economy, Cologne, 1980.

Japanese workers' wages begin at a low figure and rise with seniority. Average wages earned across the board in an industrialized economy are difficult to assess, but the official government figure for 1980 is given as Yen173,100 per month, or approximately US$752, excluding overtime.[1]

[1] *Facts and Figures of Japan*, Foreign Press Center, 1982, p. 76.

This would amount to just over $9,000 a year; but to this must be added the customary summer and winter bonuses, which usually amount to almost four months' wages, or an added $3,000, which yields a total annual wage of about $12,000.

A fourth point which distinguishes the Japanese industrial economy from those of other nations is the high rate of savings in Japan. The money saved from immediate consumption is available for re-investment in industry and leads to still further growth. The household savings rate in Japan from 1961 to 1979 was running between 18.2 percent and 22.1 percent. In the same years in the United States the high figure was 8.8 percent and the low 5.4 percent.

The ploughing back of profits into new capital equipment has had a direct effect upon productivity, and every year has seen a steady rise in the productive capacity of Japanese industry. To secure the needed capital various means have been used, among others heavy borrowing, payment of low dividends to shareholders and carefully planned inventory holdings. In 1971 there was a report that a typical Japanese firm owned only 20 percent of the capital it employed and borrowed on short or long terms the remaining 80 percent, a practice which would lead to executive heart attack in the United States. A study of the rates of return on stock markets in New York and Frankfurt has shown an average yield of about 4 percent in recent years, contrasted with 1.5 percent in dividends paid by major Japanese firms. Inventory overhead is also kept low. A large Nagasaki shipyard in 1971 was keeping only five days' supply of steel on hand. Apparently the steel supplier could be completely relied upon to make regular deliveries on time. These methods of operation, large loans and small stockpiles, contribute to a certain nervousness and a febrile activity among Japanese businessmen striving for ever-expanding economic growth.

A fifth key factor in Japanese industry is the close cooperation between the government, management and labor. This was a crucial necessity in the rebuilding of Japan after the war, and has continued since then. It may be now the chief form in which Japanese patriotism and solidarity display themselves since the military form fell into disfavor. Japan's success has given rise to considerable resentment abroad, and the common tendency is to blame the part played by the government in the partnership. The chief though not the only arm of government involved is the Ministry of International Trade and Industry, known in Japanese as well as in English by its acronym, MITI. It plays a role in identifying international markets and in research and development. MITI also recommends to government banks the granting of venture capital to certain industries considered vital to the national interest at a given point. The total funds expended by Japan for research and industrial expansion may be no more than that supplied, directly or indirectly, in the United States; but it is more deliberately and accurately targeted. Where MITI is most effective is in securing consensus between government, labor and management on the problems and the direction of industrial development. A cumbersome bureaucratic system at various levels proceeds through compromise to eventual agreement. But the final consensus tends to be solid and faithfully maintained.

The above holds true between the different sectors of the bureaucracy and industry. But within the industrial field itself there is often fierce rivalry and competition. The desire to get ahead, individually and corporately, has led to business scandals of considerable proportions, made worse by the very political business ties we have been discussing. The most notorious of these was the Lockheed scandal which erupted in 1976 but concerned transactions made earlier. Apparently Yoshio Kodama, a right-wing so-called "lobbyist," and incidentally a former war-criminal, had funneled from the Lockheed Corporation some $7 million to various business and political figures in order to void a McDonnell-Douglas option for the sale of civilian aircraft and to secure the contract for Lockheed Tristar planes. Prime Minister Miki had to resign over the scandal, though not himself involved, and Tanaka, the former prime minister, was among those indicted and ultimately found guilty. The Japanese took the matter seriously and tried and convicted top political and business figures. This fact should be taken into account, if we are to assess correctly Lockheed's insistence that bribery was necessary when dealing with foreign countries like Japan.

Many attempts have been made to account for the economic success of Japan in the years since 1945. One that is succinct and close to the mark is that of Ardath W. Burks: "Japan's high growth rate was a product of the rate of investment, the high quality of the labor force, the acumen in business organization, and the diffusion of technology."[2] Although the lead in many areas of science and technology has come from America and from European countries, Japan has applied and developed the techniques involved. In some fields the technological leadership remains with Western countries, but is being challenged by Japan.

Automation of the steel industry is advanced in Japan (see Plate 35). Industrial robots are in wide use in the automobile and other industries; indeed Japan is now among the leaders in their manufacture. Laser technology has also been given great attention, to the extent that some military devices embodying lasers have been acquired by the United States from Japan. The United States leads Japan in basic biological research, but the commercial application of gene-splicing techniques is being very actively pursued in Japan. This will affect the production of new drugs and foods, medical, agricultural and chemical products, and new ways to dispose of toxic waste materials. Advances in the computer field are perhaps the most notable of all. Japanese companies have moved from the 64K chip for Random Access Memory (RAM) and are already selling 256K memory chips (256,000 plus bits). The Japanese have embarked on research in the megabit range, with over a million bits, the equivalent of 22,000 words on one small chip. IBM is in the race, for they announced their megabit chip

---

[2] Burks, Ardath W. (*Japan—Profile of a Post-Industrial Power*, Boulder: Westview Press, 1981), p. 159.

in April 1984. Japan is also offering a serious challenge in the field of supercomputers, which are used at present mainly for problems in science that involve billions of calculations, and which cost anything up to $15 million. In 1983 there were only seventy-five of them in existence. The new supercomputers being designed by the Japanese will be compatible with IBM software, and will work 100 times as fast as the present machines. But if you want something smaller and less expensive, you could always ask for the latest Seiko wristwatch, which incorporates a TV screen of 1.2 inches diagonal and is activated not with a tube but with a liquid crystal video system.

High technology is not a luxury but a necessity for Japan. For an island country with limited natural resources to survive in the comtemporary world it is necessary for its manufacture to have a very high value-added factor—that is, more and more skill, knowledge and sophistication must be added to less and less raw material in the course of making a product, if that product is to be sold at a high profit. That profit is required in order to pay for the import of scarce raw materials and to maintain the standard of living to which the new society has become accustomed. This was the case in Great Britain in the nineteenth and twentieth centuries, and is the case in Japan today to an even greater degree.

Sociologists distinguish three stages of development, the primary, where work is mainly agricultural; the secondary, where it is industrial; and the tertiary, where the workers are engaged in highly skilled and service jobs such as communication, transport, finance, trade, management, information systems and so on. The first stage is labor-intensive; the second, capital-intensive; and the third, knowledge-intensive. This last stage has been named the post-industrial society.[3]

The Japanese recognize clearly that they have reached the third stage, and that other countries are pressing on their heels. Japanese labor costs have now become so high that the economy has lost the former market edge due to cheap labor. Signs of the future are to be seen in an interesting table published by the Japanese government entitled "Asian NICs Catch Up with Japan in the U.S. Market." NICs stands for Newly Industrializing Countries, and these are listed (in Asia) as South Korea, Taiwan, Singapore and Hongkong. Among the products for export in which they have caught up with Japan are toys, footwear, apparel and leather goods; those in which they are about to catch up include textiles, radios and TVs, and watches.[4] Japanese managers are now setting up branch factories in these countries in order to take advantage of lower wages combined with the traditional Asian workers' willingness to work hard and to learn new skills. Wage scales are rising rapidly in the NICs also, and other countries, characterized by the Japanese as "semi-industrializing," such as the Philippines, Thailand, and Malaysia, as well as China, are waiting in the wings.

[3] Here I am indebted to the analysis of Burks, op. cit., p. 169.
[4] MITI White Paper on International Trade, 1982.

The beginnings of Japan's remarkable industrial expansion have been briefly traced in the preceding chapter (see pp. 207–8). In the decade after 1955 growth in the gross national product (GNP) averaged over 10 percent a year, and in 1968 moved past that of West Germany, becoming second in the free world after that of the United States. In 1965 the Japanese GNP was only 10 percent that of the United States, but by 1980 had reached 40 percent of the American figure.

THE OIL SHOCK. Japan's success is the more impressive when one considers the country's heavy dependence on outside sources of raw materials, in particular oil, which must be imported. Japan's oil bill for the year 1978, for example, was $23.4 billion, and this rose the next year to $33.5 billion, because of a 14.5 percent increase in oil prices. At the point of the "oil shock" in 1973–74, Japan was receiving 83 percent of her oil supply from the Arab countries and Iran. (Later, in 1980, she secured some oil from elsewhere, notably Mexico and Venezuela.) The oil crisis and consequent inflation affected all the countries of the world, but bore very hard on Japan and entailed difficult political as well as economic choices. In November of 1973 the Arab nations tried to get Japan to cut off diplomatic and trade relations with Israel and agree to supply the Arab nations with arms. In return for this Japan would be declared a "friendly nation" and receive uninterrupted supplies of oil. Japan refused. The government had already put into operation an anti-inflation plan, tightened credit, instituted emergency petroleum regulations and frozen the price of rice. The budget for 1974 was called an "austerity budget," but did not entirely deserve the name as it was still higher than that of the previous year. Inflation, however, running at 19.1 percent, was a serious problem for Japan. It was characterized by the Organization for Economic Coop-

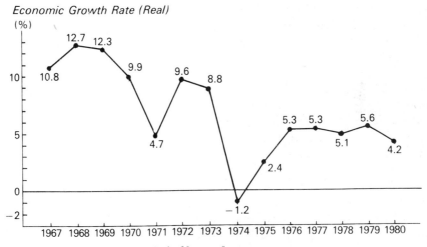

Economic Growth Rate (Real)

Comparative International Statistics, Bank of Japan, 1981.

In the accompanying graph, which shows Japan's economic growth rate between 1967 and 1980, the dip in 1971 was due largely to worldwide currency fluctuations, and the more severe drop in 1974 to the oil crisis.

eration and Development (OECD) as having reached "unprecedented and clearly intolerable rates." And in 1974 Japan had a record balance of deficit payments, due mainly to the high price of oil.

The situation improved markedly from 1976 to 1978, and inflation rates dropped to 3.5 percent. An increase in Japan's favorable trade balance even led to problems with the United States; Prime Minister Fukuda promised President Carter in mid-1978 to make "massive efforts" to reduce the trade surplus and hold down exports. Japan was doing too well. Pressure was brought to bear on her at the Bonn economic summit meeting in the same year, 1978, and these promises had to be renewed on subsequent occasions. But the oil supply was a constant problem, and the nation showed a balance of deficit payments again in 1979.

The Venice summit meeting in 1980 aimed "to break the existing link between economic growth and the consumption of oil," and stressed the necessity of expanding the use of nuclear energy. Japan already had 21 nuclear power plant units operating in 1980. Eleven additional units were then under construction and three more planned, which in all would increase output by two-thirds.

MADE IN JAPAN. After the oil crisis, exports of steel, automobiles and electrical appliances continued to climb while imports remained steady because Japan's domestic economy was recovering only slowly. This raised the favorable trade balance to levels unacceptable to other countries. Japan had made some efforts to correct the trade imbalance by reducing high import duties on steel, clothing, home appliances, cars and farm products. The last was a particularly sensitive item, and millions of signatures reached the Japanese government from farmers requesting protection. But at the beginning of the 1980's the United States and the European Community (EC) both demanded with renewed urgency that Japan narrow the gap in trade by increasing imports, especially of agricultural products, and by exercising voluntary restraints on exports. The trade surplus with the United States alone reached $13.4 billion in 1981, almost twice the level of

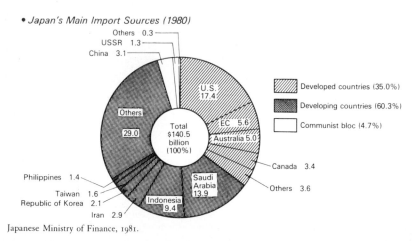

• *Japan's Main Import Sources (1980)*

Others 0.3
USSR 1.3
China 3.1

U.S. 17.4
Others 29.0
Total $140.5 billion (100%)
EC 5.6
Australia 5.0

Developed countries (35.0%)
Developing countries (60.3%)
Communist bloc (4.7%)

Canada 3.4

Philippines 1.4
Taiwan 1.6
Republic of Korea 2.1
Iran 2.9
Indonesia 9.4
Saudi Arabia 13.9
Others 3.6

Japanese Ministry of Finance, 1981.

[218]

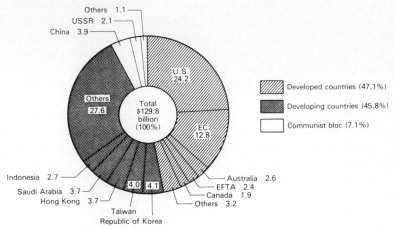

• *Japan's Main Export Markets (1980)*

Others 1.1
USSR 2.1
China 3.9

U.S. 24.2

Others 27.6

Total
$129.8
billion
(100%)

EC 12.8

Developed countries (47.1%)
Developing countries (45.8%)
Communist bloc (7.1%)

Indonesia 2.7
Saudi Arabia 3.7
Hong Kong 3.7
Taiwan
Republic of Korea
4.0 4.1

Australia 2.6
EFTA 2.4
Canada 1.9
Others 3.2

Japanese Ministry of Finance, 1981.

the previous year. In order to increase imports the Japanese government, without reducing tariffs, abolished non-tariff trade barriers in 1982 in sixty-seven different measures designed to ease customs regulations, and it opened an Office of Trade Ombudsman to handle complaints from foreign companies. This did not have much effect, for whatever reasons, since imports of U.S. goods in 1982 still went down by 4.5 percent.

Trade wars or trade disputes can be bitter and long drawn out, but they usually stop short of total breakdown in relations, since merchants are pragmatic and both sides want to continue trading. Japan's remarkable success story has brought with it numerous problems, but none of these has ended by checking her advance or rupturing relations with her trading partners. It is instructive to note both the progress and the problems in a few specific areas of trade.

First, cars and trucks. From 1955 onwards the German Volkswagen was the firm selling the highest number of cars imported into the United States. The Japanese Datsun began selling in the United States in 1960, and by 1975 had replaced Volkswagen as the leader in sales. In 1976 Japan's export of cars to all markets was the highest in the world, followed by France with a 33 percent lower total. Of the foreign cars purchased in the United States that year 62 percent were made in Japan. The U.S. Department of commerce attributed the popularity of Japanese cars to their "competitive prices, reputation for quality and efficient sales networks." At this point the U.S. production of automobiles was greater than that of Japan, but by the middle of 1980 Japan became the largest producer of cars and trucks in the world.

America, not surprisingly, reacted. Douglas Fraser, president of the United Automobile Workers, called the conduct of Toyota and Nissan "outrageous—exporting not just cars but unemployment to the United States." He said Japanese car manufacturers should be compelled by law

[219]

to build cars in the United States. Two hundred thousand American auto workers were unemployed in 1980. Douglas Fraser visited Japan to persuade firms there to set up production in the United States or limit the number of cars exported, at the same time warning them that they risked future barriers of protectionist legislation. Honda announced the planned building of an assembly plant in Ohio, and Nissan and Toyota were said to be making similar moves. The Japanese government, to stave off American legislation, announced in June of 1981 that it would place voluntary limits on car exports to the United States for two years, and this was finally extended to four years.

An American government study of the whole question released in July of 1982 stated that U.S. auto production was weakened by a management style that was basically adversarial and control-oriented, which ". . . inspires no loyalty or commitment. Japan's success in capturing so much of the U.S. car market is due less to superior technology and more to better management." The debate thus occasioned still continues.

Trade in other major Japanese products for export, such as textiles, steel and TV sets, followed a similar pattern. We shall take the United States, as Japan's largest customer, for our example. But the pattern holds true for other areas such as Europe. Japanese success and a rising U.S. demand for the product is followed by complaints from American manufacturers. The U.S. government holds an inquiry, sometimes long drawn out, and then enacts anti-dumping laws and imposes restriction and fines. Japan responds by cutting down exports or building factories in the United States, and goes on selling the product.

The height of the crisis in textile trading occurred about 1970. Major problems in steel began before 1970 and are still going on. In steel, for example, import quotas were in place in 1970, and in 1976 President Ford threatened further quotas unless negotiators on both sides could come to a rapid agreement. President Carter the next year said vigorous endorsement would be given to laws against "dumping" steel, *i.e.* selling it abroad at a price below the domestic figure. Japanese producers claimed they were able to offer steel at a lower price in America than the American firms, because their technology and their management practices were superior to those of the United States. Inland Steel, the most profitable of the U.S. firms, decided in 1977 to have Japanese experts build them a new "superfurnace." This was said to be the first entirely new furnace in the United States since World War II, while in that period Nippon Kokan had built thirteen new furnaces, each larger and more efficient than the previous one. The problem refused to go away, and in 1978 the Carter administration introduced a new device, the trigger price system for steel, based on a best estimate of Japanese production costs plus reasonable profit. If the import sale price in the United States fell below this, a process of extra heavy duties would be invoked, sufficient to make the sales in the United States unprofitable. The trigger price has from time to time been raised as production costs have risen.

As far as television sets are concerned, the electrical unions in the United States were seeking damages against Japanese TV manufacturers in 1971, and complaints widened during the next year on the grounds that Japan was granting undue subsidies to TV exporters to the United States. By 1977 three out of the five major Japanese producers already had factories in the United States. Sony, in fact, derived 67 percent of its annual sales in this period from sets made in America. Toshiba had a factory in Nashville, Tennessee, and Hitachi arranged a joint manufacturing agreement with General Electric. But all this did not prevent attempts to evade the law. The U.S. Treasury in 1979 fined thirty-eight U.S. subsidiaries and agents of Japanese firms $40.7 million for dumping.

These recurring problems in the control of trade adversely affected labor, management and shareholders in the United States; but, the general public in America gained from better quality and lower prices, while the Japanese public gained from higher living standards.

The pattern of Japanese trade expansion was, of course, to be seen not only in the United States, but also in Europe and worldwide. Japan made an agreement with the European Economic Community (EEC) in 1972 in which it was stipulated that the EEC members would permit a rise for that year only of 12 percent in the importation of Japanese textiles and would abolish arbitrary quotas. The dumping of steel was a problem in Europe as in America, and in 1978 the EEC took measures to counter it by imposing penalties. Honda entered into an arrangement with British Leyland to manufacture a model in Britain, and Nissan secured Italian government approval to operate a factory near Naples in conjunction with Alfa-Romeo. The Italian Fiat firm was not pleased.

One should not consider that these expensive mergers and joint arrangements are in any way limited to the Japanese. They are an international phenomenon in which the businesses of many nations play a part. What has attracted so much notice, favorable and unfavorable, to the operations of the Japanese is, first, their meteoric rise, concentrated in so short a period of time, and second, the energy and worldwide expansion of a country only the size of California. (Its population, however, at 119 million is by no means small.)

The Japanese have attached great importance to trade with the countries of Latin America. Many of them were granted development loans and technical assistance by Japan, but Peru appears to have been given more than usual attention. Oil in Peru, Mexico, Venezuela and elsewhere was for obvious reasons a high priority. The other countries bordering the Pacific are naturally of great importance to Japanese business. Australia is in a sense a special case, as an instance of a country in the Western group that supplies Japan with raw materials and foodstuffs only, and receives technology and investment from Japan. This was the rationale of agreements between prime ministers Whitlam and Tanaka in 1973, and again between Fraser and Ohira in 1980. Australia has been for a long time Japan's chief supplier of meat and wool, and has also shipped large quantities of wheat.

Australian coal and iron ore are vital elements in the supply of Japanese industry. In the other direction, Mitsubishi was a major partner in the building of a pipeline serving the city of Sydney, New South Wales. The same firm in 1979 acquired a one-third share in Chrysler Australia. Toyota produces auto engines in Australia, and Nissan built a plant there under a rule that requires 85 percent of products sold to be made in Australia. Japan is Australia's largest trading partner, and this is greatly to Australia's advantage. The steady Japanese demand for coal, for example, enabled the Australians to open new coal mines in Queensland and Western Australia.

The trade of Japan with the U.S.S.R. and Eastern Europe is not of major importance in terms of quantity. Exports to these countries comprise only 3.2 percent of Japan's total, and imports from them 1.6 percent. Difficulties arise even with this small amount of trade, as in a quarrel over exploration for oil and natural gas in Sakhalin. The channels of trade do not run smoothly.

The situation with trade between China and Japan is different. The two countries have had a long love-hate relationship, and yet they belong together and have a deep, underlying consciousness that they need each other. When the Tokugawa regime effectively closed Japan to outside intercourse in the seventeenth century, our history books stress that only the Dutch were allowed to trade from the little enclave of Deshima. We tend to forget that trade with China and Korea continued through Japan's southern island, Kyushu, although under stricter supervision than before. In the contemporary period the feelings engendered by the long and bitter struggle between the two nations before and during World War II made the resumption of relations difficult. But Japan's desire for trade and investment opportunities, and her paramount thirst for oil, along with China's recent determination to modernize, with the accompanying need for technology and capital, have combined to promote a growing interchange of trade. The contrasting Japanese views of Russia and China are revealed in a paragraph from an official publication:

> The Soviet Union and the East European countries are plagued with stagnating investment and production bottlenecks. On the other hand, China is vigorously pushing ahead with an economic adjustment program.[5]

China announced in 1975 that she was prepared to increase sales of petroleum to Japan, and later to export natural gas. The importation of oil from China was soon great enough to offer serious competition to another of Japan's suppliers, Indonesia.[6] Trade between China and Japan declined by 20 percent in the slump of 1974 to 1976, but by 1978 both powers had entered into an ambitious new trade pact. This was further

[5] Japanese MITI White Paper, 1982, p. 12.
[6] Japanese trade with South-East Asia has been significant for several centuries and into modern times. Imports into Japan from Indonesia, mainly oil, now amount to almost 10 percent of total imports.

discussed the next year when Prime Minister Ohira visited Peking. The talks covered economic, technical and cultural fields. Preferential tariff treatment was extended to China as a developing country. Japan announced she was prepared to grant loans and technical assistance for railway, port and hydro-electric construction, and for the development of offshore oil drilling. This, in turn, would enable Japan to import more coal and oil from China. In 1980 Japan was China's largest trading partner with 32.6 percent of China's export trade. Yet Japan's exports to China comprised only 3.9 percent of her large world trade.

But the trading road became rather rocky. China did not have much modern experience in estimating and contracting. The Japanese were shocked in early 1981 when China cancelled a $1.5 billion contract for steel and petrochemical plants owing to shortage of oil revenues. China was unwilling to abandon the projects altogether, and after some delay Japan agreed to a loan of $1.38 billion for a steel mill and a petrochemical plant.

POLITICS. The present prime minister of Japan, Nakasone Yasuhiro, when elected in 1982 announced as his policy, "to foster ties with the United States," and "to strengthen national defense." If these two aims are combined with a third, the strong emphasis of early postwar prime ministers on building up economic strength and increasing the GNP (see pp. 207–8), one has a summary of the main objectives of the ruling Liberal Democratic Party over the years. These objectives can be seen as a natural development of LDP policy, and one which enjoys sufficient support from the people of Japan to have remained generally steady over nearly 40 years.

The turn after World War II towards a general agreement with the United States and the free enterprise system follows logically from Japan's recent past. Once again it is evident that history determines politics, even though the participants, the people and their leaders, may be only subliminally influenced and scarcely aware of what is going on. Japan at the very end of the sixteenth century, with civil war threatening ruin to her economy, submitted finally to the Tokugawa regime, which brought peace at the price of severe standardization and control over a period of two and a half centuries. Japan in this way had a chance to recover and build inner reserves of strength and leadership. When contact with the West and modernization began in the mid-nineteenth century, there was already a trend towards commercial development and capital formation (see p. 170). Even in the militaristic period of the 1930's and 1940's, which so confused and angered the West, a search for raw materials, new markets, and commercial opportunities was a part of the drive for empire. Once peace was restored and the economy rebuilt with some help from America, it was highly likely that Japan would continue on the path of modernization and economic growth, and almost as a corollary, alliance with the Western democratic nations.

Thus the Liberal Democratic Party, conservative despite its name, was constantly returned to power. The party standings in the Diet in 1982 were as follows:

Diet Members by Party (February 1, 1982)

HOUSE OF REPRESENTATIVES		HOUSE OF COUNCILLORS	
PARTY	MEM-BERS	PARTY	MEM-BERS
Liberal Democratic Party	287	Liberal Democratic Party	136
Japan Socialist Party	104	Japan Socialist Party	47
Komeito	34	Komeito	27
Democratic Socialist Party	32	Japan Communist Party	12
Japan Communist Party	29	Democratic Socialist Party	11
New Liberal Club	} 13	Shinsei Club	7
United Social Democratic Party[1]		Dainiin Club	3
Independent	7	Ichi no Kai	3
Vacancies	5	Independent	3
		Vacancies	3
Total	511	Total	252

[1] Note: These two parties have joined forces within the House of Representatives.

Facts and Figures of Japan, Foreign Press Center, 1982, p. 32.

Comparing this table with the figures for the Lower House in 1970 (see p. 209), it is clear that the Liberal Democrats and the Komeito have suffered a decline in numbers, while the Socialist and Communist parties have gained. In any event, the Liberal Democrats have been able to control the government continuously from shortly after the end of World War II until the present.

This control of late has not been easily maintained. The chief opposition has come from the Socialists, usually supported by the trade unions. The opposition would have been more effective had there not been such division within its ranks. But the opposition has also drawn strength from other varied sources: youth disillusioned with old-style establishment politics; those concerned with the rise of defense forces, which they feel is contrary to the Peace Article 9 in the constitution; environmentalists opposing pollution; some small businessmen and government employees; those protesting political and business scandals; and a considerable proportion of women who feel the effects of inflation.

Opposition members of the Diet boycotted the sessions in 1973 and forced the resignation of two members of government, while in 1980 the LDP was defeated in a confidence motion in the Lower House for failing to deal with inflation and government corruption. The most violent action against the government occurred in protests by farmers and students over the expropriation of land for the building of the new Narita Airport outside Tokyo. A concrete redoubt and a steel tower on a runway were built by the demonstrators, and a pitched battle with the police took place, reminiscent of the 60's, in which 5,000 on each side used clubs, shields, stones, spears and bottles of gasoline, resulting in heavy casualties. The airport was eventually opened to traffic. The elections of 1983 registered another loss for the LDP. They required the help of a small, splinter conservative group and some independents to remain in power.

The brokerage of power goes on in Japan, as it does everywhere in one form or another. In Japan, although the LDP continues as the dominant party, power groups within it rise in turn to the surface, headed by eminent political figures, each with their loyal following. The leaders are men such as Sato Eisaku (the longest-serving postwar prime minister), Fukuda Takeo, and Ohiro Masayoshi allied with Suzuki Zenko, among others. One of the most powerful, to whom the present prime minister, Nakasone Yasuhiro owes much, is Tanaka Kakuei. Tanaka has been involved in several scandals (see p. 217), and once had to resign as prime minister. But he has used patronage skillfully and has bluff qualities that appeal to his followers and his constituency. After the lengthy Lockheed trial he was found guilty in the fall of 1983 and condemned to four years' imprisonment and a fine in the official amount of the bribes received, $2 million, but appealed the sentence. In spite of nationwide protests he has refused to resign his seat in the Diet, and continues to be an influential political figure. Yet, because the press is powerful and the Japanese are the greatest newspaper reading public in the world, none of the above should be interpreted as the demise of democracy in Japan. On the contrary, the popular will is able to assert itself in Japan as in no other Asian country.

FOREIGN RELATIONS. Japan's foreign relations are intimately bound up with her economic expansion, already discussed. There are also purely diplomatic aspects. After the war Japan maintained what her own leaders called a "low posture." But in recent years the nation has shown much more confidence and assertiveness based on solid performance, while at the same time experiencing admiration, misunderstanding and resentment, in varying degrees, from other nations. There is an increasing desire in Japan for independence from the United States, although the government recognizes the need to maintain close ties. The decennial question of renewal of the U.S.-Japan security treaty was controversial in 1960 (see p. 209) and in 1970. In the latter year the government of Japan raised no objection to the treaty's automatic extension, but there were nine days of large-scale and violent demonstrations nationwide by 750,000 people, and 600 were arrested. Then came the "Nixon shock," when President Nixon visited China without any prior consultation with or warning to the Japanese. A chagrined Prime Minister Sato, watching Nixon's arrival in Peking on television, remarked in an acid tone, "It must be an historic event, since he himself says so."

But there were solid reasons for a rising morale. Japan was admitted as a full member to the Asia Development Bank and then to the International Development Bank. In a major address in New York, Henry Kissinger proposed "a new Atlantic Charter," which "creates for the Atlantic nations a new relationship whose progress Japan can share." The Atlantic community cannot be "an exclusive club," and Japan must be "a principal partner in our common enterprise." It mattered not that these words contained no concrete proposal; they were what Japan needed and deserved to hear.

The relations of Japan with the People's Republic of China, as indicated above, were cautious for some time. Zhou Enlai then said, in 1971, that the Japanese must recognize the People's Republic as the sole legitimate government of China, that Taiwan was a part of the sacred territory of the PRC, and that the Japan-Taiwan treaty must be abrogated without fail. These conditions were met by Japan the next year and the two countries agreed to end a state of war and enter into diplomatic relations. Prime Minister Tanaka expressed "regret and repentance for past aggression" against China, and said their countries should "not forever linger in the dim, blind alley of the past, but confer in the interest of tomorrow." China agreed not to make any claim on Japan for reparations.

Relations with Russia were not so cordial. Peace talks were initiated in 1972 but came to an impasse almost at once over Japan's claim to the Kurile Islands and Russia's refusal to return them, or, indeed, to give up fortifying the southern islands in the chain. Later China and Russia were rivals for a pact with Japan, and Prime Minister Miki Takeo leaned towards China. A ten-year treaty of peace and friendship between China and Japan was signed in 1978, after China had agreed to soften the wording of a clause directed against "Soviet hegemony."

FOREIGN AID. One way which Japan has abandoned her low posture and has become more active in world affairs has been in her increased budget for foreign aid. She has made large loans to South Korea, the People's Republic of China and nations in South-East Asia. As with all foreign aid and technical assistance, benefit generally accrues in the end to the donor nation, and so Japan has been particularly interested in her Pacific neighbors. But aid has also been given to Latin American countries, to Zimbabwe, and especially to Pakistan, in rice for flood relief and in a loan and technical assistance for agriculture, fisheries and telecommunications.

The figures for an international comparison of foreign aid in 1980 show that in dollar terms Japan ranks fourth in the world among donor nations, after the United States, France and West Germany, and ahead of Great Britain and Canada. If the aid is recknoned as a percentage of GNP, there is an interesting change in the order. Then Japan is fifth, with 0.32 percent, after France (0.62 percent), West Germany, Canada and Great Britain. The United States stands low, in sixth place, with 0.27 percent.

DEFENSE. The famous Article 9 of the Constitution of 1947 (see p. 204) says, "the Japanese people, forever, renounce war as a sovereign right of the nation," but some means of self-defense was maintained from the beginning of the post-war period. In a reversal of policy at the time of the

Korean War the U.S. authorities actively encouraged a build-up of Japanese defense forces (see p. 206). By 1971 the Japanese Self-Defense Agency (SDA) had obtained from the government a promise of $14 billion for the next five years, more than double the amount spent in the previous five-year period. This raised Japan to seventh place in the world in defense expenditure.

Soon after this residents of Naganuma in Hokkaido brought a suit against the construction of a missile base in a forest preserve. The court in Sapporo found in their favor on the grounds that Article 9 contains the phrase, "land, sea and air forces, as well as other war potential, will never be maintained." The government's interpretation of the Constitution is that the right of self-defense is inherent in a sovereign state, and is recognized by Article 51 of the United Nations Charter. Armed action, however, must be purely defensive, and this precludes the use of ICBMs, long-range bombers, and the despatch of overseas forces. Japan maintains no military nuclear capability.

In 1980 the United States again urged Japan to increase expenditure for her share of the common defense above the existing 0.9 percent of GNP. But U.S. Ambassador Mike Mansfield pointed out at the same time that Japan was spending more on defense than most NATO countries. She had increased expenditure 8 percent a year for ten years, compared to 2 percent increase in NATO and 2 percent decrease in the United States over the same period, though admittedly starting from a very much lower base. The Japanese Cabinet approved an increase of 9.7 percent in defense, the only department of the goverment to exceed the 7.5 percent budget limit allowed in 1980. This increase was due to anxiety over the Soviet military build-up of land, sea and air forces in eastern Siberia, their military presence in the Kurile Islands, and their use of naval bases in Vietnam. Fear of Russia increased further in 1983 when SS-20 medium range missiles were stationed in eastern Siberia, even though Soviet officials claimed these were not aimed at Japan, but were there as a counterforce to U.S. seaborne missiles in the north-west Pacific Ocean.

A large group of business and government leaders in 1982 proposed changes in the Security Treaty with the United States to make Japan more independent of American help and to bring defense expenditure into line with the actual financial position of the two countries. They pointed out that the GNP of Japan in 1960, at the time of the original treaty, was only 8 percent of the United States, whereas now it was 50 percent. In the same year the defense budget for 1984 was set to increase by 7.34 percent, while most other sections of the budget were lowered by 5 percent.

The defense budgets and the conservative party and business support for them are very unpopular with many of the groups mentioned in the political opposition above (see p. 225). There is widespread determination that Japan will under no circumstances include nuclear weapons in her armaments. Two million people are said to have participated in over 400 rallies to protest President Ford's 1974 visit and to demand the removal of U.S. nuclear weapons from Japan. Four Hiroshima survivors gave evidence at the U.S. Senate hearing on the Kennedy-Hatfield nuclear freeze resolution in 1982. At the same time 100,000 gathered in Hiroshima itself to protest the nuclear arms race, the largest demonstration against nuclear arms ever held in Japan.

The U.S. government has on more than one occasion reminded the Japanese of their commitment to increase their forces of planes and ships so as to be able to defend the sea-lanes around Japan to a distance of 1,000 miles. These statements contained warnings of possible U.S. Congressional reprisals. But this objective is unlikely to be met until after 1990, unless defense expenditures are greatly increased. In this connection it is interesting to note a comment from the Center for Defense Information in Washington, a group which generally advocates strong American military forces. Members of the Center observed in a report that Japan is accused of "shirking its military duties," but warn that current American policy could push Japan to become an independent military power "which may not be responsive to U.S. influence, nor always support U.S. interests." The study ends by saying, in a subtle reversal of roles, "The current shapers of U.S. military policy would do well to reflect on the prescient words of Imperial Fleet Admiral Yamamoto Isoroku the day Japan attacked the United States at Pearl Harbor: "I fear all we have done is to awaken a sleeping giant and fill him with a terrible resolve:"

SOCIETY. Not many years ago the average Chinese household on the mainland desired above all things to possess "The Three Rounds," or three objects which revolve: a sewing machine, a wristwatch and a bicycle. Japan, as a post-industrial society, has gone much further in consumerism. "The Three Imperial Treasures" of the 1960's were said to be a refrigerator, a color television set and a washing machine. Now, of course, many Japanese own a car, and are looking for a second car and a house in the country.

Enough has been said of the remarkable growth in the economy of Japan. With it has gone a corresponding rise in the standard of living. With better nourishment there has also been a physical "rise"; the average Japanese twenty-year-old is two inches taller than his or her parents, and four inches taller than the grandparents. For this to occur as average growth is quite extraordinary. But progress has been costly. Japan is an expensive place. If New York's cost of living in 1981 be taken as a basic 100, then London comes in at 133, and Tokyo at 160. The overcrowding, scarcity and poor quality of housing, the time wasted in commuting to work, totalling two, three, even four hours daily, the comparative neglect of the infrastructure of roads and drainage—all these factors combine to offset some of the benefits of increased wealth. Businesses, factories and services crowd together and vie with agriculture for the scarce level land in the country. Conurbation has gone to extraordinary lengths, so that the whole stretch from northern Kyushu up to Tokyo, over 600 miles, is almost one long city, with only patches of farmland.

In 1970 in Tokyo 650 persons were treated for eye and throat irritation, and a smog warning system was set up. A bill was passed this year by the "Pollution Diet" making "the emission of materials harmful to human life" a crime for the first time, punishable by up to three years in prison. Two notorious cases followed; one, a fine of $800,000 for a leading chemical firm, where seven persons died and seventy more were affected by mercury poisoning from eating fish. The second case was worse; the Chisso Corporation was ordered to pay $3.6 million to 138 victims of mercury poisoning. It was discovered that sixty-seven persons had died and 330 became permanently disabled in the six years preceding 1973, the date of the case. *Kogai,* environmental disruption, has come to the forefront as a political issue, and the women were the first to see it clearly. Of what value was a constantly rising GNP, if they and their families were not receiving benefits in the same proportion? Inflation cut the household budget; traffic accidents killed children; cramped housing multiplied strains in family life. As a result all Japan is gradually realizing that a new concept of "net national welfare" must replace "growth of GNP" as a national goal.

EDUCATION. Japan made a fresh start with a modern type of education at the Meiji Restoration of 1868, a secular and open system, free of ties to the aristocratic elite or the Buddhist church. Compulsory education at the primary level worked so well that a century ago 45 percent of Japanese males could read, and for several generations now there has been almost universal literacy, male and female. The changes brought about in the Occupation period after World War II resulted, Reischauer said, "in a new breed of young Japanese, more direct, casual and undisciplined than their prewar predecessors, but at the same time more independent, spontaneous and lively.[7] Any lack of discipline in school has been mild in comparison to America, and educational standards have remained high. Today all children attend six years of elementary school and three years of junior high school. Almost 90 percent then enter senior high school. Those who go on to higher education comprise almost one-third of high school graduates, more than the corresponding proportion in Western Europe and less than that of the United States.

There is heavy emphasis on achievement and on making ever greater efforts to succeed in school. Children begin homework in first grade, and may end up later with four or five hours of it. The school day is longer in Japan than in the United States. The week includes a half-day on Saturday, and the school year lasts for 240 days (180 in the United States). The quality of teachers, especially on the secondary level, is high. Indeed, they are said to be better equipped and more highly motivated than their counterparts in the United States, although this would be hard to establish

[7] Edwin O. Reischauer, *Japan—The Story of a Nation* (New York: Alfred A. Knopf, 1974), p. 233.

statistically. Teachers in Japan are certainly more respected and honored, though not very highly paid. Pupil performance in mathematics and science is generally good, and the study of English is begun in seventh grade.

Such a record in the schools is clearly of great benefit to the nation, since it makes available not only leaders capable of being trained at higher levels, but also an educated labor pool, able to supply the requirements of the present post-industrial world for work which is knowledge-intensive. As to character formation, the most important factors are the support of the home and the sense of national loyalty stemming from the past of Japan. But there is an educational factor also; for the classes in ethics, abolished during the Occupation (see p. 205), were restored in 1957 in a new, less nationalistic form, stressing respect for the common good. Japan has a remarkably homogeneous, non-pluralistic society, and this approach appears to suit the national ethos.

There is, however, a darker side to the educational picture, and the Japanese themselves are well aware of it. Start from the end of the equation—lifetime employment. The business firm or government bureau you enter, perhaps for life, is determined to a great extent by the university you attend. Your grades while at that university do not even matter so much. Only about 38 percent of applicants get into university on their first try; so high school preparation is vital. Although high schools are in actuality fairly uniform, some are perceived as being better than others, hence competition for those is severe. Thus competition is extended all the way down through elementary school. Many parents want their children to get a flying start in kindergarten. All this means that regular schooling is not enough, and many children are sent to *juku,* or cram schools, in the afternoon, as well as doing homework at night. It is the role of the mother, *kyoiku mama,* "education mom," to see that the child puts forth the necessary effort. She will not only attend parent-teacher meetings, but even take notes in class if her child is sick. The supportive parental role may be a help, but the accompanying expectations may place extra strain on the child.

This is summed up in the phrase, "examination hell," the examination to gain entrance to the university. "Four hours sleep, you pass. Five hours, you fail." In addition to the psychological damage to the students, there are also harmful side effects on the curriculum. Although study of English, for example, starts early, the stress on fine points of grammar required by the examination means that thorough reading in the English language is neglected, and fluency in speaking, even the comprehension of spoken English, is often extremely poor. It is not unknown to find a student learning the contents of a small dictionary by heart. More serious is the fact that stress on standardized material and memorization by rote means that creativity, imagination, critical thinking and the ability to enter into independent discussion tend to be sacrificed. The gradual acquisition of a love of learning, on which civilization is built, is an early casualty; but the problem is not confined to Japan.

Once a student has gained access to university on a first, second or third try, he or she tends, understandably, to relax, do little study, and turn to sport or take up political activism. (Activists in the student Left have opposed the government on such controversies as oppression of the *eta* [untouchables] and the Korean minority, the exploitation of women, disruption of the environment, and the re-militarization of Japan.) Poor class attendance is attributed by many to the lack of intellectual stimulation in the university. A trenchant criticism of the system comes from the writer, Eto Jun, who said, "The contemporary Japanese university ... is a dry, sterile world where true education is seldom dispensed or desired."[8] The four years of university are thus not fully utilized, though students rarely drop out.

There are currently 1,834,000 students in university, of whom 22.6 percent are women. Of the 379,000 students in junior colleges the vast majority, almost 90 percent, are female. A great increase in students entering private universities occurred after 1950, and their enrollment now accounts for 80 percent of all students, with the remaining 20 percent enrolled in goverment sponsored universities. The majority of students in most industrial countries are in government supported universities, and in the United States the proportion is 75 percent. Budgetary problems in Japan are severe, especially in private universities which depend largely on student tuition and examination entrance fees. The government, though spending 10 percent of the GNP on education as a whole, more proportionately than in the United States, has not made sufficient provision for university expansion. Japan lacks a tradition of large private benevolence to education, and therefore the pressure on private universities is excessive. The following table makes this clear:

UNIVERSITIES

	PUBLIC	PRIVATE
Teacher-student ratio	1:8	1:31
Physical space per student	1.0 as base	0.33
Tuition fees per student	1.0 as base	7.0

One great benefit which the government supported universities offer to society is that their standards are the highest and their fees the lowest; hence they recruit students from all strata of society with remarkable equality.

The favorite undergraduate major is social science (39 percent), while for the doctorate the highest numbers are in medicine and dentistry. There has been an increase of late in the number of students doing post-graudate work, but less higher level research is now done in universities and more in business and government facilities. The civil service departments and

[8] *Journal of Social and Political Ideas in Japan,* 1967, p. 179f.

firms send representatives to universities to recruit recent graduates. After they pass yet another examination, they are given in-service training; or they may be sent to graduate school in Japan or abroad for further study. Whatever the route followed, status in Japan is determined largely by education, less by class or background.[9]

WOMEN AND THE FAMILY. Today in Tokyo it is possible for a Japanese woman to ask a bewildered tourist if he wants help, and to have a short conversation without any sense of restraint or awkwardness. This could never have happened in Japan before World War II. Women have emerged from the status of vassals, but due to old prejudices and the sporadic and untidy nature of life, much remains to be done. Half of the married women in Japan now have a job outside the home.

Women are freer to go out to work because there are markedly fewer children. Parents desire with a new intensity to see that their children are well brought up and well educated, so they do not have too many. Abortion laws in Japan are neither strict nor strictly enforced, and birth control is widely practiced. There was an increase in childbearing after the war, but Japan at 1 percent per annum now has one of the lowest rates of population growth in the world. One measure of the increasing satisfaction Japanese women find in the control of their own lives is to be seen in a survey, in which the question posed to women was: If you could be born again, would you rather be as a man or as a woman? The percentages answering "as a woman" were

in 1958, 27%   in 1963, 36%   in 1973, 51%

Among the reasons for the increase in female preference were awareness of outside pressures on men, satisfaction at the important status of the Japanese family, largely controlled by women, and real enjoyment in childrearing, including responsibility for education.[10] However, 89 percent of the men interrogated said they would rather be reborn as men.

It is a mark of Japanese thoroughness as well as of their concern for image that they have such enthusiasm for statistics. The Office of the Prime Minister issues a number of surveys which include opinion polls as well as hard statistics. One such poll contrasts the attitudes of men and women on their concern for national vs. private interests. Both men and women in their twenties are concerned, not surprisingly, with private interests, but this preoccupation declines through life. Women's concern for national interests remains at a low level throughout (about 20 percent), but the concern of men for national interests rises steadily until their sixties (33 percent). It exceeds the interest they showed in youth for their own affairs. Women are not very interested in national affairs, presumably because they feel they have little chance to make their influence felt.

[9] I am indebted for some of the above information to Edwin O. Reischauer, The Japanese, (Cambridge, Mass.: Belknap-Harvard University, 1978).

[10] Burks, op. cit., pp. 210–11.

Japanese business, as we have seen, makes heavy demands on men, and leaves little time for husband and father to be at home with the family. The father will often leave home on weekdays before the children are awake and return long after they are asleep. The pattern, of course, is not unknown in commuter America or other countries. The situation for the Japanese family is worse because of the tradition of the use of leisure in a male-oriented society. Japanese businessmen will often spend the evening in restaurants with colleagues until ten or eleven o'clock at night, and sometimes will not even bother to telephone home. The story goes that if a man comes home early, his wife will ask him what is wrong.

Japan, along with other countries, now has a society in which youth predominates, for 50 percent of Japanese living are under the age of thirty-two. But the trend is towards an increase in the older section of the nation. In 1950 those under fourteen formed 35 percent of the population, greatly outnumbering the 5 percent who were over sixty-five. but in the year 2000 it is expected that the two groups will be approximately equal at 18 percent and 16 percent respectively. Is there therefore a generation gap in empathy and understanding? It exists in Japan, as everywhere, but evidence suggests it is decreasing. It is certainly less prevalent where women are concerned, perhaps because of the important nurturing role of the mother at home.

RELIGION. The Japanese people today seem to be basically of a pragmatic, rational or scientific turn of mind. Less than one-third profess a personal religious faith, yet most think, paradoxically, that a religious attitude is important. Shinto, the original native religion, imparts to the Japanese ethos a happy, if not very profound or moral tone. (Morality derives rather from the Confucian element in Japan's past and from the group responsibility which it fosters.) Shinto festivals punctuate the year with holidays which derive from the cycle of Nature. Buddhism, whose importance is abundantly illustrated in Japan's history, today counts over 83 million adherents out of a population of 119 million, but not all of these can by any means be reckoned as devout. Shinto overlaps with Buddhism and no numbers of Shinto believers can be given with any accuracy. Japanese may employ Shinto rites when they marry, and Buddhist funeral rites when they die. Or a family may, without feeling of contradiction, go at midnight of the New Year in Kyoto to receive a light for their hearth at the sacred fire of the Shinto shrine, and go on the same night to hear at the Buddhist temple the boom of the great bell which drives away the 108 evil passions.

Christians, divided approximately equally between Protestants and Catholics, are said to number 883,000. But they probably exert a greater influence than their small number would indicate, since many leaders in public life have imbibed Christian ideas in their general outlook and particularly in their attitudes to education and social welfare.

A postwar phenomenon has been the rapid growth of the "new religions" in the wake of the defeat and disillusionment of World War II.

The sects were so numerous that a book appeared with the title *The Rush Hour of the Gods*. Most of these new religions were founded in the nineteenth century or early twentieth century, but showed a great increase after 1946. The combined adherents claimed are now 14 million, or 12 percent of the population.

Two of the more popular religions are Tenrikyo and Soka Gakkai. Tenrikyo, the religion of the heavenly principle, generally Buddhist in background, was founded by a housewife and stresses simple and joyful service and cleanliness. Believers run spotlessly clean work camps, and as an act of service join in large numbers in front of the Emperor's palace to clear the whole area of litter. To Westerners this emphasis on cleanliness may seem superficial, but for the Japanese the notion of ritual purity extends far back in history. Shinto worshippers rinse hands and mouths before approaching the shrine; and everyone who visits Japan comments on the constant bathing and personal cleanliness of the people.

The religious movement that has shown the most rapid growth of all has been the Soka Gakkai, Value-Creating Society. This is a militant Buddhist group, founded by a schoolteacher, which draws its inspiration from the Buddhist patriot saint of the thirteenth century, Nichiren. Intolerant of other religions and of other Buddhist sects, it promises health and well-being to all who will embrace its tenets and work actively for its extension. The movement makes a special appeal to the twenty to thirty age group and to small businessmen, many of whom have found their capital insufficient and have gone bankrupt in the competition of modern commerce. It also appeals to the downtrodden and to those in the lower classes seeking security, such as domestic servants who are alienated in the towns and cannot claim membership in a labor union or other similar group. Soka Gakkai makes use of paramilitary methods to incite mass enthusiasm by parades, marching bands and sports. It has been accused of using brainwashing and strong-arm methods to gain converts. The political arm of Soka Gakkai is called Komeito, or Clean Government Party. The adherents of the new religions feel that their beliefs foster self-confidence, are more in tune with modern times than the tenets of Shinto and Buddhism, and more adapted to Japanese life than those of Christianity.

ARTS AND LEISURE. The Japanese, who can be withdrawn and meditative as well as outgoing and energetic, are nourished and sustained by a sense of their own past to a degree not found elsewhere. They go out to seek the new, the latest, in style and taste, yet know the value of ancient forms in art and have sedulously conserved them. This fertilizing effect of traditional forms upon modern art and design is not susceptible of easy explanation, but must be felt and experienced through a study of Japan's cultural past. Nevertheless such is its intrinsic appeal that Japanese design in furniture, gardens and architecture is having an increasing influence upon Western styles. The Japanese have long known the value of simplicity and clean lines, of the asymmetrical and informal. They are adept at the use of materials which they allow to preserve their original nature—stone, wood, bamboo, thatch—often untreated and unpainted. They value texture as much as shape and color; and in this respect particularly their architects and craftsmen have helped to raise the level of international taste.

The Japanese architect who is at present best known in the West is Tange Kenzo. One of the most noteworthy of his buildings is the Swimming Arena for the 1964 Tokyo Olympics, which, when seen from above exhibits swinging curves reminiscent of a leaf or a clam shell. Japanese influence on the arts in the West is not seen so much in direct imitation. The Western tradition is too far apart from the Oriental for that approach to be successful today. Subtle penetration and cross-fertilization is more sophisticated and more successful. Interior gardens on the ground floor of city skyscrapers, and gardens in minimal space owe much to Japanese design in architecture. Astringent (*shibui*) taste and intentionally rough texture and irregularity in pots have exerted an influence in ceramics, as have Japanese woodblock prints and calligraphy in graphics and design.

The Japanese are passionate readers of the printed word. The three largest Tokyo daily newspapers are *Yomiuri* (combined morning and evening circulation 13.6 million), *Asahi* (12.1 million) and *Mainichi* (6.9-million). *Yomiuri,* largest newspaper in the world, has an editorial staff of over 3,000, prints many regional editions and is read in more than one-third of the households in Japan. *Yomiuri* also runs a first-rate symphony orchestra, a professional baseball team and a TV network. Television in Japan, with two national networks (one is educational) and five commercial ones, maintains a generally high standard and commands an enormous audience. Adult comic books have become a public passion, to a degree which alarms the scholars and the conservatives. Traditional Japanese music has maintained its place in Japanese life, partly because of its use in *kabuki* and the world of the geisha. But classical and popular music from the West are to be heard everywhere, and there are nine symphony orchestras in Tokyo alone.

The great days of Japanese filmmaking were in the 1950's, with the work of such directors as Ozu Yasujiro (*Tokyo Story,* the conflict between the traditional and the modern within a family), and Mizoguchi Kenji (*Ugetsu,* a medieval love story, in which the real and the unreal merge). One of the greatest of all the film directors and the best known in the West is Kurosawa Akira (*Rashomon, To Live,* and *Seven Samurai*). The warlike samurai themes are shot through with constant, subtle reminders of enduring human values. Superb use of the camera lens blends humanity with nature in the steady and ineluctable flow of time. After a number of years of much less distinction, Japanese filmmaking is beginning to revive with the work of such directors as Oshima and Nigisa.

The sensitivity to nature and its moods seen in Kurosawa's films has from the dawn of literature been an integral part of the Japanese imagination (see pp. 29–30). In ways reminiscent of the brief poems of the *Manyoshu* and scenes in *The Tale of Genji* the modern novelists at moments of great poignancy break off the narrative to speak of trees in the rain, sunlight, the caprices of the wind, especially the clouds and their changing moods. Nature brings calming relief from unbearable tension, somewhat in the manner of a chorus in the plays of Euripides.

The Japanese novelists also blend with past tradition in their episodic writing. There are brief scenes with skillful and minute observation of detail, then loose ends. Much space is left for the imagination, as space is intentionally left in Japanese painting. One seems to be left hanging; but a personality is built up; the plot does resume. The method is particularly effective for delineating the compulsive, obsessive characters which fill the pages of such novels as Mishima's *Temple of the Golden Pavilion.*

But writers also react violently against the tradition in their refusal to conform to the group and group mentality. They search for and pursue the mind and the destiny of the individual, often through the individual they know best in the so-called I-novel. Here is a struggling spirit, set off alone by itself, through heredity or through outward circumstances, often apparently trivial. The writer follows with minute care that person's joys and sorrows, purely interior and often contrary to all "normal" expectation. The most powerful, internal emotions concern love and death. These basic themes are common to all modern writing, but the treatment of them in Japanese literature leaves the impression that it stems from inherently Japanese roots.

In Japan a decisive factor in modern literature is, of course, "the war." By that is meant the long, slow, bleeding China Incident (1937–1941) followed by the great adventure of the war in the Pacific and its gruesome ending. The ending involved not only the atomic bombs, but also the humiliation and suffering which came from the first experience in the whole of Japanese history of invasion and defeat on her own sacred soil. This meant utter despair. But here and there in postwar writing beauty and ordinary human affection re-assert themselves.

A few names and examples may be taken as illustrative of these varied themes. Tanizaki Junichiro (1886–1965) was known as one of the "aesthetes," or "decadents." He wrote of the conflict between the past and the present in a psychologically involved tale *The Makioka Sisters,* considered one of the best of the modern novels. Abe Kobo (1924–) is concerned, among other things, with individualism against conformity, and with the two faces of freedom. A man trapped in a sandpit (*The Woman in the Dunes*) longs to escape, but is in no hurry to do so when the chance comes. So humankind longs to be free, yet is afraid of freedom. Kawabata Yasunari (1899–1972) was the first Japanese to receive the Nobel prize for literature in 1968. One of his best known novels is *Snow Country,* published before the war. To say that it is the story of a sophisticate from Tokyo who goes to see a geisha he once knew, now at a hot springs resort in the high mountains, is to give no idea of its baffling imaginative power. Kawabata felt deeply the despair which followed the war. The title of one of his books, *Beauty and Sadness,* indicates his spirit and hints at the inspiration he found when he returned from an early preoccupation with the West to the old literary tradition of Japan. Kawabata was a mentor to Mishima Yukio (1925–1970), a complex and intriguing writer, more influenced by foreign ideas than Kawabata, but also one who turned back to his native roots. His *Confessions of a Mask* brought him fame as a young man, but he reacted against the confessional, egocentric tradition of the I-novel. He wrote on varied themes, such as a tale of young lovers in a fishing village in the delightful *Sound of Waves,* and realistic portrayal of an old-fashioned, aristocratic politician and a charmingly practical restaurant owner cum businesswoman in *After the Banquet.* Mishima commited suicide at the height of his powers, as did also two other modern writers, the romantic nihilist Dazai Osamu (at the fifth attempt) and Akutagawa Ryonosuke, author of the story behind the film *Rashomon.*

It would be a mistake, nevertheless, to deduce the whole mood of a country from the sensitive, often tortured, spirits of writers who look further into life than the man in the street. The limited leisure of present-day Japanese is often devoted to the eager pursuit of sports, for example. One meets crowds of students, men and women, traveling long hours on the train into the mountains for a weekend's skiing. Golf is a popular rich man's game and is used for making deals as well as scores. Volleyball, table tennis, mountain climbing—everything known to the West—is also practiced in Japan. But the two greatest favorites are baseball and traditional *sumo* wrestling.

MOOD AND CONCLUSION. Is it possible to catch and hold on mere paper the mood of a country at one moment of time? That question must perforce hang in the air. There is great diversity in modern Japan. Development is now pluralistic as never before. There is a youth culture, for one thing, nonchalant, not living mainly for the family or the firm, as their elders did. And yet it is also true that after the disturbances of the 60's there was a discernible trend in the 70's toward return to traditional values. Even in the 60's, "the Japanese were able to carry with them a large measure of traditional behavior to protect themselves against the shocks of change."[11] The use of statistics to convey something as subjective as the self-image of a whole people has an element of the absurd; yet polls have their impressionistic uses. It seems that 66 percent of the Japanese see themselves as "diligent," 52 percent as "persistent," 37 percent as "polite," and only 31 percent as "kind."

How patriotic are they, and what do they think of their country? They are proud of Japan (according to the Prime Minister's Office in a 1983 sample of 7,700 persons) for the following reasons, in order of importance: industry and ability of the people, long history and tradition of the country, beautiful natural features of the landscape, well maintained public order, and a high standard of education. There are other reasons; but low on the list comes economic prosperity, and at the bottom, solidarity

[11] Burks, op. cit., p. 131.

as a nation. The last is a view of the Japanese which many in the West would place near the top. The three worst impressions the Japanese have of their own society, according to this survey, are its self-centeredness, irresponsibility and restlessness. When asked, "Do you want to render service to the State, or to be served by it?" forty-four percent said they wanted to serve, 12 percent said they wanted to be served, and 31 percent had evenly divided feelings on the matter. One wonders what the replies would be in Europe, in Russia and in the United States of America.

In conclusion, Japan has chosen the way of free enterprise and has been phenomenally successful at it. Her people are more confident than they were after the war but are aware of deep, inner anxieties, for which material success does not hold the answer. With outstanding economic expansion they inherit the accompanying problems, with which the United States and other nations are familiar—pollution, traffic jams and the malaise of youth. The more sensitive are aware of demonic elements of frenzy and cruelty beneath the surface. As in the emotional tension of a *No* play, there is a longing for the calm the Buddha promises.

Japan has emerged as a world power. Hard though it is to generalize on the reasons for this, one or two factors seem clear. First, the Japanese have energy, drive and the capacity for hard work. They show immense application, an indifference to fatigue and an expectation of hardship far above most Western tolerance. Second, they have discipline, leading to a capacity to act together. The Greeks were glad they did not have to be whipped into battle like the slave soldiers of the Great King of Persia, because they were free men and fought willingly for their liberty. The Japanese never spoke of freedom, but their warriors were always free men. They fought, strove, out of loyalty, and expected to act under discipline, under an obligation to nation, clan, family, and indeed to themselves and their personal honor. The forms have changed; the force seems still to be there. This makes them a powerful people.

Third, they have curiosity, insatiable curiosity. "How does the thing work?"—a musket, a steamboat, an electron, an enzyme. Find out and do it better. Fourth, they have a certain artistic style. Here we are on the thin ice of speculation. Yet the natural aesthetic taste of the Japanese seems to surface not only in the creations of great artists but also in the ancient traditions of an instinctive folk art. Perhaps it is not fanciful to see this artistic heritage emerging in the ways in which the Japanese have put together the pieces of modern electronics, a viable economic system, and even a life-style.

When the Japanese military trumpeted their right to be leaders in Asia, they found few willing followers in other nations. Many are still suspicious and afraid of Japanese economic domination; but it is evident that Japan has given solid proof of the capacity to change, to offer valuable patterns for modernization, and to work constructively and cooperatively for the advancement of the Pacific area and the world.

GLOSSARY

ashigaru	foot-soldier, light infantry
aware no mono	the sadness of things
bakufu	tent government, military rule
be	corporation
biwa	lute
buke sho-hatto	ordinances for military houses
bunraku	puppet stage
bushido	the way of the warrior
bussangaku	science of production
butsu	Buddha
daikan	deputy
daimyo	lit., great name, territorial lord
daikon	giant radish
dainagon	great councillor
dajo-daijin	chancellor
dajo-kan	department of state
fudai	hereditary vassals
fokoku-kyohei	rich country—strong army
fumi-e	lit., treading picture, sacred emblem used to test Christians
genro	elder statesman
giri	right, obligation, duty
go	intricate Japanese board game
go-kenin	house men
gonin-gumi	five-man group
go-sanke	three houses of Tokugawa Ieyasu's sons
go-tairo	five (great) elders
haikai	chain poem
haikara	lit., high collar, fashionable
haiku	poem of seventeen syllables
haniwa	clay funerary figures
harakiri or seppuku	formal suicide by slitting the belly
hatamoto	bannerman
hitatare	ceremonial robe

hyojosho	Judicial Council
ikki	league, revolt promoted by a league
ikko	lit., single-minded, name for Shinshu sect of Buddhism
insei	cloister government by a retired emperor
jidai	period, era in history
jingi-kan	department of worship
jito	steward
kabuki	a popular form of drama
kageyushi	Board of Audit
kaidan	ordination platform
kambun	written Chinese
kami	gods, those above
kamikaze	lit., wind of the gods, typhoon during Mongol attack, suicide pilots in World War II
kampaku	regent after an emperor came of age, or civil dictator
kana	Japanese syllabary
kebiishi-cho	Commissioners of Police
kega	wound, defilement
kempeitai	military police, secret police
kirisute	to cut down and leave, the right to kill with impunity
koan	nonsense puzzle, used in Zen Buddhism
kokutai	national polity
kurando-dokoro	Bureau of Archivists
kyogen	lit., mad words, farcical interlude, comedy
kyuba-no-michi	the way of the horse and the bow
mandokoro	Secretariat, Council
matsurigoto	religious affairs, government
metsuke	censors, secret police
mobo	modern boy
moga	modern girl
monchujo	Board of Inquiry
moningu	morning coat
monogatari	tale, story
no	classical Japanese drama
rangaku	lit., Dutch learning, European knowledge
ritsu	disciplinary and penal regulations
roju	Council of Elders
ronin	lit., wave men, masterless warriors
ryo	administrative and civil code
sadaijin	minister of the Left
sake	a spirit made from rice

samurai	lit., one who serves, retainer, warrior
samurai-dokoro	orderly room, Board of Retainers
sankin-kotai	alternate attendance (at the shogun's court)
sarugaku	lit., monkey music, comic performance
sebiro	Savile Row, business suit
sei-i tai-shogun	barbarian-subduing generalissimo
sessho	regent during an emperor's minority
shibui	astringent, understated, quiet (in art)
shiki	rights or shares in the produce of an estate
shikken	director, equivalent to regent for the shogun
shimpan	related or collateral fiefs
shinto or kami-no-michi	the way of the gods, native Japanese religion
shite	principal actor in a *No* play
shoen	tax-free manor
shogun	generalissimo, supreme military commander
shonagon	lesser councillor
shugo	protector (a Kamakura official)
sonno-joi	honor the emperor, expel the barbarians
tairo	Great Elder
tanka	poem of 31 syllables
tokaido	the eastern sea road
tomo	attendant
tozama	outside lords, *i.e.*, not Tokugawa vassals
tsuibushi	constable
tsumi	crime, sin
udaijin	minister of the Right
uji	clan
ukiyo-e	pictures of the floating world, of the transient scene
waki	second actor in *No* play
yamato-damashii	the spirit of Old Japan
za	seat or pitch in a marketplace, guild
zazen	sitting in meditation
zaibatsu	financial clique, large industrial combine

ChRONOLOGY

YEAR	POLITICAL	MILITARY	CULTURAL
B.C.			
from 3,000			Jomon culture
660	Traditional date of accession of first emperor, Jimmu		
300–100			Yayoi culture and Tomb culture
A.D.			
57	Envoy sent to Han court		
369		Japanese conquests at Mimana in Korea (held until 562)	
391			Scholars from Korea entered Japan, introducing writing
552			Buddhism officially introduced to Japan; image sent from the king of Paikche in Korea
586			Emperor Yomei supports Buddhism
587		Battle at Shigisen— Soga Umako against Mononobe over Buddhism	
592–628	Reign of Empress Suiko		
593–622	Regency of Prince Shotoku—supporter of Buddhism and Chinese learning		
604	"Constitution" cf Prince Shotoku		
607	Ono-no-Imoko on first official embassy of united Japan to China		Horyuji monastery built

YEAR	POLITICAL	MILITARY	CULTURAL
630	Embassy to T'ang China		
645	Taika Reform		
661–671	Reign of Emperor Tenchi—the former Prince Naka-no-Oye		
663		Defeat of Japanese army in Korea and destruction of ally Paikche by Silla and T'ang	
669	Granting of surname Fujiwara to Nakatomi Kamatari before his death		
702	Taiho Law Code		
708	First issue of copper coinage		Horyuji monastery rebuilt
710	Location of capital fixed at Nara		

NARA PERIOD 710–794

YEAR	POLITICAL	MILITARY	CULTURAL
712			Compilation of *Kojiki*, "Record of Ancient Things"
720			Compilation of *Nihongi* or *Nihonshoki*, "Chronicles of Japan"
724 749	Reign of Emperor Shomu (d. 756)		
729–749			Tempyo Period—great era of Buddhist statuary
738–756			Tachibana-no-Moroye collection of poems, *Manyoshu*, "Collection of Myriad Leaves"
752			Dedication of Daibutsu (Great Buddha) at Todaiji Temple in Nara
781–806	Reign of Emperor Kammu		
784	Move of capital to Nagaoka		
794	Heian capital established at Kyoto		

HEIAN PERIOD 794–1158

EARLY HEIAN PERIOD 794–857

YEAR	POLITICAL	MILITARY	CULTURAL
800–803		Defeat of Ainu in northern Honshu by Sakanouye Tamura Maro—he receives title sei-i tai-shogun, "barbarian-subduing generalissimo"	
805			Returning monk from China, Saicho, introduces Tendai sect with headquarters at Enryakuji on Mount Hiei
806			Monk Kukai, having studied in China, introduces Shingon sect, establishing center at Mount Koya
838	Last embassy to T'ang China		

LATE HEIAN OR FUJIWARA PERIOD 858–1185

YEAR	POLITICAL	MILITARY	CULTURAL
858–872	Fujiwara Yoshifusa as first Regent not of the imperial family		
891	Sugawara Michizane in power		
899	Removal of Michizane to a post in Kyushu by Fujiwara Tokihira		
905			Compilation of Kokinshu by Ki-no-Tsurayuki and others
930–49	Fujiwara Tadahira as Regent and Chancellor		
935–40		Revolt and execution of Taira Masakado	
995–1027	Supremacy of Fujiwara Michinaga		
c. 1002			Writing of *Makura no Soshi* (Pillow Book) by Lady Sei Shonagon
c. 1008–20			Writing of *Genji Monogatari* ("Tale of Genji") by Lady Murasaki Shikibu
1017–1068	Fujiwara Yorimichi as Regent and Chancellor		

YEAR	POLITICAL	MILITARY	CULTURAL
1051–1062		Early Nine Years' War	
1053			Byodo-in (temple) erected by Fujiwara Yorimichi
1068–1072	Reign of Emperor Go-Sanjo (d. 1073)		
1072–1086	Reign of Emperor Shirakawa		
1083–1087		Later Three Years' War	
1086–1129	Shirakawa abdicates, but rules from the cloister, establishing custom of *insei,* rule by a retired emperor		
1107–1123	Reign of Emperor Toba		
1129–1156	Insei of Toba		
1156–1158		Hogen Insurrection led by Fujiwara Yorinaga	
1159–1160		Heiji War: destruction of Minamoto Yoshitomo and Fujiwara Nobuyori by Taira Kiyomori and his son Shigemori	
1167	Taira Kiyomori as Prime Minister		
1175			Founding of the Jodo (Pure Land) sect in Japan by Honen Shonin
1180–1185		Gempei Wars, between Minamoto and Taira forces

1180. Minamoto Yoritomo defeated at Ishibashiyama. Yoritomo successful at battle of River Fujikawa

1184. Battle of Ichi-no-tani—Minamoto victory

1185. Yoshitsune victorious over Taira at Yashima. Battle at sea near Dan-no-ura, final Taira defeat, and death of child emperor Antoku | |

KAMAKURA PERIOD 1185-1336

YEAR	POLITICAL	MILITARY	CULTURAL
1185	Constable and Steward system set up by Minamoto Yoritomo		
1189	Death of Minamoto Yoshitsune		
1191			Zen sect (Rinzai Branch) introduced from China by Eisai
1192	Yoritomo granted title of Shogun by Emperor		
1199	Death of Minamoto Yoritomo; power passes to Hojo family through wife Hojo Masako and father-in-law Hojo Tokimasa		
1203	Assumption of post of *shikken* (head of Council) by Tokimasa		
1221		Shokyu (Jokyu) disturbance—retired emperor Go-Toba tries to assume real power	
1224–1242	Hojo Yasutoki as *shikken*		
1224			Jodo Shinshu (True Pure Land) or Shin sect founded by Shinran
1227			Zen (Soto branch) introduced from China by Dogen
1232	Promulgation of Joei Shikimoku— Kamakura law code		
1246–1256	Hojo Tokiyori as *shikken* (d. 1263)		
1253			Founding of Nichiren sect by Nichiren
1274		First Mongol attack— Hakata Bay, northern Kyushu	
1281		Second Mongol attack —*kamikaze*, "Wind of the Gods," saves the Japanese	
1297	Law of "virtuous administration"		

YEAR	POLITICAL	MILITARY	CULTURAL
1318–1339	Reign of Emperor Go-Daigo		
1331–36		Genko War	
1333		Ashikaga Takauji captures Kyoto in Go-Daigo's name	
1335		Destruction of Kamakura by Nitta Yoshisada	
1335		Revolt of Takauji against Go-Daigo	
1336	Rival emperor placed on throne by Takauji; flight of Go-Daigo to Yoshino		

ASHIKAGA PERIOD 1336–1573

NAMBOKUCHO PERIOD 1336–1392
(SOUTHERN CAPITAL AT YOSHINO, NORTHERN CAPITAL AT KYOTO)

YEAR	POLITICAL	MILITARY	CULTURAL
1338	Assumption of title of Shogun by Takauji		
1339	Death of Go-Daigo		
1358–1367	Shogunate of Yoshiakira		
1365–1372		Battles on Kyushu between rival forces of Prince Kanenaga and Imagawa Sadayo	
1368–1394	Shogunate of Yoshimitsu (d. 1408)		
1378			Building of Hana-no-Gosho
1384			Death of Kanami, who developed *No* drama

MUROMACHI PERIOD 1392–1573

YEAR	POLITICAL	MILITARY	CULTURAL
1392	Regalia brought back to Kyoto; Southern Court to have alternate succession		
1394–1423	Shogunate of Yoshimochi (d. 1428)		
1397			Building of Kinkakuji by 3rd Shogun, Yoshimitsu
1404	Trade agreement with Ming China		
1429–1441	Shogunate of Yoshinori		

YEAR	POLITICAL	MILITARY	CULTURAL
1443–1473	Shogunate of Yoshimasa (d. 1490)		
1444			Death of Zeami, who perfected *No* drama
1467–1477		Onin War—Ashikaga cease to be effective	
1483			Construction of Ginkakuji by 8th Shogun Yoshimasa
1485		Peasant uprisings in Yamashino Province	
1488		Members of Shin sect (Ikko-ikki) in control of Kaga and Echizen provinces	
1506			Death of painter-monk Sesshu (b. 1420)

1534–1615 SENGOKU-JIDAI: PERIOD OF COUNTRY AT WAR

1534–1582 ODA NOBUNAGA
1536–1598 TOYOTOMI HIDEYOSHI
1543–1616 TOKUGAWA IEYASU

YEAR	POLITICAL	MILITARY	CULTURAL
1542	Arrival of Portuguese at Tanegashima; firearms introduced		
1549			Arrival of the Jesuit St. Francis Xavier in Kyushu
1560		Battle of Okehazama; Oda Nobunaga's move on capital	
1568		Seizure of Kyoto by Nobunaga	
1571		Destruction by Nobunaga of Enrya-kuji	
1573	Imprisonment of last Shogun Yoshiaki; end of Ashikaga Shogunate		
1576–1579	Transfer of Nobunaga to his castle at Azuchi on Lake Biwa		
1579–1598			Azuchi-Momoyama "Peach Mountain" period in art
1580		Surrender of Osaka castle-monastery of Shin sect to Nobunaga	
1582	Death of Nobunaga at the hands of Akechi Mitsuhide		

YEAR	POLITICAL	MILITARY	CULTURAL
1583–1598	Land Survey commissioned by Hideyoshi		
1587	Confiscation of arms of peasantry—the "Sword Hunt"		Promulgation of decree ordering expulsion of Christian missionaries
1590		Destruction of Hojo family of Odawara and installation of Tokugawa Ieyasu in Edo castle as master of Kanto	
1592		Hideyoshi invaded Korea	
1593		Truce with Chinese armies in Korea and withdrawal of Japanese forces to extreme south	
1597		Resumption of Korean campaign. Hideyoshi ordered death of 26 Christians near Nagasaki	
1598	Death of Hideyoshi and withdrawal of troops from Korea		
1600		Victory of Tokugawa Ieyasu at Battle of Sekigahara, last battle of civil war	
1603	Ieyasu granted title of Shogun		
1605–1623	Shogunate of Hidetada (d. 1632)		
1614		Seige of Osaka castle by Ieyasu	Edict suppressing Christianity

TOKUGAWA PERIOD 1615–1867

YEAR	POLITICAL	MILITARY	CULTURAL
1615	Promulgation of *buke sho-hatto*, "ordinances for military houses"		
1622–1638			Period of greatest Christian persecutions
1623–1651	Shogunate of Iemitsu		
1636	Ban on Japanese travel abroad		
1637–1638		Shimabara Rebellion	
1638	Expulsion of Portuguese traders		
1641	Dutch traders confined to Deshima island in Nagasaki harbor		

YEAR	POLITICAL	MILITARY	CULTURAL
1651–1680	Shogunate of Ietsuna		
1657	Great Edo fire		Death of Hayashi Razan (Doshun), adviser to Ieyasu and proponent of Neo-Confucianism (b. 1583)
1680–1709	Shogunate of Tsunayoshi		
1688–1704			Genroku Era—new urban culture
1693			Death of Ihara Saikaku, novelist (b. 1642)
1694			Death of *haiku* poet Matsuo Basho (b. 1644)
1697	Dojima Rice Exchange founded in Osaka		
1701–1703			Chushingura incident (*Forty-Seven Ronin*)
1707	Last eruption of Mount Fuji		
1714			Death of Hishikawa Moronobu, first great *ukiyo-e* artist (b. 1638)
1716–1745	Shogunate of Yoshimune (d. 1751)		
1720			Ban lifted on importation of foreign books, on condition that they are not Christian
1724			Death of Chikamatsu Monzaemon, playwright (b. 1653)
1745–1760	Shogunate of Ieshige (d. 1761)		
1758			Aoki Konyo introduced sweet potato, and published first Dutch-Japanese dictionary
1760–1786	Shogunate of Ieharu		
1779			Death of Hiraga Gennai (b. 1728) who made contributions in botany, mining, electricity, and oil painting
1787–1837	Shogunate of Ienari (d. 1841)—instituted Kansei Reforms		

YEAR	POLITICAL	MILITARY	CULTURAL
1793	Visit of Russian Lt. Adam Laxman to Hokkaido		
1798			Completion of commentary on *Kojiki* by Shinto scholar Motoori Norinaga (d. 1801)
1806			Death of Utamaro, wood-block artist
1808	British ship *Phaeton* arrives at Nagasaki		
1811			Translation bureau established for foreign books
1837	Rice riots in Osaka		
1837–1853	Shogunate of Ieyoshi		
1852	Visit of Russians to Shimoda		
1853	Commodore Matthew C. Perry arrives at Uraga		
1854	Treaty of Kanagawa with United States		
1857	Townsend Harris' visit to Shogun's court		
1858	Commercial treaty with the United States		Death of wood-block artist Hiroshige
1858–1868	Rivalry between imperial court, Shogunate, Choshu and Satsuma clans, and foreign powers		
1859	Foreign trading community established at Yokohama		Death of Yoshida Shoin (b. 1830), teacher of *samurai* and exponent of role of emperor
1860	Exchange in Washington of treaty ratification by first embassy to U.S.		
1862	First Japanese embassy in Europe		
	Murder of Englishman Richardson at Namaugi by Satsuma *samurai*		
1863		Bombardment of foreign vessels by Choshu forts at Shimonoseki	

YEAR	POLITICAL	MILITARY	CULTURAL
		Bombardment of Kagoshima, capital of Satsuma, by British	
		Expulsion of Choshu forces from Kyoto	
1864		Bombardment of Shimonoseki by British, French, Dutch, and American ships	
1866	Satsuma and Choshu clans agree to join against Shogunate		
1866–1867	Shogunate of Yoshinobu (Keiki d. 1913)		
1867	Enthronement of Mutsuhito (Emperor Meiji)		
1868	JAN. 3. Proclamation of imperial restoration	JAN. 27. Capitulation of Shogun's forces at Fushimi and Toba	

MEIJI PERIOD 1868–1912

YEAR	POLITICAL	MILITARY	CULTURAL
1868	APR. 6. Emperor's Charter Oath		
	NOV. 26. Tokyo (Edo) established as new capital		
1869	MAR. 5. Return of lands by Satsuma, Choshu, Tosa, and Hizen to emperor		
	JULY. Appointment of *daimyo* as governors of their former fiefs		
1871	NOV. 20. Departure of Iwakura Mission for America and Europe		SEPT. 2. Ministry of Education established. Postal service instituted. First daily newspaper published
1872	Railway opened between Tokyo and Yokohama		
1873	New land-tax system	Universal military service	OCT. End of ban on Christianity. Gregorian calendar adopted
	SEPT. Return of Iwakura mission		
	OCT. Peaceful policy toward Korea decided upon		

YEAR	POLITICAL	MILITARY	CULTURAL
	Yamagata Aritomo becomes minister of army		
1874	Kobe-Osaka Railroad (1877 to Kyoto)	MAY. Victory of expeditionary force in Taiwan under Saigo Tsugumichi	
1875–1888	Civil legal code—final draft with German additions in 1896		
1876	MAR. 28. Prohibition of carrying swords by *samurai*		
	AUG. 5. Compulsory commutation of *samurai* pensions		
1877		FEB.-SEPT. Satsuma Rebellion and death of Saigo Takamori— last stand of *samurai*	
1878		Adoption of German General Staff organization in army	
1879	MAR. Beginning of elected prefectural assemblies		
1881	Emperor promises constitution by 1890 Political parties formed		
1882	Ito Hirobumi sent to Europe to study constitutional systems		
1884	Creation of peerage		
1885	DEC. 22. Adoption of cabinet system with Ito as first premier		
1887	DEC. 26. Peace Preservation Ordinance		
1888	Creation of Privy Council		
1889	FEB. 11. Promulgation of Meiji Constitution		
1890	JULY 1. First election for Diet (convened Nov. 25)		OCT. 30. Imperial Rescript on Education
1892	Ito as premier (resigned Aug. 31, 1896)		

YEAR	POLITICAL	MILITARY	CULTURAL
1894		JUNE 5. Uprising in Korea.	
		AUG. 1. Declaration of War on China (Sino-Japanese War)	
		NOV. 21. Capture of Port Arthur	
1895		APR. 17. Treaty of Shimonoseki, concluding Sino-Japanese War	
		APR. 20. Japanese decision to return Liaotung Peninsula to China after interventions of Russia, France, and Germany	
1900		JUNE-AUG. Participation of Japanese forces in relief of Legation Quarter, Peking, during Boxer Uprising	
1902	Anglo-Japanese Alliance signed		
1904		FEB. 9. Attack on Russian navy	
		FEB. 10. Declaration of War on Russia (Russo-Japanese War)	
		SEPT. 4. Liao-yang captured	
1905		JAN. 1. Port Arthur captured	
		MAR. 10. Mukden captured	
		MAY 27-28. Destruction of Russian fleet at Battle of Tsushima Straits	
		SEPT. 5. Treaty of Portsmouth	
1906	MAR. Nationalization of railways		
	NOV. South Manchuria Railroad completed		
1909	OCT. 26. Assassination of Prince Ito in Harbin by a Korean		
1910	AUG. 22. Annexation of Korea by Japan		
1912	JULY 30. Death of Meiji Emperor, accession of son, Yoshihito		

PERIOD OF TAISHO EMPEROR 1912–1926

YEAR	POLITICAL	MILITARY	CULTURAL
1914		AUG. 23. Japanese declaration of war on Germany (World War I)	
		NOV. 7. Capture of Tsingtao	
1915	JAN. 18. Twenty-One Demands on China presented to Yüan Shih-k'ai		
1917	NOV. 2. Lansing-Ishii exchange of notes with U.S., recognizing Japan's special interests in China		
1918	SEPT. 29. Hara Kei of Seiyukai party became premier, first commoner in post	APR. Japanese and British forces landed at Vladivostok	
1920	JAN. 10. Peace concluded with Germany. Japanese given mandate over former German Pacific islands		
1921	NOV. 4. Assassination of Premier Hara		
	NOV. 12. Washington Conference		
	Formation of Japanese Communist party		
1922	Nine Power Treaty and Open Door Policy		
	OCT. Withdrawal from Vladivostok		
	NOV. Return of Kiaochow (Tsingtao) to China		
1923	SEPT. 1. Tokyo and Yokohama earthquake		
1925	MAR. Universal manhood suffrage and Peace Preservation Law		
1926	DEC. 25. Death of Taisho Emperor, accession of Emperor Hirohito		

PERIOD OF SHOWA EMPEROR 1926–

YEAR	POLITICAL	MILITARY	CULTURAL
1928	FEB. 20. First general election under universal manhood suffrage	JUNE 4. Bomb attack on Chang Tso-lin in Manchuria	
1930	APR. 22. London Naval Treaty		
1931		SEPT. 18. Manchurian Incident	
1932	FEB. 18. Creation of Manchukuo	JAN. 28-MAR. 3. Shanghai campaign	
1933	FEB. 24. Lytton Report on Manchuria adopted by League of Nations		
1935	NOV. East Hopei Autonomous Regime set up		
1936	NOV. 25. Anti-Comintern Pact	FEB. 26. Assassination of government ministers in Tokyo by troops of First Division	
1937		JULY 7. Outbreak of war with China. Clash at Marco Polo Bridge, near Peking DEC. 13. Capture of Nanking	
1938	MAR. 24. National Mobilization Law	OCT. 21. Capture of Canton	
1939	JULY 27. Denunciation of 1911 Trade Treaty by U.S.A. AUG. 23. German-Soviet non-aggression pact	APR.-JULY. Fighting on Manchukuo-Outer Mongolia border SEPT. 1. Outbreak of war in Europe (World War II)	
1940	MAR. Wang Ching-wei puppet regime set up in Nanking JULY 6-AUG. 15. Dissolution of political parties SEPT. 27. Tripartite Alliance with Germany and Italy OCT. 12. Inauguration of Imperial Rule Assistance Association	SEPT. 23. Entrance of Japanese troops into French Indo-China	
1941	MAR. 8. Cordell Hull and Ambassador Nomura Kichisaburo began conversations	JULY 24. Occupation of southern Indo-China	

YEAR	POLITICAL	MILITARY	CULTURAL
	APR. 13. Soviet-Japanese neutrality pact	DEC. 7. Attack on Pearl Harbor and start of Pacific War	
	OCT. 18. General Tojo as premier		
1942	NOV. 1. Greater East Asia Ministry set up	JUNE 3-5. Battle of Midway	
		AUG. 7-FEB 9., 1943. Guadalcanal campaign	
1943	JAN. Casablanca Conference		
1944		JUNE 19-JULY 9. Saipan in Marianas fell to U.S. forces: Japan within bombing range	
		NOV. 24. B-29 bombings of Japan begun	
1945	JULY 26. Potsdam Proclamation	FEB. 5. Fall of Manila	
		APR. 1-JUNE 23. Okinawa campaign	
		MAY 8. Germany surrendered	
		AUG. 6. Atomic bomb, Hiroshima	
	AUG. 14. Japan accepted terms of Potsdam Proclamation	AUG. 8. U.S.S.R. entered the war	
	SEPT. 2. Formal surrender received on U.S.S. *Missouri*	AUG. 9. Atomic bomb, Nagasaki	
	DEC. 15. Disestablishment of Shinto		
1946	JAN. 1. Emperor's denial of his own divinity		
	OCT. Land Reform Law enacted		
1947	MAY 3. New Constitution		
1948	DEC. 23. Gen. Tojo and six others executed as war criminals		
1949	MAY 12. Announcement made of ending of removals for reparations and of limitations on industry by Oct. 1.		
1950	AUG. 10. National Police Reserve created	JUNE 25. South Korea invaded by North Korea	

YEAR	POLITICAL	MILITARY	CULTURAL
1951	APR. 11. Gen. Mac-Arthur dismissed, Gen. Matthew Ridgway appointed Supreme Commander SEPT. 8. Peace Treaty signed with 48 nations U.S.-Japan Security Pact signed		
1952	FEB. 28. Agreement regarding U.S. bases in Japan		
1953		JULY 27. Cease-fire in Korea	
1955	DEC. U.S.S.R. veto on Japan's membership in UN		
1956	MAY 9. Japanese-Soviet fisheries agreement DEC. 12. Japan admitted to UN		
1957	DEC. 6. Treaty of Commerce signed with U.S.S.R.		
1959	APR. 10. Crown Prince and Shoda Michiko (commoner) married		
1960	JAN. 19. Treaty of Mutual Security and Cooperation with U.S.		
1964			Tokyo Olympiad
1965	Japan joined Asian Development Bank		Death of Tanizaki Junichiro, novelist (b. 1886)
1969	NOV. Premier Sato Eisaku visited Washington: negotiated return of Okinawa, effective 1972		JUNE. Final link of Tokyo-Kobe auto expressway opened
1970	Law passed in the Diet, making pollution a crime		MAR. 15. Expo '70 opened in Osaka
1972	SEPT. Peace Treaty with China signed		Death of Mishima Yukio, novelist, (b. 1925)
1973	Beginning of the oil crisis		Death of Kawabata Yasunari, novelist, (b. 1899)

SELECTED READINGS

Beasley, W. G. *The Modern History of Japan.* New York: Praeger, 1963.

Burks, Ardath W. *Japan—A Postindustrial Power,* 2d rev. ed. Boulder: Westview Press, 1984

Craig, Albert M., ed. *Japan, A Comparative View.* Princeton: Princeton University Press, 1979.

Fairbank, John K., Reischauer, Edwin O., Craig, Albert M. *East Asia, Tradition and Transformation.* Boston: Houghton Mifflin, 1973.

Hall, John Whitney. *Japan from Prehistory to Modern Times.* New York: Dell Publishing Co., 1970.

Hall, John W. and Beardsley, Richard K. *Twelve Doors to Japan.* New York: McGraw-Hill, 1965.

Hollerman, Leon, ed. *Japan and the United States: Economic and Political Adversaries.* Boulder: Westview Press, 1979.

Jansen, Marius B., ed. *Changing Japanese Attitudes Towards Modernization.* Princeton: Princeton Universty Press, 1965.

Keene, Donald. *Anthology of Japanese Literature from the Earliest Era to the Mid-nineteenth Century.* New York; Grove Press, 1955.

Keene, Donald. *Modern Japanese Literature.* New York: Grove Press, 1956.

Kitagawa, Joseph M. *Religion in Japanese History.* New York: Columbia University Press, 1966.

Lockwood, William W., ed. *The State and Economic Enterprise in Modern Japan.* Princeton: Princeton University Press, 1965.

Nakane, Chie. *Japanese Society.* Berkeley and Los Angeles: University of California Press, 1970.

Reischauer, Edwin O. *Japan—The Story of a Nation,* rev. ed. New York: Alfred A. Knopf, 1974, formerly titled *Japan: Past and Present.*

Reischauer, Edwin O. *The Japanese.* Cambridge, Mass.: Belknap Harvard University Press, 1978.

Sansom, G.B. *Japan—A Short Cultural History.* rev. ed. New York: Appleton-Century, 1944.

Seidensticker, Edward G., trans., Murasaki. *Tale of Genji.* New York: Alfred A. Knopf, 1976. See also translation by Arthur Waley, Boston: Houghton Mifflin, 1925-33.

Storry, Richard. *A History of Modern Japan,* rev. ed. Baltimore: Pelican, 1965.

Tiedemann, Arthur E., ed. *An Introduction to Japanese Civilization*. New York and London: Columbia University Press, 1974.

Tsunoda, Ryusaku, de Bary, William Theodore, Keene, Donald. *Sources of the Japanese Tradition*. New York: Columbia University Press, 1958.

Varley, H. Paul. *Japanese Culture—A Short History*, 3rd expanded ed. New York: Praeger, 1984.

Vogel, Ezra. *Japan as Number One: Lessons for America*. Cambridge, Mass.: Harvard University Press, 1979.

Waley, Arthur. *No Plays of Japan*. New York: Alfred A. Knopf, 1922, and Grove Press.

Ward, Robert E., ed. *Political Development in Modern Japan*. Princeton: Princeton University Press, 1968.

Warner, Langdon. *The Enduring Art of Japan*. New York: Grove Press, 1952.

INDEX